Muhammad

CAMPAIGNS & COMMANDERS

GREGORY J. W. URWIN, SERIES EDITOR

CAMPAIGNS AND COMMANDERS

GENERAL EDITOR

Gregory J. W. Urwin, *Temple University, Philadelphia,*
Pennsylvania

ADVISORY BOARD

Lawrence E. Babits, *East Carolina University, Greenville*
James C. Bradford, *Texas A & M University, College Station*
Robert M. Epstein, *U.S. Army School of Advanced Military Studies,*
Fort Leavenworth, Kansas
David M. Glantz, *Carlisle, Pennsylvania*
Jerome A. Greene, *National Park Service*
Victor Davis Hanson, *California State University, Fresno*
Herman Hattaway, *University of Missouri, Kansas City*
Eugenia C. Kiesling, *U.S. Military Academy, West Point, New York*
Timothy K. Nenninger, *National Archives, Washington, D.C.*
Bruce Vandervort, *Virginia Military Institute, Lexington*

MUHAMMAD

Islam's First Great General

Richard A. Gabriel

UNIVERSITY OF OKLAHOMA PRESS : NORMAN

Library of Congress Cataloging-in-Publication Data

Gabriel, Richard A.
  Muhammad : Islam's first great general / Richard A. Gabriel.
    p.   cm. — (Campaigns and commanders ; v. 11)
  Includes bibliographical references and index.
  ISBN–13: 978-0-8061-3860-2 (hardcover : alk. paper)
  1. Muhammad, Prophet, d. 632—Military leadership. I. Title. II. Series.

  BP77.7.G34 2007
  297.6'3—dc22

                                                            2007000690

Muhammad: Islam's First Great General is Volume 11 in the Campaigns and
Commanders series.

The paper in this book meets the guidelines for permanence and durability of
the Committee on Production Guidelines for Book Longevity of the Council
on Library Resources, Inc. ∞

1 2 3 4 5 6 7 8 9 10

For pretty Susan,
the one who sees the dream
and whom I love beyond all measure

and

In memoriam

Professor John Daniel Windhausen
(1932–2006)

"Here is your servant John . . .
Take him, Lord.
But never take him lightly."

All well-armed prophets have conquered and the unarmed failed.

Machiavelli, *The Prince*

The number of combatants in Muhammad's battles never exceeded a few thousand, but in importance they rank among the world's most decisive battles.

Alfred Guillaume, *Islam*

No great man lives in vain. The history of the world is but the biography of great men.

Carlyle, *On Heroes*

CONTENTS

Maps

Important Dates

August–September 625   Siege and Exile of Beni an-Nadir
March 626   Second Battle of Badr
June 626   Dhat al Riqa Raid
August 626   Dumat al-Jandal Raid
March–April 627   Siege of Medina
April 627   Extermination of Beni Qurayzah
January 628   Beni Lihyan Raid
March 628   The Truce of Hudaibiya
September 628   Conquest of Kheibar
September 629   Battle of Mu'ta
February 629   Muhammad's *Omra* Pilgrimage to Mecca
January 630   Capture of Mecca
February 630   Battle of Hunayn
February–March 630   Siege of Ta'if
September–October 630   Expedition to Tabuk
631   Year of Deputations
632   Muhammad's Farewell Pilgrimage
June 632   Death of Muhammad
632–633   The *Riddah*

ACKNOWLEDGMENTS

I am indebted and deeply grateful to the following individuals who gave graciously of their time and expertise in reading the manuscript and offering their advice and criticism. Joe Spoerl, professor of philosophy at St. Anselm College and an expert on Muslim religion and philosophy, deserves a special note of thanks for his efforts on my behalf. It was he who first suggested the idea for a military biography of Muhammad. His substantive comments were indispensable to my understanding of the currents of Muslim religious and philosophical thought that provided the larger context against which the military events of Muhammad's life must be understood. Jim Coyle, my old friend and colleague from our days together at the U.S. Army War College, was invaluable in making certain that I was attentive to the sensitivities of Muslims in the manner in which I addressed certain controversial aspects of Muhammad's life. Before assuming his position at Chapman College in California, Jim spent more than twenty years as an analyst for one of the country's premier intelligence agencies. He is fluent in Arabic, Farsi, and Urdu, and a student of Arab and Muslim history for more than thirty years. Joel Klein, who holds a doctorate in ancient languages and also is fluent in Arabic and Hebrew, helped me improve the accuracy of the Arabic terms contained herein. David Lufkin, a professional writer and author, did much to tighten and focus the manuscript making it accessible to both academic and general readers. Steve Weingartner, military history editor for Greenwood-Praeger and a fine writer in his own right, also read and edited the manuscript. I am especially grateful to Salem Jubran, a Christian Arab living in Nazareth, and to Col. Salim Al-Salmy of the Army of Oman, a devout Muslim, for their valuable advice and insight into the complexities of Arab and Muslim culture and psychology. While this book could never have been written without the aid and comfort of all these fine people, responsibility for any errors rests with me alone.

INTRODUCTION

It is always difficult to be objective about the life of the founder of a great religion. His personality is blurred by an aura of the miraculous, enhanced almost inevitably by the needs of his believers to believe. The earliest biographers, those closest to his lifetime, are often preoccupied not with historical fact, but with glorifying in every way the memory of one they believe to have been the Messenger of God or even God himself. The result is a rich accretion of myth and miracle, mysterious portents and heavenly signs, of residues from other religions and traditions. The biographies of saviors and messiahs cannot usually pass as history; they are rather the propaganda of an expanding faith.[1] It is the task of the historian to locate and explicate the truth that lies behind the myth. At the root of the effort rests the historian's faith that the task can be accomplished at all.

This book is about the military life of Muhammad, the founder of the great world religion of Islam. Any work about Muhammad confronts all of the problems noted above. Despite Muhammad's outstanding military accomplishments, there is no biography of this great man that examines his military life in detail. Extant biographies of Muhammad have focused on his role as a great seer who founded the religion of Islam, or his achievements as a social revolutionary, or his abilities as a statesman and administrator who created new institutions to govern the peoples of Arabia.[2] There is no biography written from the perspective of Muhammad's role as Islam's first great general and leader of a successful insurgency.

Those biographies that do treat of Muhammad's military achievements do so mostly in passing so that his role as a competent military commander has been largely overlooked, or treated as a matter of secondary importance, or, as with some biographies written by Muslim scholars, even attributed to miracle and divine guidance.[3] This is a curious state of affairs in light of the fact that had Muhammad not succeeded as a military commander Islam might have remained but one of a number of interesting religious sects relegated to a geographic backwater, and the conquest of the Byzantine and Persian Empires by Arab armies might never have occurred. Samuel P. Huntington has remarked in this regard that Muhammad is the only founder of a great religion who was also a military commander. Previous generations of Western scholars often took note that Muhammad was a military man. James L. Payne, writing in 1899, said that "Muhammad is remembered as a hard fighter and skillful military commander."[4] This memory persists in the minds of modern *jihadis*. This book is the first military biography of Muhammad and has as its goal a detailed treatment of Muhammad's military life and accomplishments that transformed the armies and society of the Arabs. This transformation made possible the conquest of two of the greatest empires of the ancient world by the armies of Islam in the space of only a few years.

While this book is a *military* biography, the social, economic, and cultural environments in which Muhammad lived are also addressed insofar as they had an important influence on his military life. This, of course, includes Muhammad's religious experience. But this, too, is addressed only when it is relevant to military history. Muhammad's reform of the marriage laws, for example, permitting each man four wives was, at least in part, motivated by the need to find husbands to care for the widows and orphans of his troops killed at the Battle of Badr.[5] The book is careful to avoid religious analysis or conclusions, elements that have sometimes made biographies of the Prophet partisan and unreliable.

To think of Muhammad as a military man will come as something of a new experience to many. And yet Muhammad was truly a great general. In the space of a single decade he fought eight major battles, led eighteen raids, and planned thirty-eight other military operations where others were in command but operating under his orders and strategic direction. He was wounded twice, suffered defeats, and twice had his positions overrun by superior forces before rallying his troops to victory. But Muhammad was more than a great field general and tactician. He was a military theorist, organizational reformer, strategic thinker, operational level combat commander, political and military leader, heroic soldier, revolutionary, and inventor of the theory of insurgency and history's first successful practitioner. Like some other great commanders in history—Moses, Subotai, and Vo Nguyen Giap—Muhammad had no military training before actually commanding an army in the field. As an orphan he had no opportunity to learn military skills at the hands of an Arab father, the usual means of acquiring military training among the Arabs in his day. His only early exposure to warfare came at the age of fourteen when he witnessed a skirmish between two clans in which he retrieved arrows for his uncle. Yet, Muhammad became an excellent field commander and tactician and an even more astute political and military strategist.

Muhammad proved to be a master of intelligence in war, and his intelligence service eventually came to rival that of Rome and Persia, especially in the area of political intelligence. He often spent hours devising tactical and political stratagems and once remarked that "all war is cunning," reminding us of Sun Tzu's dictum that "all war is deception." In his thinking and application of force Muhammad was a combination of Clausewitz and Machiavelli for he always employed force in the service of political goals. He was an astute grand strategist whose use of nonmilitary methods (alliance building, political assassination, bribery, religious appeals, mercy, and calculated butchery) always resulted in strengthening his long-term strategic position, sometimes at the expense of short-term military considerations.

Muhammad's unshakable belief in Islam and in his role as the Messenger of God revolutionized warfare in Arabia in many respects and created the first army in the ancient world motivated by a coherent system of ideological belief. The ideology of holy war (*jihad*) and martyrdom (*shahada*) for the faith was transmitted to the West during the wars between Muslims and Christians in Spain and France, where it changed traditional Christian pacifistic thinking on war, brought into being a coterie of Christian warrior saints, and provided the Catholic

Church with its ideological justification for the Crusades.[6] Ideology of the religious or secular variety has remained a primary element of military adventure ever since.

It was Muhammad who forged the military instrument of the Arab conquests that began within two years of his death by bringing into being a completely new kind of army not seen before in Arabia. As a military innovator Muhammad introduced no fewer than eight major military reforms that transformed the armies and conduct of war in Arabia. Just as Philip of Macedon transformed the armies of Greece so that his successor, Alexander, could employ them as instruments of conquest and empire, so Muhammad transformed the armies of Arabia so his successors could use them to defeat the armies of the Persian and Byzantine Empires and establish the core of the Empire of Islam. Had Muhammad not transformed the armies, the Arab conquests would likely have remained a military impossibility.

Muhammad the Insurgent

Although his reforms and military achievements give him much in common with the greatest generals in antiquity, Muhammad was not a conventional field general. He was, instead, a new type of warrior, one never before seen in antiquity. Muhammad was first and foremost a revolutionary, a fiery religious guerrilla leader who created and led the first genuine national insurgency in antiquity that is comprehensible in modern terms, a fact not lost on the *jihadis* of the present day who often cite the Quran and Muhammad's use of violence as justification for their own. Unlike conventional generals Muhammad's goal was not the defeat of a foreign enemy or invader but the replacement of the existing Arabian social order with a new one based on a radically different ideological view of the world. To achieve his revolutionary goals Muhammad utilized all the means recognized by modern analysts as characteristic of and necessary to a successful insurgency. Although Muhammad began his struggle for a new order with a small guerrilla cadre capable of undertaking only limited hit-and-run raids, by the time he was ready to attack Mecca a decade later that small guerrilla force had grown into a large conventional armed force with integrated cavalry and infantry units capable of conducting large-scale combat operations. It was this conventional military instrument that Muhammad's successors used to forge a great empire. It was the first truly national military force in Arab history.

Beginning with a small band of believers, Muhammad undertook a guerrilla war in which he waged a campaign of ambushes and raids to erode the economic and political base of his enemy's power. He introduced new social programs and a politico-religious ideology that attracted others to his cause, expanding his base of military manpower and making it possible to recruit and deploy larger military forces. After years of guerrilla war Muhammad finally defeated his enemies by drawing them into a series of set-piece battles, eventually capturing Mecca itself. Supporting the military effort was the political dimension of the insurgency that used political alliances to deprive his enemy of a source of military manpower and to erode the enemy's popular base of support. Political maneuver and negotiation, intelligence, propaganda, and the judicious use of terror and assassination were employed to wage a psychological warfare campaign against those potential sources of opposition that could not yet be won over by calculations of self-interest or ideology.

Muhammad's rise to power was a textbook example of a successful insurgency, indeed the first such example in history of which I am aware.[7] Modern insurgents like Mao Zedong, Ho Chi Minh, Jomo Kenyatta, Fidel Castro, and perhaps, George Washington would easily have recognized Muhammad's strategy and methods in their own revolutionary struggles. The West has been accustomed to thinking of the Arab conquests that followed Muhammad in purely *conventional* military terms. But the armies that achieved those conquests did not exist in Arabia before Muhammad. It was Muhammad's successful *unconventional* guerrilla operations, his successful insurgency, that brought those armies into existence. Thus, the later Arab conquests, as regards both strategic concept and the new armies as instruments of military method, were the consequences of Muhammad's prior military success as the leader of an insurgency.

This aspect of Muhammad's military life as a guerrilla insurgent is likely to strike the reader as curious and, as such, is worth exploring in some detail. If the means and methods used by modern military analysts to characterize insurgency warfare are employed as categories of analysis, it is clear that Muhammad's campaign to spread Islam throughout Arabia fulfilled each of the analytical criteria. The first requirement for an insurgency to succeed is a determined leader whose followers regard him as special in some way and worthy of their following him. In Muhammad's case his own charismatic personality was enhanced by his deeply held belief that he was indeed God's Messenger, and that to follow Muhammad was to obey the dictates of God himself. Insurgencies also require a messianic ideology, one that espouses a coherent creed or plan to replace the existing social, political, and economic order, usually seen as unjust, with a new order that is better, more just, or ordained by history or even by God. Muhammad used the new religious creed of Islam to challenge central traditional Arab social institutions and values as oppressive and unholy and worthy of replacement. To this end he created the *ummah*, or community of believers, God's community on earth, to serve as a messianic replacement for the clans and tribes that were the basis of traditional Arab society. One of Muhammad's most important achievements was the establishment of new social institutions that greatly altered and in some cases completely replaced those of the old Arab social order.

Successful insurgencies also require a disciplined cadre of true believers to do the work of organizing and recruiting new members. Muhammad's revolutionary cadre consisted of the small group of original converts he attracted in Mecca and took with him to Medina. These were the *muhajirun*, or Emigrants. The first converts among the clans of Medina, the *ansar*, or Helpers, also filled the ranks. Within this revolutionary cadre was an inner circle of talented men, some of them much later converts. Some, like Abdullah Ibn Ubay and Khalid al-Walid, were experienced field commanders and provided a much needed source of military expertise. Muhammad's inner circle advised him and saw to it that his directives were carried out. Not surprisingly, some of his advisers came to hold key positions during the Prophet's lifetime and fought among themselves for power after his death.

Once Muhammad had created his cadre of revolutionaries, he established a base from which to undertake military operations against his adversaries. These operations initially took the form of ambushes and raids aimed at isolating Mecca, the enemy's main city, and other trading towns that opposed him. Only one in six Arabs lived in a city or town at this time; the others resided in the "countryside" or desert living as enclosed pastoral nomads.[8] Muhammad chose Medina as his base of operations. Medina was strategically located in that it was a short distance from the main caravan route from Mecca to Syria that constituted the economic lifeline of Mecca and other oases and towns that depended on the caravan trade for their economic survival. Medina was also sufficiently distant from Mecca to permit Muhammad a relatively free hand in his efforts to convert the bedouin clans living along the caravan route. Muhammad understood that conversions and political alliances with the bedouins, not military engagements with the Meccans, were the keys to initial success.

Insurgencies require an armed force and the manpower to sustain them. It was from the original small cadre of guerrillas that the larger conventional army could be grown that would ultimately permit the insurgency to engage its enemies in set-piece battles when the time and political conditions were right. Muhammad may have been the first commander in history to understand and implement the doctrine that General Vo Nguyen Giap of North Vietnam later referred to as "people's war, people's army."[9] Muhammad established the idea among his followers that God had commandeered all Muslims' purposes and property and that all Muslims had a responsibility to fight for the faith. Everyone—men, women, and even children—had an obligation for military service in defense of the faith and the ummah that was the community of God's chosen people on earth. If this is not properly understood, then it will be difficult to grasp that it was the attraction of the ideology of Islam more than anything else that drew together the manpower that permitted Muhammad's small revolutionary cadre to grow into a conventional armed force capable of large-scale engagements.

The growth of Muhammad's insurgent army is evident from the following figures. At the Battle of Badr (624 C.E.) Muhammad could put only 314 men in the field. Two years later at Second Badr (626 C.E.), 1,500 Muslims took the field. At Kheibar in 628 C.E., the Muslim army had grown to 2,000 combatants. When Muhammad mounted his assault on Mecca (630 C.E.) he did so with 10,000 men. And at the Battle of Hunayn a few months later the army numbered 12,000. Some sources record that Muhammad's expedition to Tabuk later the same year comprised 30,000 men and 10,000 cavalry, but this is probably an exaggeration.[10] What is evident from the figures, however, is that Muhammad's insurgency grew very quickly in terms of its ability to recruit military manpower.

Like all insurgent armies, Muhammad's forces initially acquired weapons by stripping them from prisoners and the enemy dead. Weapons, helmets, and armor were expensive items in relatively impoverished

Arabia, and the early Muslim converts—drawn mostly from among the poor, orphaned, widowed, and otherwise socially marginal—could ill afford them. At the Battle of Badr, the first major engagement with an enemy army, the dead were stripped of their swords and other military equipment, establishing a practice that became common. Muhammad also required prisoners to provide weapons and equipment instead of money to purchase their freedom. One prisoner taken at Badr was an arms merchant and was required to provide the insurgents with a thousand spears as the price of his freedom.[11] In the early days at Medina Muhammad purchased what arms he could from one of the Jewish tribes in the city that were armorers. Later, when he drove this tribe from the city, he was careful to require that they leave behind their metalworking tools so that the Muslims could now manufacture weapons for themselves. Muhammad was eventually able to supply weapons, helmets, shields, and armor for an army of ten thousand for his march on Mecca.

Muhammad's ability to obtain sufficient weapons and equipment had another important advantage. Many of the insurgency's converts came from the poorest elements of the bedouin clans, people too impoverished to afford weapons and armor. Muhammad often supplied these converts with expensive military equipment, immediately raising their status within the clan and guaranteeing their loyalty to him, if not always to the creed of Islam. In negotiations with bedouin chiefs Muhammad made them gifts of expensive weaponry. Several pagan clans were won over to Muhammad's insurgency in this manner, although they did not convert to Islam. Horses and camels were equally important military assets, for without them raids and the conduct of operations over distances were not possible. Muhammad obtained his animals in much the same manner as he did his weapons and with equal success. At Badr the insurgents had only two horses. Six years later at Hunayn Muhammad's cavalry squadrons numbered eight hundred horses and cavalrymen.[12]

An insurgency must also be able to sustain the popular base that supports the fighting elements. To accomplish this Muhammad changed the ancient customs regarding the sharing of booty taken in raids. The chief of a clan or tribe traditionally took one-fourth of the booty for himself. Muhammad decreed that he receive only one-fifth, and even this he took not for himself but in the name of the ummah. Under the old ways individuals kept whatever booty they had captured. Muhammad required that all booty be turned in to the common pool where it was shared equally among all combatants who had participated in the raid. Most importantly, Muhammad established that the first claimants on the booty that had been taken in the name of the ummah were the poor and the widows and orphans of the soldiers killed in battle. He also used the promise of a larger share of booty to strike alliances with bedouin clans, some of whom remained both loyal and pagan to the end fighting for loot instead of Islam. Muhammad's later military successes against towns, oases, and caravans provided an important source of wealth to supply the insurgent popular base with the necessities of life.

The leader of an insurgency must take great care to guard his power from challenges, including those that come from within the movement itself. Muhammad had many enemies, and he was always on guard against an attempt on his life. Like other insurgent leaders, Muhammad surrounded himself with a loyal group of men who would act as his bodyguard and carry out his orders without question. Muhammad created the *suffah* precisely for this purpose. The suffah was a small cadre who lived in the mosque next to Muhammad's house. They were recruited from among the most pious, enthusiastic, and fanatical followers, and were generally from impoverished backgrounds with no other way to make a living. The members of the suffah spent their time studying Islam and leading a life of spiritual avocation. They were devoted to Muhammad and served not only as his life guard but as a secret police that could be called on at a moment's notice to carry out whatever task Muhammad set for them. These tasks included assassination and terror.

No insurgency can survive without an effective intelligence apparatus, and the Muslim insurgency was no exception. As early as when Muhammad left Mecca he left behind a trusted agent, his uncle Abbas, who continued to send him reports on the situation there. Abbas served as an agent-in-place for more than a decade until Mecca itself fell to Muhammad. In the beginning Muhammad's operations suffered from a lack of tactical intelligence. His followers were mostly townspeople and had no experience in desert travel. On some of the early operations Muhammad had to hire bedouin guides to show him the way to where he wanted to go. As the insurgency grew, however, Muhammad's intelligence service became more organized and sophisticated, using agents-in-place, commercial spies, debriefing of prisoners, combat patrols, and reconnaissance in force as methods of intelligence collection.

Muhammad himself seems to have possessed a detailed knowledge of clan loyalties and politics within the insurgency's area of operations and used this knowledge to good effect when negotiating alliances with the bedouins. Muhammad often conducted an advance reconnaissance of the battlefields upon which he fought, and only once in ten years of military operations was he taken by surprise. In most cases Muhammad's intelligence service was able to provide him with sufficient information as to the enemy's location and intentions in advance of any military engagement. We have no knowledge of how Muhammad's intelligence service was organized or where it was located. That it was part of the suffah seems a reasonable guess.

Insurgencies succeed or fail to the degree that they are able to win the allegiance of the great numbers of the uncommitted to support the insurgents' goals. Muhammad understood the role of propaganda in the struggle for the hearts and minds of the uncommitted and went to great lengths to make his message public and widely known. In an Arab society that was largely illiterate, the poet served as the chief conveyor of political propaganda. Muhammad hired the best poets money could buy to sing his praises and denigrate his opponents. He publicly issued proclamations regarding the revelations he received as the Messenger of God, and remained always in public view to keep the vision of the new order and the promise of a heavenly paradise constantly before his followers and those he hoped to convert. He sent "missionaries" to other clans and tribes to instruct the pagans in the new faith, sometimes teaching the pagans to read and write in the process. Muhammad understood that the conflict was between the existing social order and its manifest injustices and his vision of the future, and he surpassed his adversaries in spreading his vision to win the struggle for the loyalty and support of the Arab population.

The use of terror seems to be an indispensable element of a successful insurgency, and no less so in Muhammad's case. Muhammad used terror in two basic ways. First, to keep discipline among his followers by making public examples of traitors or backsliders. It is sometimes forgotten that in Muhammad's day the penalty for apostasy in Islam was death. Muhammad also ordered the assassination of some of his political enemies, including poets and singers who had publicly ridiculed him. Never one to forget a slight, when his armies marched into Mecca Muhammad's suffah set about hunting down a list of old enemies marked for execution. Muhammad also used terror to strike fear into the minds of his enemies on a large scale. In the case of the Jewish tribes of Medina, Muhammad seems to have ordered the death of the entire Beni Qaynuqa tribe and the selling of their women and children into slavery before being talked out of it by the chief of one of his allies. On another occasion, again against a Jewish tribe of Medina, he ordered all the tribe's adult males—some nine hundred—beheaded in a city square, the women and children sold into slavery, and their property distributed among his Muslim followers. Shortly after the conquest of Mecca, Muhammad declared "war to the knife" against all those who remained idolaters, instructing his followers to kill any pagans they encountered on the spot! Such public displays of ruthlessness and brutality, as with all insurgencies, strengthened Muhammad's hand when dealing with opponents and allies.

When examined against the criteria used by modern analysts to characterize an insurgency, Muhammad's military campaign to establish Islam in Arabia seems to qualify in all respects. Nothing in this conclusion detracts from the substance and value of Islam itself as a religion any more than the history of the Israelite military campaign to conquer Canaan detracts from the substance and value of Judaism. Over time the violent origins of a religion are forgotten and only the faith itself remains, with the result that the founders of creeds come to be remembered as untinged by the violence of the historical record. In Muhammad's case the result has been to deemphasize the military aspects of his life and his considerable military accomplishments. One purpose of this book is to reilluminate the historical record of Muhammad's military life. We leave the religious history of Islam's first great general to others.

RESEARCH SOURCES

Any attempt to write a military biography of Muhammad is forced to rely on only a few reliable sources of information. The first is the Quran itself, that scriptural collection of moral rules, instructions, and interpretations of events believed by Muslims to have been revealed by God to Muhammad. Whenever Muhammad experienced a revelation he would repeat its instructions to his followers who committed them to memory. Some of these listeners may have taken notes, but the low level of literacy and scarcity of writing materials in Arabia at the time would have made this a rare occurrence. Devout Muslims believe, however, that the words of Muhammad were written down immediately after his revelations. The fact that Muhammad's words were recorded immediately is taken as proof to Muslims that the Quran contains the unadulterated word of God. By contrast, the failure of Christians and Jews to write down God's revelations immediately is viewed as permitting human experience to corrupt His divine words. For Muslims, belief in the immediate recording of Muhammad's words is a major article of faith. Theology aside, it is likely that the Quran is the best source of the words spoken by Muhammad himself. But as a source document for the writing of military history, the Quran is only marginally useful for the pertinent information it provides. It was not collated into a single document until some twenty years after Muhammad's death and was never intended as a narrative of the Prophet's life. The Quran is not arranged in chronological order of the occurrence of the events recorded within it. It is instead arranged in order of the length of the discourses themselves, beginning with the longest and ending with the shortest. For our purposes its most valuable contribution remains as a source of Muhammad's words in those instances where they are relevant to his military life.

The most useful source of information about Muhammad's life is Ibn Ishaq's great work, *The Life of Muhammad*, written about ninety years after the Prophet's death, and translated into French and English by the great Arabic scholar, Alfred Guillaume, in 1955. Ishaq's work was edited later by Ibn Hisham, and it is the edited version that has survived. Despite Ibn Hisham's admission that he has purposely omitted "things which it is disgraceful to discuss" and "matters which would distress certain people," his work has no serious rival as an original source of information about Muhammad and the events, especially the military events, surrounding his life. Guillaume's translation is regarded as the "gold standard" of translations of this source. Anyone writing about Muhammad's life must rely heavily on Ibn Ishaq or fail to do so at great risk.

Ibn Ishaq's biography of the Prophet was constructed from the *maghazi*, the earliest accounts of Muhammad's life written within a hundred years of his death. None of the maghazi has survived in usable form; only a single fragment of one book exists. The maghazi were based on oral accounts of individuals who knew the Prophet, took part in battles with him, or were close relatives of those who did. These accounts were passed down from one generation to the next in the oral tradition typical of Arab culture to this day. Ibn Ishaq is careful to cite the names of the sources of his accounts for most major events in his book, sometimes tracing a source to its previous one and to the one before that. That these oral accounts should have survived for almost a hundred years before Ibn Ishaq collected them and wrote them down is not surprising in a culture where the exploits of tribal, clan, and family heroes were memorized, recited, and passed to the young as a matter of common practice.

Ibn Ishaq's biography also includes additional original material in the form of poems about the raids and battles written shortly after the events themselves, sometimes by actual participants. Ishaq's efforts thus preserved another valuable source of oral tradition that otherwise might have been lost. The poems are often excellent sources of detail about military equipment and tactical events. Ibn Ishaq's *Life of Muhammad*, whether in Arabic or in Guillaume's definitive translation, remains the most basic work used by *all* biographers of Muhammad, including those writing in Arabic.

The academic concern for "original" sources might lead some to criticize the material on which this study relies as "secondary" sources and thus not sufficiently scholarly. If by original sources we at least mean that the materials ought to have been written as close as possible to the events they address, then Ibn Ishaq's work certainly qualifies. He is writing only ninety years after the events he is recording. Compared to the "original" sources often cited by ancient historians in the West, Ibn Ishaq's work is almost contemporaneous with the events themselves. Plutarch, for example, wrote about events that occurred two hundred to six hundred years before he wrote; Arrian's *History of Alexander* was written five hundred years after Alexander's death; Curtius's history of Alexander was written between three hundred and five hundred years after the events it records; and Livy, the old reliable, wrote of events that occurred two centuries before he was born. Only a few ancient historians—Tacitus, Polybius and Suetonius to name the most obvious—wrote about events that actually took place during their lifetimes. By any fair standard of proximity to events Ibn Ishaq qualifies as an original and reliable source.

A second criticism will likely be that the work relies on translations of its "original" sources and not on the original Arabic versions.[13] But only rarely do the language skills of any researcher equal those of a scholarly translator, so that one can be as certain as one can be in

these matters that works by scholarly translators of Guillaume's standing are more reliable than those produced by a researcher simply because
the researcher reads Arabic. As regards military history, a knowledge of
the subject and context of the materials in the target language are more
important than linguistic skills in the source language. Otherwise, the
literal use of language will likely mislead the translator. Reading Arabic
does not make one a translator of Arabic military history. One must be
a military historian first. Moreover, modern translations of classic
works are far more likely to be free of the ideological, cultural, and religious bias characteristic of those produced earlier when such prejudices
commanded more attention. Whenever I have used materials from other
Western or Arabic scholars (Becker, Caetani, Glubb, Hitti, Hourani,
Lewis, Lings, Rodinson, Shoufani, Watt, and Wellhausen) I have been
careful to rely on only those who themselves read Arabic and whose
published works have already been subjected to academic scrutiny and
found acceptable. I have not used scholarly Arabic transliterations for
the various names and places mentioned herein, but have relied on the
spellings used by my sources. Wherever applicable I have also noted in
the relevant footnotes the original Arabic sources on which the accounts
of these scholars were based.

The Arabic words that appear in the manuscript were taken directly
from the academic sources in which they appear. As such, they should
all be correct. Some people might find fault with the Arabic transliterations because they are not expressed in *classical* Arabic. This is an
inevitable risk of reading translations, but hardly a fatal flaw as long
as the meaning is not changed by the spelling. These problems have
been minimized through manuscript review by the four Arabic experts
mentioned in the acknowledgments.

The third source of research material on which this work relies is
the *hadith* (narrative or account); that is, verbal reports or conversations
comprising the compilations of the "traditions" of Muhammad gathered
some 120 years after the Prophet's death. These traditions are extrapo-
lations of various "sayings, words, deeds, and tacit approvals" of the
Prophet accompanied by interpretations by lawyers, religious authorities, and others, including political factionaries with influence at any
given time. The hadith represents the *sunna*, or tradition—the customs
and practices attributed to the Prophet Muhammad. As a historical source
this compilation can at best be regarded as repetitious of those accounts
within Ibn Ishaq's work or at worst as misleading and inaccurate

because of the bias of the extrapolators themselves who interpret the reports. A major difficulty in using works published in Arabic after Ibn Ishaq's work is that Muhammad's utterances and oral accounts of events surrounding his life quickly became thickly entangled in the various interpretations of Quranic law that were used as propagandistic weapons in theological and political disputes by various factions to favor themselves and discredit their opponents. As Guillaume has noted in this regard, "Apostolic tradition in Islam is the battlefield of warring sects striving for the mastery of men's minds and the control of their behavior with all the weight that Muhammad's presumed or fabricated example could bring to bear. The earlier the tradition . . . the less this tendency is in evidence."[14] Much of what was written about Muhammad in Arabic in later periods following Ibn Ishaq's work is often so culturally, ideologically, legalistically, or theologically partisan as to be useless as reliable research material. In any case precious little of it addresses Muhammad's military exploits.

This book is the first military biography of Muhammad in English written by a military historian. It is free from the religious and political bias often found in previous Muslim biographies. The conclusion that Muhammad was a military reformer is new to Muhammad scholarship, as is the conclusion that he shaped the rise of a new kind of army and style of warfare in Arabia. Had these military reforms not brought into being a new military instrument, it is unlikely that the Muslim conquests would have been militarily possible. Of great significance is that Muhammad was the inventor of the methodology of insurgency and that he was its first successful practitioner. I have tried to make the descriptions of Muhammad's battles more complete and empirically detailed than previous efforts have made them, with the hope that scholars will have to reexamine their assumptions about how these battles were fought and what their effects were. Finally, because of all these conclusions I have tried to place the life of Muhammad in a completely new context. That Muhammad succeeded as a Prophet is undeniable, but I suggest he might not have done so had he not been a great soldier first. This presents a new challenge to the extant scholarship in interpreting Muhammad's life and place in history.

MUHAMMAD

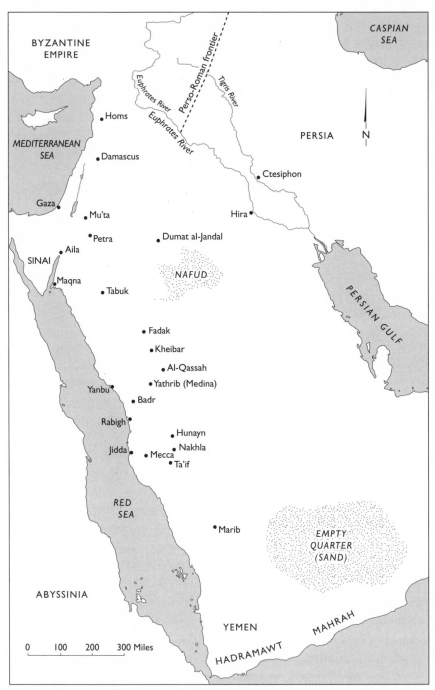

Map 1. Important Places in Muhammad's Arabia

1

THE LAND OF ARABIA

The Arabs call their land *Jazirat al-Arab*, the "island of the Arabs," and it is indeed an island surrounded by water on three sides and by sand on the fourth. The land is harsh, and until modern times when armies could take advantage of motorized transport, history knew of no invader who had succeeded in penetrating the country's sandy barriers to establish a permanent presence in the land. Arabia comprises the Arabian Peninsula and its northern extension, the Syrian Desert, a vast landmass that encompasses almost 1.5 million square miles, an area slightly larger than all of western Europe including Scandinavia.[1] The ground itself is made up of a single uniform block of ancient rock called the Arabian Shield and consists mostly of desert and steppe. The climate is uniformly hot, dry, and harsh, except for Yemen, which is blessed by monsoon rains and is fertile. The rest of the country is almost completely barren, receiving on average only six inches of rain per year.

Arabia is divided into four geographic regions. One is *Al Hijaz* (Hejaz), consisting of the western highlands that parallel the coast of the Red Sea. The mountains themselves reach as high as four thousand feet and separate the narrow coastal plain from the steppe land of the interior. A number of valley passes make it possible to travel from the interior to the coastal strip with only little difficulty. But the passes are few and of some distance between, making the mountains a formidable

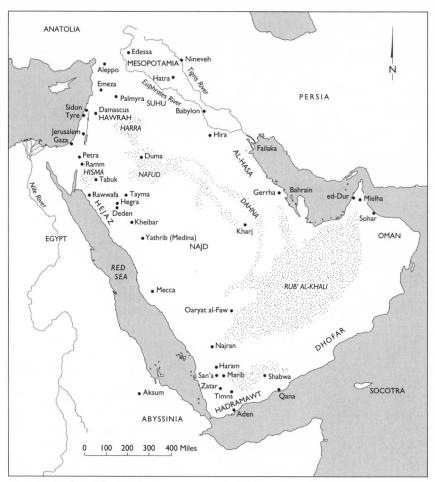

Map 2. Arabia: The Land

obstacle to military passage. Running sometimes along the coast and sometimes on the interior side of the mountains is the famous Arabian spice road, the route connecting the ports at the southern tip of the peninsula with the road to the north and the former Byzantine border provinces, including Palestine and Egypt. Ships from India and Africa unloaded their cargoes in these ports, where they were transferred to camel caravan trains and carried northward to Mecca, the commercial center located halfway between the ports and the markets farther north. This road was the commercial lifeline of Mecca and the entire westernmost area of the country.

The second geographic zone is the interior, largely stony, sandy wastes and desert. The Rub' al-Khali, or Empty Quarter, is a vast desert in the south that has large sand dunes sometimes reaching more than a hundred feet high and running on for miles at a stretch. In the center of Arabia are the Nafud and Dahna Deserts, which constitute formidable barriers to west–east travel. In the north lies the great Syrian Desert and the smaller wastes of Hisma and Hamad. The routes used by the Meccan caravan trains skirted these desolate areas; it was impossible for man or beast to attempt a crossing and survive. The third zone lies far to the east and comprises the hot and humid coastal lands of the Persian Gulf where agriculture is possible due to abundant groundwater.

Far to the south is Yemen, the fourth zone, the famous land of antiquity from which the prized aromatic plants that produced frankincense and myrrh were found. Yemen is a land of towering mountains, fertile valleys, and coastal plains. The monsoon rains make the ground fertile and well suited to agriculture. The people of Yemen were mostly settled rather than nomadic and were skilled in the building of dams and irrigation systems that made large-scale agriculture feasible. One of these dams, at Marib, was said to have made possible the cultivation of more than twenty thousand square acres of land. So large was the population supported by these lands that when the dam broke sometime near the beginning of the second century C.E., a great number of people were forced to migrate to the north.

There are no permanent rivers anywhere in Arabia, and rainfall is sparse and limited to certain times of the year. In the south the rains come in the spring and summer; in the north winter and spring are the rainy seasons. The rains can be heavy at times and are often accompanied by gale-force winds that can turn the wadi beds into raging torrents that wreak havoc on the mud-brick houses and walled gardens. Driving rains have been known to turn mud-brick walls into mud, sweeping away the liquid mass in a localized flood.[2]

During Muhammad's time five-sixths of the population of Arabia was bedouin and permanent settlements were few.[3] Ptolemy, writing in his *Geography* sometime around 150 c.e., listed only 218 settlements in Arabia, of which more than 150 were small villages. Only six "cities" were listed, and all of these were in Yemen where the land was sufficiently fertile to sustain large populations.[4] Most of these "cities" were relatively small in both area and population, and only two were surrounded by walls of mud-brick and stone. The length of the walls permit a rough estimate of the size of the populations. The walls of Qarnaw were 1,150 meters in length, and those of Timna were 1,850 meters long.[5] Walls of this size can enclose, on average, about eight to nine acres of land.[6] Using Yigael Yadin's estimate of approximately 240 persons per urban acre as the average population density for cities of the Middle East in antiquity, one might reasonably guess that the size of these cities was around two thousand souls.[7] The language of Arabia itself reflects the lack of urbanization in the land, for there is no word for city in classical Arabic. The most commonly used term in this context is *hagar*, a word that connotes the fortified assembly place or compound of a tribe where its clans are brought together for war or other purposes.

Muhammad spent most of his life in the Hejaz. With the exception of the mountains, the land of the Hejaz consists of desert and steppe. The steppe (*darah*) forms itself into vast circular plains lying between hills covered with sand. Large tracts of the steppeland are covered by fissured fields of hardened lava overlying sandstone. These lava fields are important barriers to military and commercial movement since neither horse nor camel can negotiate them without great risk of the animal's falling and breaking its limbs or falling on its rider. There are few trees, and only the acacia and the tamarisk seem to thrive. The Hejaz is a rocky and harsh place given to drought, with the land often going without rain for three years at a time. Deeply dug wells and cisterns are the main means of water supply. Cisterns are cavelike holes dug in the ground, the walls of which are sealed with stucco and into which water is diverted or caught from rainstorms. The cistern is then sealed until its contents are needed. It is an old ÿayÿuin custom to construct cisterns along a planned route of march so that the clan can be supplied with water as it moves over the desert. It was not unusual for bedouin raiders to construct and fill a cistern in some desolate location from which they could undertake raids against caravans. Without a source of water themselves, the caravan guards were unable to pursue the raiders.

In a few places groundwater seeps to the surface forming a fetid, swamplike area called an oasis. Most of the oases in the Hejaz are located north of Medina, itself the largest oasis in the region. The second-largest oasis in the Hejaz is only ten square miles in area. Although malaria is endemic, the oases are valuable for their water supply and their ability to sustain substantial agriculture. Agriculture was probably introduced to the area sometime around the first century c.e., most probably by the Jewish tribes. The origins of the Jewish tribes in the Hejaz are obscure. One possibility is that the Jews that settled there were refugees from Roman suppression of the Bar Kokhba Revolt in Israel in the early 130s c.e. or from the prior Jewish War. Another is that the Jews migrated from Yemen after the destruction of the great dam at Marib about a hundred years later. By Muhammad's time the Jewish tribes of the area were indistinguishable from the Arab tribes in structure, ethos, and behavior. Only their religious observance distinguished them from other Arab clans.

Barley and millet were the major grain crops grown in the oases and were used to make small breadlike cakes for human consumption. Among the animals only horses were sometimes fed on grain as a supplement to their grazing. Grapes were introduced sometime during the fourth century c.e.; the olive tree was unknown. The Jews and Nabataeans were likely responsible for the importation of fruit trees to the area, and apples, oranges, lemons, watermelons, pomegranates, and bananas were cultivated.[8] The most important of all Arabian crops was the date palm. It is likely that the date palm was introduced from Mesopotamia during very ancient times. The fruit of the date palm (tamr), together with the milk of camels and goats, is the chief food of the bedouin. The date is often mixed with flour or roasted barley or millet and washed down with milk or water. It is the wish of every bedouin to have "the two black ones," that is, plenty of dates to eat and water or camel milk to drink. Except for the flesh of a camel slaughtered for food when its useful life was at an end, the date fruit was the bedouin's only solid food.[9] Muhammad took note of the importance of the date to the Arab way of life when he said, "Honor your aunt, the palm, which is made of the same clay as Adam."[10]

In the harsh land of the Hejaz only the bedouin was truly at home. Those who lived in the oases or the few towns often had to hire bedouin guides to travel from one place to another or hire them as personal and caravan guards to ensure a safe journey. The heat, trackless roads, lack of food, scarcity of water, and the general discomfort of life in the desert, while problematic during times of peace, became the allies of the bedouin in times of war. His daily ration of dates and water would bring any other army to its knees in a few days; but the bedouin could subsist on this diet forever. Living on dates, water, and the very camels that carried them, Arab armies were far more mobile than those of their adversaries. During the first battles of the Arab conquests Arab armies chose battlefields that were close to the desert so that in the event of a defeat they could retreat into the desert where the enemy could not follow. Perhaps it was this capability that King Faisal of Saudi Arabia had in mind when he responded to Secretary of State Henry Kissinger's threat that the U.S. Army might be forced to seize the Saudi oil fields if the Saudis did not bring down the price of OPEC oil to ease the energy crisis of 1973. Confronted with Kissinger's threat, Faisal is said to have smiled and replied, "We are Arabs. We will return to the desert and live on camel milk and dates . . . and fight you from there forever."

The Arabs of Muhammad's day wore clothing that was well suited to the harsh Arabian environment. Men wore a long shirt called a *thawb* tied with a belt around the waist. A long flowing robelike garment that reached almost to the ground called an *'aba* was worn over the thawb. The head was covered with a kind of shawl called a *kufiyah* held in place with a cord or *iqal*. Trousers were not usually worn, and most people went barefoot, although the later use of stirrups may have required sandals or some other form of footwear when riding. Arab clothing made an ideal military uniform given the climatic conditions. The loose-fitting garments provided adequate protection against the sun and helped to hold in the body's moisture. Tents and blankets made of goat's or camel's hair afforded excellent protection against the cold of the desert night. The military kit of the Arab made it possible for Arab armies to move unencumbered by heavy baggage trains and gave the armies of the later Arab conquests a mobility, speed, and range unmatched by their enemies.

The bedouin nomads of the Hejaz moved with their flocks on a regular basis searching for pasture and water for their animals. These

Arab nomads usually practiced a form of enclosed nomadism, that is, movement in a regular pattern that brought them close to settlements and towns where they could trade or purchase goods with the few meager resources that they possessed. The relationship between nomads and the settled populations was genuinely symbiotic in that neither could survive without the products of the other. The grain and dates that were staples of the nomads' diets were obtained in the oases where they grew; saddles, weapons, cloth, and other goods were manufactured in the towns. In return the nomad provided the town dweller with goats, sheep, and camels as well as the materials from which tents and blankets might be woven. Most bedouins were desperately poor and were almost always on the brink of malnutrition. Among bedouins in times of drought or starvation, it was a not uncommon practice to bury their female babies alive in order to free up resources for the surviving adults and male infants. Moreover, spending long days watching animals graze made for stultifying boredom. It is not surprising that the *ghazw*, or raid, became a way of bedouin life.

Raiding the camps and flocks of other bedouin or the outskirts of the towns where the horses and camels were usually set to grazing served two important functions. First, it provided a needed form of social stimulation, the only way in which the bedouin could practice the manly virtues of the warrior. For the most part these raids were more a rough sport than real conflicts. Pitched battles were usually avoided and casualties few. Raids sometimes resulted in individual combats between chiefs, but even these rarely resulted in death. The object of a raid, after all, was to steal the flocks. The second function of the raid was to act as a form of redistributing the wealth, a means of obtaining goods that would otherwise be unattainable by some bedouin families. In a poor country like Arabia where malnutrition was endemic, raiding was often the only way a man could improve his lot in life. Finally, the competition for water and grazing often led to skirmishes between bedouin clans. In difficult climatic times these skirmishes could become very intense since to be defeated meant to be driven from the water and grass and risked the destruction of the flocks. Still, it is hard to escape the impression that raiding was more a social enterprise than either a military or an economic one. Arabs often explain raiding in the following terms. "Our business is to make raids on the enemy, on our neighbor, and on our brother, in case we find nobody to raid but our brother."[11]

The basis of bedouin society was the clan. Every tent represented a family; an encampment of tents was a ÿay. The members of an hayy made up a *qawm*, or clan. A number of clans related by blood and kin formed a *qabilah*, or tribe. All members of the same clan considered themselves as of one blood and submitted to the authority of a single chief called a sheikh, whose power to command was limited by the fact that all males in the tribe were considered equals who might reasonably disagree and even resist the sheikh in important matters. As an old Arab proverb put it, "A man's clan are his claws." Loyalty to one's clan was unconditional. Anyone committing a crime inside the clan was either banished or killed by the clan members themselves. The murder of a clan member by someone outside the clan required all males to avenge the crime in any manner possible, the usual rules of chivalry and combat being ignored in favor of treachery and ambush. This was the *asabiyah*, or blood loyalty, that rendered anyone outside the clan devoid of any moral standing that might place limits on revenge. During Muhammad's day the clan was the center of the Arab's moral universe. Only members of the clan had any claim to ethical treatment, and even this bound only fellow members of the clan. Those outside the clan lacked any moral standing and were treated accordingly.

The Arabs of Muhammad's time lived in a harsh society in a harsh land. There were few laws and no institutions to afford justice or restrain violence. Only the blood feud and its threat of retaliation against a wrongdoer provided a rough balance of power to limit violence. Blood feuds were not to be taken lightly since the feud did not end until the wrongdoer was dead or some member of his tribe had been killed as compensation. Later, it became a common practice to limit the feud by paying the blood-wit (*diya*), financial compensation usually in the form of a number of camels, to the person or clan against whom the wrong had been committed. This aside, anyone outside the clan remained without moral standing. When Muhammad divided the ethical world between believers and unbelievers in which the latter might rightly be enslaved or even killed by the former, he was only extending the morality of the blood feud to religion. The religious community of believers to which absolute loyalty was owed and outside of which there were no obligations simply replaced the old clan community of blood and kin.

2

THE STRATEGIC SETTING

Luck and timing often determine the success or failure of great causes. So it seems to have been in the case of Muhammad and the new religion of Islam. The initial success and survival of both depended on a favorable array of strategic circumstances that occurred far from Mecca and Medina and were quite beyond the control of Muhammad himself. Muhammad (570–632 C.E.) lived when political and social circumstances inside and outside Arabia were creating a dynamic that favored the religious and military success of Islam. It is pointless to question whether success would have been possible under another set of counterfactual circumstances. What is important is to understand the circumstances within the Arabian strategic environment that influenced the outcome of Muhammad's life and how these circumstances contributed to his military success and the establishment of Islam.

Much is sometimes made of the isolation enforced by Arabia's deserts and the remoteness of places like Mecca and Medina. Such portrayals are accurate only in a geographic sense. In the broader social and political sense, however, Arabia during Muhammad's day was not isolated from the geopolitical and strategic forces that were influencing the great Byzantine and Persian Empires that bordered Arabia. By the time of Muhammad's birth, Arabia was being strongly influenced by and entangled in Byzantine and Persian politics. The Arabian merchant class enjoyed frequent contact with both empires and had visited the towns and courts of the great powers in pursuit of their economic interests. The caravans that left Mecca for Damascus or Aila on the Gulf of Aqaba, the latter ultimately bound for Gaza and Egypt, or traveled northeast across the desert to Hira in Iraq and the towns along the Persian Gulf brought the traders of Mecca into direct contact with the Byzantine and Persian officials. Mecca sent at least two large caravans a year to the imperial markets, and many smaller ones traveled there more frequently. Imperial influences in the form of religious and political ideas were everywhere in evidence in Arabian trading towns during Muhammad's lifetime. There is no reason to assume that Muhammad was any less aware of them than were other members of the merchant class to which he came to belong. Even the idea that a new prophet was about to appear somewhere in Arabia was perpetrated by various Christian sects in both the Byzantine and Persian Empires. The native Arabian religion of the day consisted mostly of idol worship, and it is likely although not certain that one of the idols, Hubal, worshipped for at least a century at the sacred *ka'ba* (Kaaba) in Mecca before Muhammad was born, had been purchased by Meccan merchants and brought to the city by an Arab caravan returning from Nabataea, where the idol was widely worshipped.[1]

The Arabian merchant class was also aware of the interests and machinations of the imperial powers as they pertained to Arabia. Both security and economic concerns compelled the imperial powers to look to their interests there. The farms and towns of both empires bordering Arabia had long been raided by bedouin tribesmen who struck quickly and retreated into the desert wastes where neither Persian nor Byzantine troops could follow. Both powers were deeply involved in the tribal politics of their respective border zones in the search for reliable Arab allies that could be used to patrol and defend the imperial borders against these desert raiders. Imperial ambitions ran further than border security, however. Persia had frequently encouraged the pretensions of some Arab tribes deep in the interior as a way of increasing its own influence in the rich spice trade. Persian ambitions were mostly focused in the south, in Yemen, where Persia sponsored unrest aimed at establishing a friendly regime there. The Byzantines countered these ambitions by using Abyssinia as a strategic platform from which to launch allied armies into Arabia to counter Persian influence.

With Byzantine support an Abyssinian army invaded Arabia and attacked Mecca in 570 c.e., the year of Muhammad's birth. This event was recorded in Arab memory as "The Year of the Elephant." No Meccan had ever seen an elephant, and the appearance of one at the head of an invading army stunned the Meccans. There was no Meccan force capable of resistance, and defeat seemed certain. What happened next is unclear. Arab texts tell the tale of a great flock of birds that blackened the sky flying over the enemy dropping stones in their faces as the soldiers looked up. These pebbles struck with such force as to leave pockmarks. Wounded and bleeding, the Abyssinian army withdrew and Mecca was saved.[2] Instead of a miracle, it is more likely that the invaders suffered an outbreak of disease, perhaps smallpox, that devastated the Abyssinian army and forced it to withdraw.

The central players in the great game of power politics in Arabia and elsewhere at the beginning of the seventh century c.e. were the Byzantine and Persian Empires. For more than five hundred years these two powerful states shared a common border creating problems of imperial security that were mirror images of one another. An increase in the strength of one was necessarily perceived as a threat to the other, and one's weakness often proved an irresistible temptation to the predations of the other. This proximity produced continuous political, commercial, and military rivalry that resulted in wars and military clashes of considerable magnitude. Despite more than a half millennium of rivalry and war, the frontier between the two great powers had remained almost unchanged, neither side gaining more than a short-term tactical advantage for its efforts.

The collapse of the Roman Empire in the West at the hands of barbarian invaders had resulted in the loss of imperial control in the western provinces of Italy, Gaul, Spain, Britain, and much of what is now eastern Europe to. The center of imperial government shifted to the eastern Roman capital of Constantinople. Despite the devastating blow to the western empire, Rome lived on at Constantinople for another thousand years until it finally met its end by military defeat at the hands of the Ottomans in 1453.[3] At the time of Muhammad's birth the Eastern Roman Empire was still a great power comprising Greece, Asia Minor, Syria, and Egypt. It included substantial territory along the North African littoral as well. These provinces formed a continuous defensive arc bordering the eastern Mediterranean Sea, which was controlled by the Byzantine navy. Directly to the south lay

the desert of Arabia. The border raids to which the southern frontier had
been subjected for centuries were more of a nuisance than a strategic
threat. The most serious threat to Byzantine security came from whence
it had always come, from Persia to the east.

The loss of the Roman West paralyzed the emperors of Constantinople into inaction for more than fifty years during which no substantive attempt was made to reestablish Roman control over the lost
provinces. When Emperor Justinian (527–565 C.E.) rose to the purple he
set about changing Roman policy and undertook a military campaign to
recover the western lands. Led by the great field commander Belisarius,
the eastern Romans managed to reestablish control over large tracts of
North Africa and parts of Italy. The difficulty was that the balance of
military power on the Perso-Roman frontier had always been precarious
at best, the advantage of manpower and internal lines resting usually
with the Persians. To wage his campaign in the West Justinian had to
strip the Persian border defenses of much of their manpower and
resources leaving the border open to Persian attack. The temptation
proved too much for the Persians, and a series of large-scale military
clashes took place along the border. Justinian, always the strategic
realist, recognized the danger of a Persian invasion and moved to forestall it through negotiation and concession. He negotiated a peace
with the Persians to remove the invasion threat. While there is no
doubt that the treaty was seen as temporary by both sides, the Romans
surrendered some border towns and lands and promised to make
financial payments to keep the Persians at bay. In exchange, the Persian
armies stood down.

The Persian Empire was enormous, stretching from Afghanistan to
the Oxus River to the far reaches of the modern region of Kurdistan. It
was governed by a Sassanid dynasty whose capital lay at the narrowing
of the Rivers Tigris and Euphrates at Ctesiphon, south of modern Baghdad. Constantinople's uneasy peace with Persia held until Justinian's
death in 565. The empire then fell into a period of crisis brought on
by a series of weak rulers that led to a military revolt in 602 that
produced more confusion and weakness. The Persian emperor, Chosroes
II, had never taken his eyes off the rich Roman cities, and in that same
year he launched an invasion of the Roman territories. In 613 Persian
armies captured Damascus, and a year later Jerusalem fell. The True
Cross, Christendom's holiest relic, was carried off by the Persians,
themselves Nestorian Christians. In 616 Persian armies occupied

Egypt and substantial parts of Asia Minor. The Byzantine Empire seemed on the verge of collapse and occupation, unable to reverse its military defeats.

This serious set of circumstances caused elements of the Roman army in the East to rebel against the capital's corrupt rulers, a rebellion that proved ultimately to be Rome's salvation. One of the leaders of the rebellion, Heraclius (575–641 C.E.), would become one of the empire's greatest emperors. Heraclius had deposed the Byzantine emperor, Phocas, and assumed power in 610. By now almost all of the eastern provinces were in Persian hands. Heraclius set out to recapture the occupied lands and destroy the Persian armies. In four major battles—Issus (622), the Halys River (623), the River Sarus (625), and Nineveh (627)—Heraclius cut off the Persian armies, invaded Persia itself, and destroyed what was left of Persian military might, a series of defeats that ended the war.[4] In 628 Chosroes was assassinated and the Persian Empire collapsed into anarchy and dynastic struggle. Chosroes's successor, Kavadh II, made peace with the Romans. The war had gone on for twenty-six years and exhausted both imperial powers. The boundaries agreed to in the peace treaty were essentially the same as had separated the two powers before the war began.

The exhaustion of the major powers coincided with the period in which Muhammad undertook his insurgency. The significance of this coincidence lies in the limitations the weakness of the imperial powers placed on their ability to influence events in neighboring Arabia. Both powers had pursued their interests in Arabia for centuries. At times these efforts were pursued by proxy wars using rival coalitions of Arab tribes; at other times, by outright invasion. By the time Muhammad began his insurgency, all these efforts had come to nothing. The ability of the great powers themselves and what few of their proxies remained to influence events in Arabia was seriously diminished. The important consequence was that there was no one in a position to oppose Muhammad's insurgency.

The ties between the great powers and their proxies were strongly rooted in religious affiliation. This was especially so within the Byzantine realm where the Orthodox faith was the official religion of the state and where persecution of heretical Christian sects had reached alarming proportions. The Persians had adopted Nestorian Christianity after it had been declared a heresy by Byzantine emperors, and its persecuted adherents had taken refuge in Persia. Syrians, Palestinians,

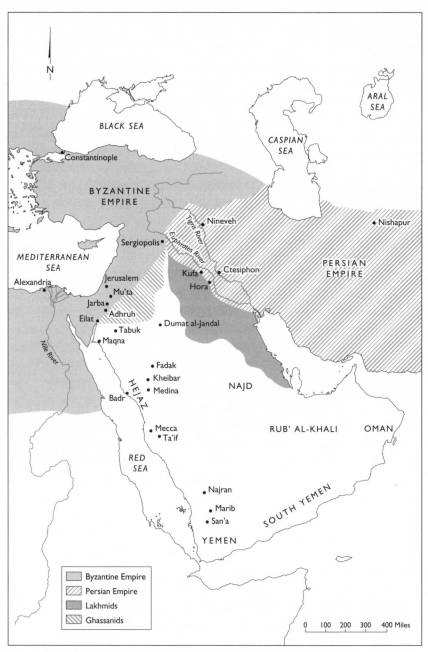

Map 3. Strategic Setting during Muhammad's Life, 570–632 C.E.

and Egyptians were mostly Monophysite Christians, another sect considered heretical by the Byzantine rulers. All these sects were associated in one way or another with imperial ambitions. Christianity had made some limited inroads in Arabia, the tribal clans often adopting the creed of their imperial allies. By Muhammad's time the weakness of the imperial powers had also loosened their ties with their respective Arab allies with the result that whatever religious influence had once been present was almost completely lost as the tribes reverted to their traditional idol worship. Without imperial support none of Christian sects or their allies in Arabia had the power or inclination to see Muhammad's religious movement as another dangerous heretical sect that had to be suppressed. There was no organized *religious* opposition from anywhere in Arabia to Muhammad's new creed. Had Muhammad attempted to establish Islam within the borders of either imperial realm, he would have encountered strong opposition from the sacerdotal classes and their allies that might have resulted in the suppression of the new religion and the execution or imprisonment of its messianic leader.

Arab allies were an important element in the strategy of the great powers to protect their borders from bedouin raids. Both empires created strong coalitions of Arab tribes led by powerful chiefs to protect the imperial borders. These chiefs were paid and given lavish gifts and official titles to increase their standing with their clan chiefs who, in turn, depended on them for the patronage required to keep their own clans loyal. Had the imperial powers been able or inclined to oppose Muhammad as a threat to Christianity, they could have used these tribal allies to do so. Many of the Arab allies had become Christians themselves and could have been employed to crush Muhammad and his insurgency on the grounds of heresy. They might have done so with comparative ease.

The Arab Beni Ghassan family, or Ghassanids, served in the pay of the Romans to protect the southern border of Syria and Jordan from the bedouins. The Ghassanids were Monophysites, a fact conveniently ignored by the Orthodox rulers of Constantinople who required their services as border guards. To the east the Persians pursued the same policy of hiring Arab allies to protect their border with Arabia. The Nestorian Christian Lakhmid tribes were Persian allies. So long as these tribal coalitions remained loyal to their respective clients, the desert frontiers were relatively safe from Arab raiders. These loyal Arab tribes were also the first line of *strategic* defense against any large-scale invasion attempted from the desert, an invasion that Muslim armies successfully carried out shortly after Muhammad's death. These imperial alliances with the Arab tribal coalitions had been the successful basis of imperial border defense for more than a hundred years before Muhammad's birth.

For reasons that are unclear, both great powers committed the same strategic mistake that resulted in each exposing their desert flanks to the same invader. In 581 the chief of the Ghassanids was arrested and imprisoned as a Monophysite heretic. This resulted in an open revolt by the Ghassanids who now became raiders themselves. In 605 the Persian emperor quarreled with the chief of the Lakhmids and rescinded the chief's payments, position, and privileges. The Lakhmids went over to revolt and began sacking the towns along the Persian-Arabian border. The consequence of these short-sighted actions was to strip the imperial borders of both great powers of their respective protective military forces and expose them to Arab attack.

The strategic danger was not immediately obvious, however. Muhammad was in the midst of his insurgency, and Islam was still in its infancy. There was as yet no Arab army capable of attacking the great powers. For the foreseeable future the problem of border security remained one of defending against small-scale, sporadic bedouin raids. By the time of Muhammad's death in 632, however, the strategic situation had changed considerably. One of Muhammad's greatest legacies was a large, trained, and well-led military force motivated by religious zeal and ready to exploit the only source of pillage and loot available to Arabs whose new religion forbade attacks on one another. Islam's armies were ready to reach beyond the borders of Arabia, bringing the new Islamic faith to the East and West in their wake. Exhausted and bankrupt by years of pointless warfare, the Persians and Byzantines found themselves suddenly confronted with a grave military threat from Arabia itself.

It was these circumstances of the larger strategic, religious, and social situation that formed the backdrop for Muhammad's life and prophethood and increased his prospects for success. The movement toward Christian monotheism within the Byzantine and Persian Empires had penetrated Arabia long before Muhammad was born. The idea of a single God and even the coming of a new prophet were widely held at the time of Muhammad's insurgency. The religious persecution fiercely practiced by the Byzantines but less so by Persians against so-called heretical sects, and sometimes against their own Arab allies, made it impossible for the great powers to project force against the new creed of Islam, thus permitting Muhammad a free hand to begin his insurgency and establish the new religion free from outside interference. At the same time regular commercial contacts between Arab merchants and imperial markets spread tales of the great wealth of the two empires making the towns and cities of the empires tempting targets for looting when the time was right. The traditional raids against fellow Arabs that had provided Arabs with loot and stimulation for centuries were now forbidden by the Islamic creed. United, the Arab armies turned outward against the Byzantines and Persians for new outlets for the manly practice of war and needed sources of booty.

The armies of Islam attacked the border provinces of the Byzantine Empire in the winter of 633–634. Three columns staging from Medina invaded Palestine and Syria, taking the small Byzantine border garrisons by surprise and overrunning them. At the same time another Arab army struck at Damascus. A Byzantine relief force coming to the aid of the city was engaged and forced to withdraw. All Palestine was left defenseless to Arab raids, and a year later Damascus fell to the Arabs. To the east, in Iraq, the Lakhmid tribes moved up the River Euphrates and seized the important commercial town of Hira. On August 26, 636, the last remaining Byzantine force in Syria suffered a crushing defeat on the banks of the Yarmuk River, and all Syria to the Taurus Mountains fell to the Arab invaders. Two years after the battle of the Yarmuk River, Jerusalem and Caesarea surrendered to the Arabs. In 640 Arab armies attacked Egypt and defeated the Byzantines again. By September 642 the occupation of Egypt was complete. By 646 the last vestiges of Byzantine rule in what had been Roman Mesopotamia were eradicated, destroying the unity of the ancient Mediterranean world forever.

To the east a series of Arab victories spelled the end of the Persian Sassanid Empire. The Persians were brought under attack in 634, and within three years Arab armies had pushed to the edge of Iraq. The Persians withdrew beyond the Zagros Mountains leaving the door open to Iraq. A year later, in February 637, a large Persian army was destroyed south of Hira at Qadasiya. Within a few months all of Iraq had fallen to the Arabs including the imperial capital at Ctesiphon. In

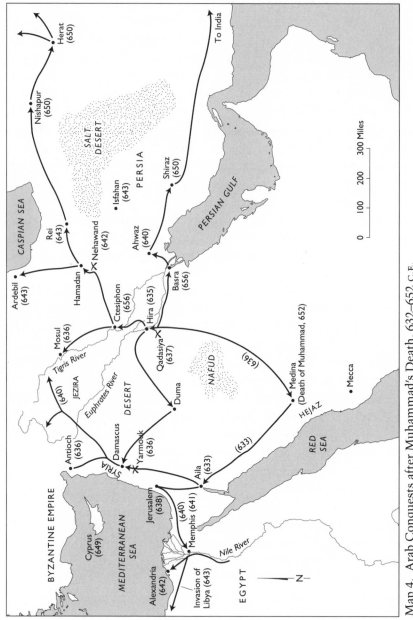

Map 4. Arab Conquests after Muhammad's Death, 632–652 C.E.

that same year a Persian army was destroyed at Nehawand. By 642 a new Arab advance across the River Tigris was under way, and within eight years all of Persia was under Arab rule. The Arab armies prepared to push farther east across the Oxus River, reaching ultimately to India. Far to the west, Alexandria in Egypt became a major Arab naval base, extending the influence of Islam to the Mediterranean Sea. In 661 with the rise of the Umayyads the Arab assault turned west again, occupying Tunisia and the coast of Morocco. At the end of the seventh century Arab armies crossed into Spain. In less than forty years Arab armies had grown from little more than tribal coalitions to masters of an extensive empire.

Within Arabia itself the traditional religion of idol worship had never produced a sacerdotal class and state institutions that might have defended the old religion against the challenge of Islam. Had there been some form of religious institutional resistance as was faced by the heretical Christian sects of the imperial realms, often with murderous consequences, it is unlikely that Islam would have succeeded as readily as it did within Arabia. The inability of religious sects outside Arabia to project their influence and oppose Muhammad further facilitated the success of Islam. Other circumstances contributed as well. The social unrest within Medina provided the opportunity for Muhammad to move there and quickly become an influential figure, something that would never have happened in the normal course of tribal custom had the weariness and fear of continual warfare not been so overpowering in the city at that time. Muhammad preached the need for a new community, the *ummah*, at a time in Arabian history when the system of tribal obligations and protection was breaking down. The wealth and economic competition of the rising mercantile society were eroding the traditional bases of social status and obligation. It was no accident that many of Muhammad's early followers were those who had been dispossessed or oppressed by the new conditions.

The emphasis placed here on the larger forces shaping Arabia at the time of Muhammad's insurgency ought not to be taken to suggest that Muhammad's success was inevitable or that anyone but Muhammad could have achieved it. Nothing in this analysis detracts from Muhammad's brilliance in recognizing these forces and using them to his advantage. The ultimate compliment to be paid to the successful revolutionary is that he was able to recognize the tide of history building to its crest and ride that wave until it carried him and his cause to victory.

As the following analysis will demonstrate, Muhammad was no "accidental" prophet. He was a brilliant revolutionary fighter who understood the nature of the environment in which he fought and used it to his advantage at every turn.

3

ARAB WARFARE

The conduct of war usually reflects a society's values at least as much as the capabilities of its military technologies. History is full of examples where the killing power of weaponry has been either limited or has permitted its full range of lethality depending on what values the society used to guide its conduct of war. The armies of ancient India were governed by scores of specific rules forbidding the killing of prisoners and requiring humane treatment of civilians that served to limit the brutality of war.[1] The Japanese ordered the firearms imported by the Jesuits destroyed and forbade the manufacture of guns to preserve the traditional role of the *bushi* warrior in war.[2] The Swiss armies of the fourteenth century, on the other hand, made it a common practice to take no prisoners, killing even the wounded—practices that convinced the pope to hire Swiss mercenaries as his personal bodyguard.[3] The Israelite armies of the Old Testament were instructed to "leave nothing that breathes alive" in their attacks on the settlements of Canaan.[4] It is often a society's values more than its killing technologies per se that govern its conduct of war.

THE MORAL BASIS OF ARAB WARFARE

This was no less true of the Arab society into which Muhammad was born. Being a brave warrior had always been a central virtue in the

Arabs' idea of what constituted a good man. This warrior ethos was expressed in the Arabic terms *muruah* and *ird*. Ird is understood as honor, and honor was closely tied to the obligations to avenge any wrong done to a man personally, to any others to whom he had extended his protection, or to his clan. Muruah literally means virility or manhood. While hospitality, generosity, and protection of the weak were all important Arab virtues as well, no virtue was held in higher regard than a man's courage in war.[5]

An Arab injured or insulted was not expected to forgo revenge but to extract either blood or compensatory payment. Failure to do so exposed him to charges of weakness, contempt, and dishonor, perceptions that exposed him to further insult and attack. The notion that one ought to forgo revenge or that revenge itself is unethical per se is an idea that comes mostly from Christianity. The Arab view of revenge was more like that of the ancient Greeks for whom it was the duty of a good man "to be sweet to friends and bitter to enemies; honorable to the first and terrible to the latter."[6] One's honor backed by the readiness to resort to individual combat in its defense or to redress a wrong was the central military virtue of Arab men. Every male was given military training in weapons and combat from an early age and instructed in the moral code of the warrior. This code of military prowess in defense of a warrior's honor was passed to the West during the Arab wars with the Franks and later became part of the chivalric code of the medieval knight.[7]

The Arab emphasis on warrior virtues sometimes led to the misperception that Arabia was a bloodthirsty land where war and conflict were endemic, and that the brutality sometimes shown by the armies of the Arab conquests was but a natural extension of these violent conditions. This is an erroneous view, probably the result of Western propaganda generated by almost four hundred years of war during which Western armies fought the armies of Islam. Any reasonable examination of the conduct of Western and Arab armies during the Crusades would likely conclude that the brutality of the Western armies was by any measure at least equal to that of their Arab adversaries and, perhaps, even more brutal. Richard the Lion Hearted, to take but one example, routinely slaughtered Muslim prisoners, women, and children, and had the unnerving habit of riding around with the decaying severed heads of Arab victims tied to his saddle. Saladin, the great Muslim general, was appalled at the behavior of the Christian knights after Richard killed twenty-two hundred Muslim prisoners at Acre.[8] The truth is that Arabia before Muhammad's time was a land neither torn by warfare nor populated by warriors accustomed to killing one another on the slightest pretext.

The Arab warrior's courage and honor were most commonly demonstrated by his performance in the ghazw, or raid, in which a group of bedouins would attack another clan to steal their flocks, camels, or women. This was not "war" in any real sense of the word since the object of the raid was to steal and not kill. The raid usually ended quickly enough once the alarm was sounded and the warriors rushed to protect their flocks. Often the two sides would merely shout obscenities at one another. Given the distances over which Arab bedouins roamed, these raids were usually infrequent, involved only a few men on each side, and the shedding of blood, to say nothing of actual killing, was rare. Given the terrain of the desert and the general scarcity of goods to be had by even a successful raid, these Arab "wars" were more entertainment and rough sport than genuine combat. They were not unlike the "wars" fought among Native American tribes in which the idea was to steal the enemy's horses, goods, and women.

In those instances where Arab clans actually fought one another in some numbers, neither the term "war" nor "army" would be appropriate. If by armies one means some form of standing organization with a formal command structure that fought as a unit and was capable of tactical application, there were no armies as such. Arab "armies" were collections of individual warriors fighting for their own honor and opportunity to acquire loot. In this regard they were not unlike the gatherings of warrior knights that comprised the armies of medieval Europe. Arab clan battles were usually fought on some agreed-upon ground. Both sides formed up on the open field. Rival champions sallied forth and challenged the champions of the other side to individual combat. Often the death of a chief or even a few lesser men was sufficient to call off the fight, with the side suffering the casualties withdrawing from the field without being pursued. The formal nature of Arab battles was also evident in the practice of taking the clan women along to play instruments and sing songs encouraging their men to fight. Occasionally, of course, things got out of hand and a general melee might result that lasted until one side had had enough and withdrew. In most cases, however, casualties were likely to be light.

The Arab "wars" of the pre-Islamic period seldom lasted long and were never fought for what we would call today strategic objectives, such as the enslavement or destruction of a rival tribe or the occupation of their lands, which, in any case, would have been meaningless in a nomadic society where the value of the land shifted with the climate. Arab wars were primitive by the standards of warfare practiced at the time by almost any society outside Arabia itself, and were so in terms of scale, tactics, logistics, and level of casualties. These "battles" were tactical engagements only. There were no larger purposes to war other than to demonstrate honor and courage. No attempt was made to achieve strategic victory. Arab wars of the pre-Islamic period were highly ritualized and symbolic affairs and lacked any ideological, religious, ethnic, or strategic dimension.

The Arab reputation for bloody warfare even in the pre-Islamic period stems from the confusion of Arab warfare per se with the conduct associated with and morally permitted when two clans engaged in a blood feud. A person killed or done serious harm or insult by a member of another clan had to be avenged by a member of the tribe to which the harm was done. It must be remembered that in Arabia before Muhammad there were no state or civic institutions, law, police forces, or courts to protect the weak or render justice for harm suffered. The Arab relied solely on his kin, clan, and tribe to protect him; thus, the old Arab proverb that "a man's clan are his claws." The clans were democratic in that all members were equally part of the clan and enjoyed its protection. The strong protected the weak, and once separated from the clan or tribe the individual was at great risk indeed. If the blood feud did not exist, there would have been no social mechanism to bring even a rough justice to the Arabs' world. The weak or helpless would have been easily killed or enslaved. The blood feud acted as a check against this behavior by entitling any kin or clan member of the victim to strike down the killer or any member of the killer's family. The blood feud ended when the victim's family agreed to accept financial compensation for its loss, often a number of camels or other goods. If no agreement could be concluded, the feud went on if need be until the perpetrator himself was killed. In this way a rough justice was brought to Arab conflicts in the absence of any other social institution to protect the weak. The blood feud was a deadly serious affair. It put everyone on both sides at risk, and could go on for a very long time, sometimes even generations. One had to think long and hard before killing a man since the consequences could be deadly for everyone involved.

In Arab warfare other than the blood feud, then, there were rules of chivalry in which one's opponent possessed equal moral standing and worth. A warrior did not slay the wounded or kill cruelly or unnecessarily. The long Arab tradition of ransoming prisoners also limited the killing as the victorious warrior had much to gain by treating the wounded well and keeping them alive to be sold back for ransom. The result of these values was that Arab warfare in the pre-Islamic era was limited in scope, scale, frequency, and brutality. The blood feud, by contrast, knew no such rules or limitations. No restrictions were placed on how and when a man might be killed—in his sleep, by treachery, poison, or betrayal. In a blood feud no moral standing was granted one's enemy, and torture, cruelty, and brutality were often inflicted. Even under these conditions the blood feud was aimed at the individual wrongdoer. There was no thought of attempting to kill the whole clan or even large segments of it, an attempt that would certainly have created a new blood feud with the former victims and aggressors trading places. The blood feud aimed at the proportional response of "an eye for an eye," and not at a disproportionate response to a wrong.

Had the moral basis of Arab warfare remained unchanged, it is unlikely that Arabia would ever have produced the large, disciplined, and highly motivated armies that it did in the Islamic era with the consequence that the Muslim conquest of much of the ancient world would probably never have occurred. It was Muhammad who changed the traditional moral basis of Arab warfare, removing the traditional restraints on killing and bringing to Arabia a truly modern method and moral perception of war.

Unlike the old clan warriors, Muslim warriors were not primarily motivated by clan rivalries or the desire for loot, although both surely played a role. Muhammad's objective was to destroy the old Arab social order based on clan and kin and replace it with a new type of society, the ummah, made up of a community of believers. The model for the new community was not the clan per se, but the clan *as it operated when engaged in a blood feud.* Any rules of ethical behavior applied only to the community of believers; those outside the ummah were held to possess no moral standing and could be killed or enslaved without moral consequences. In the community of believers Muslim warriors fought because God had commanded them to do so or had delegated them to fight and destroy His enemies. Whereas the blood feud had proposed a life taken for a life lost, Muhammad redefined moral killing as a life taken for political purposes. The idea of exterminating an entire town or a tribe was beyond the imagination of those engaged in a blood feud. Under Muhammad it became a common practice. Even murder became acceptable under the new rules, providing the victim was either a nonbeliever or an enemy of the faith. Murder had, of course, occurred in Arabia before Muhammad, but not for ideological, religious, or other reasons of state; in short, assassination and massacre were not the usual tools of Arab political conflict. The difference between the traditional Arab view of killing and the new Islamic view is clear insofar as in all the accounts of the Prophet's life there is no mention of anyone else besides Muhammad sending someone to murder anyone.[9] On the other hand, "Muhammad had at his disposal a number of fanatical young henchmen who were virtually prepared to strike down any opposition whenever necessary."[10]

The new moral basis of war led to a more violent form of warfare—political/ideological warfare—conducted on a larger scale with ever increasing casualties and consuming far more innocents than traditional Arab warfare had consumed. At times war attempted and achieved the wholesale destruction of rival clans and tribes, as when Muhammad destroyed one of the Jewish tribes of Medina to a man. It was Muhammad who introduced the connection between tactics and strategy to Arab warfare; that is, the connection between the use of violence as a means to the achievement of larger politico-religious objectives. Muhammad sought nothing less than the subordination of the traditional clan-based society that Arabs had known since time immemorial and its replacement by a new society based on religious belief in which the moral relationship of the individual to the tribe and clan was radically changed. These strategic objectives dictated the violent tactics used by Muhammad's insurgency and then adopted by Arab armies after his death.

Muhammad's adoption of the code of the blood feud as the basis of the new morality of war was a momentous decision that justified the use of violence against nonbelievers on a scale and frequency that had never before been seen in Arab warfare or social life. It also cast Islamic forces as inhumane in their conduct of war, something the enemies of Islam in the West were quick to capitalize on to portray Muslims as bloodthirsty barbarians.[11] But Muhammad's adoption of the code of the blood feud becomes understandable when we realize that he never saw himself as a conventional general commanding a conventional army. Muhammad was first and foremost a religious revolutionary, the commander of an insurgency that had yet to create a military force that could bring his new social order into being. The old rules of war had to be changed because they were ineffective in achieving the revolutionary goals that Muhammad had set for himself. If he was to achieve his end of creating a new society governed by new ethical precepts, then a new military mechanism was required, one that served his strategic ends by expanding its repertoire of military capabilities. This required a complete change in the traditional values that had governed Arab warfare.

Weapons and Equipment

The Arab society of Muhammad's day was a warrior society in which all males were armed and trained to fight. Weapons were highly valued, and soldiers took great pride in keeping their weapons in fighting condition. Clans that settled in towns and oases usually lived in fortified compounds within which the clan's arsenal of weapons was kept in the care of the clan chief. Often these arsenals were located in stone towers or brick keeps that also served as the last defensive position in the event of attack. Weapons were acquired either through local manufacture, taken as booty or tribute, or purchased. Prior to the rise of Islam, Syria and India were the most common external sources of Arab weaponry. Local manufacture was mostly confined to those weapons that required little technical skill to make, and included slings, hide shields, short spears, javelins, and the bow and arrow. Weapons that required metalworking to manufacture—swords, helmets, metal shields, lance and spear heads, and chain mail—were almost always imported. It was in the towns and settlements that the local armorers practiced their skills. Medina, for example, was famous for its arrows, and one of the Jewish tribes there specialized in the making of metal weapons.[12] Iron arrowheads were being manufactured in Arabia as early as Hellenistic times, and some bronze manufacture seems to have been used in swords as early as the first millennium B.C.E.[13] Metalworking in Arabia seems to have lagged considerably behind its development elsewhere, however. Locally manufactured steel weapons seem to have been completely absent during Muhammad's day. Only after the Arabs had conquered the Persian and Byzantine Empires, where steel weapons were in common use, did "Arab" weapons made of steel begin to become famous for their quality.[14]

The basic infantry weapons of the Arab warrior were the bow and arrow, sword, sling, and *harbah*, or thrown javelin, this latter probably introduced either by black mercenaries or slaves from Abyssinia.[15] The chief weapons of the cavalry were the sword and the long lance, or *rumh*, and the short, stabbing spear similar to the javelin carried by Alexander's cavalry. The stabbing spear was five cubits in length (a cubit is the length of a forearm), or about six feet long. The rumh was about eleven feet long.[16] The shafts of the cavalry lances are referred to in Arabic literature as *khatti*, named after the *al-Khatt*, the coast of *al-Bahrayn* where the bamboo was grown to make the shafts of the lance. By Muhammad's day most of the bamboo was imported from India, but the old source of the materials lingered in Arab memory.[17] Arab cavalry also carried the sword for close combat. Thus, "I thrust him with my spear, then came on top of him with a trenchant Indian blade," is an accurate description of a cavalryman in the attack.[18]

Examples of Arab bows that have survived indicate that some probably were recurved bows similar to those of Persian design. If this type of bow was typical, then it was probably manufactured outside of Arabia since there is very little wood of the kind required for this type of bow in Arabia. It would also have been very expensive. Along with the sword, the bow and arrow were the national weapons of Arabia, something we would not expect to find if the bow was of foreign manufacture and considerable expense. The simple bow, on the other hand, could easily have been made locally out of palm or acacia wood, varieties native to Arabia. The simple bow would have had a more limited range and less direct penetrating power than the recurved bow, but given the manner in which the Arabs employed the bow in battle, usually firing it in volleys and not at individual targets, the simple bow would have served adequately. After the Arab conquests the bow and the manner of its use in battle initially followed Byzantine practice. Over time, however, the Arabs adopted the Persian recurved bow and learned the skill of firing the bow from horseback.[19]

The Arab warrior's most prized possession was his sword. The sword was regarded as the most noble of the warrior's weapons, and prowess with it in hand-to-hand combat was the highest military skill. Because the sword was also used for slaughtering animals to host a dinner for valued guests, the weapon became associated with the other

Arab moral virtues of generosity and hospitality. Archaeological evidence suggests that the sword made its appearance sometime in the second millennium B.C.E. when it was a long, two-piece weapon (handle and blade were separate) fashioned of bronze. By the first millennium B.C.E. it had become a short straight sword of bronze cast in a single piece. By the Roman and Persian periods the typical Arab sword had become a long straight heavy weapon made of iron.[20] By Muhammad's day these clumsy weapons had given way to the Indian swords, the famous *hindi*, made of excellent steel and imported from India.[21] Indian swords were also called *Muhannad* and were distinguished from the *Mashrafiya* swords manufactured in Syria.[22] The Indian sword was about a meter in length and straight with a double edge. After the Arab conquests, the sword began to acquire a slight curve to become the curved scimitar, still in use today. This change in design probably occurred as a result of the influence of the horsemen of Central Asia who harassed the borders of the new empire. The Arab sword was carried in a scabbard slung over the right shoulder in the manner of a baldric.[23]

A poem describes the defensive armament of the Arab warrior in the following terms. "We wore helmets and Yemeni leather shields . . . and glittering coats of mail having visible folds about the belt."[24] The helmets were fabricated of hammered iron or cast bronze and were of either Byzantine or Persian design; they were no doubt imported. Metal helmets were very expensive and were affordable only by the wealthy. Those of lesser standing usually had only a thick cloth turban for head protection. Later it became the Arab habit to wrap a cloth turban around the metal helmet worn underneath. Muhammad himself always seems to have worn a helmet in battle. Shields were made mostly of leather stretched over a wooden frame and were carried by both infantry and cavalry. Poor soldiers often had shields made of camel leather. Arab shields were small, round, light, and easy to maneuver. In hand-to-hand combat they were used mostly to block and parry sword thrusts while the other arm wielded the sword.

The most important defensive equipment was the armor coat of chain mail made of individual metal rings set closely together and bound with nails so as to make the chain mail almost impenetrable to missile or assault. Arab mail coats were wide and loose fitting and often longer than those found on Byzantine or Persian soldiers. Later, when the horse became a basic instrument of Arab warfare, shorter mail coats were the style. The shorter coat made mounting and riding the animal easier. Chain mail was most effective against the Arab simple bow with arrows tipped with iron. The Byzantine or Persian compound or recurved bow firing steel-tipped arrows was far more powerful and much more likely to pierce chain armor. Arab armor was primarily effective against sword cuts and thrusts, thrown javelins, and glancing spear or lance thrusts, weaponry used most commonly in Arab wars until the time of Muhammad's death. Arab poets referred to a warrior's chain mail as "made of David's weave," a reference to a legend also found in the Quran that King David of Israel was once an armorer. A well-made coat of mail "will seem to shimmer and ripple like a silvery pool blown by the wind and glitter like lightning."[25]

TACTICS

The tactics of pre-Islamic armies were primitive at best. Each clan's warriors usually formed up opposite one another. Judging from the few reliable accounts of these engagements, there does not appear to have been any standard formation. One text describes the formation as "a compact array," but there is no evidence either of the tightly packed spear phalanx typical of armies in antiquity or of the open flexible sword infantry formation of the Romans. The long Arab sword would have made it difficult for any sword formation to be closely packed. Unlike the Roman *gladius*, which was shorter and wielded as a stabbing weapon—a design that permitted each Roman legionnaire to occupy five square meters of ground within the *quincunx* formation—the length of the Arab weapon and its employment as a slashing weapon would have required a much looser formation for it to be used effectively. Most likely, then, these early Arab infantry formations were open and loosely packed and permitted little tactical relationship between individual swordsmen. One text describes an infantry engagement: "When the ranks stand apart from us we thrust with spears, and we strike with swords when they are upon us."[26]

Arab battles began with each side sending forth its champions to fight with the best warriors of the other side. These champions were often chiefs or other high-ranking persons. Once a few of these warriors had been killed, wounded, or captured, it was not unusual for the "battle" to end and one side to withdraw. Other times one side sought to take advantage of its superior position and went over to the attack.

The result was a general melee among individual soldiers with nothing in the way of tactics evident.

Muhammad may have recognized the weakness of the traditional Arab infantry and organized his infantry differently. His armies fought in disciplined groups of sword infantry, perhaps organized around the clan or subclan or even individual family members.[27] This organization would have greatly increased unit cohesion, morale, and the general sense of sharing a common fate within the unit. The formation would also possess greater bulk, making it more difficult for the enemy to penetrate. Muhammad also formed up his infantry in ranks committing them on command in contrast to the general melee that was the usual Arab form of fighting. Muhammad's infantry became famous for its discipline and ability to outfight its enemies man for man. On more than one occasion Muhammad's infantry appeared defeated only to fall back, rally, and reenter the fight.

Cavalry was the combat arm of the wealthy town dwellers or bedouins because of the expense of purchasing and maintaining horses. Horses were so expensive and prized that warriors were loath to risk them in close combat, especially against archers who could easily kill or wound the animal with their arrows. There is little evidence of any tactical integration between cavalry and infantry until Muhammad attempted it with some success. The evidence from pre-Islamic accounts suggests that cavalrymen fought as individual champions rambling about the battlefield spearing or striking down soldiers who had become separated from their units rather than in units acting in concert. As with cavalry everywhere in the ancient world at this time, the lack of a proper high-backed saddle and stirrups made fighting from horseback difficult, especially with the lance whose impact with the victim could unseat the rider from his saddle. As far as we are able to determine, the stirrup did not become a standard piece of Arab military equipment until well after Muhammad's death. It was probably during the wars of the Arab conquests that the stirrup was adopted from the Persians. Even then Arab poets denigrated the stirrup as encouraging effeminacy in the soldier since it seemed to diminish the traditional Arab practice of mounting the horse from the back or side with a single bound![28] These conditions left the cavalry with little role to play on the battlefield so long as the infantry retained its cohesion. There are no Arab accounts of cavalry attacking a fixed infantry formation in the pre-Islamic period or even during Muhammad's lifetime. Cavalry could be used for reconnaissance, to attack stray soldiers, or in the pursuit once the opposing infantry had abandoned its formations and taken to rout, but for little else.

Every Arab warrior was skilled with the bow as well as the sword, and archers often played an important role in the battle. Archers sometimes acted as skirmishers deploying in front of the main battle line to shoot and harass the enemy before the main engagement began. Javelin throwers also performed as light infantry skirmishers. The more common role for archers was to protect against cavalry and to deny an axis of advance to the enemy. An Arab poem describes archery performing this tactical role: "now my horse darts forth for the lance-thrusting / now retreats to the great host of archers."[29] At the Battle of Uhud Muhammad positioned his archers on a hill controlling a critical axis of advance to his rear with the instructions that they were to use arrow fire to close off this avenue. The archers left their post to sack the Meccan camp, and the Meccan cavalry attacked along the open road taking Muhammad's army from the rear and almost killing Muhammad in the process. Probably the most valued quality of the bow, however, was that it was able to kill from a distance without much risk to its user.

Pre-Islamic armies were composed of clans and tribes, each of which fought under the command of its own leaders and flew its own banner. These banners were attached to a lance and carried by one of the clan's bravest warriors, a circumstance that made him a marked man on the battlefield! The clan and tribal organization continued under Muhammad, but in a much different manner. For the first time Muhammad's army had a single commander who could enforce his authority on his subordinate commanders. The old habits of clans refusing to meet the muster, deserting on the eve of battle, and even fleeing in battle at the order of their clan chief came to an end under Muhammad. Muhammad retained the old organizational form of the pre-Islamic army, however. Arab armies were divided into a center, two wings, a vanguard, and the rear guard. This organization was used by the Yemenis long before Muhammad's day and may be attributed to Persian influence. In Arabic this formation was known as *khamis*, or five.[30]

The following poem offers an account of a typical Arab fight between two clans. It also provides an accurate portrayal of some basic military practices other than warfare itself commonly used by Arab armies of the period.

We led the horses alongside (while riding our camels)
from the sand-hills of Ghamra and of Lubna . . .
Then when the hills of Qanan and Sara came into sight
and we were in the neighborhood of the highland to
the east of Salma,
We made the camels lie down and offered the horses the
remains which were in the water skins,
some drinking, others not at all
They were compelled to have the bit of the bridle
put into their mouth
(their necks outstretched) like a palm-trunk having its top
loped off,
And the grooms made the saddles firm; then they were
handed to the men armed for war, accustomed to making raids
in the morning.
Those on lookout do not see them till they are upon
them in a wadi bordered by acacia, into which
streams drain . . .
Our infantry shot from *maskikhi*-bows,
the best that can be bought in Yathrib . . .
When the supply of arrows in the quivers was exhausted,
they took to sword-play on shields
made from the hides of well-bred camels

Al-Tufayl 1[31]

Note, for example, that the horses are not ridden to the battlefield but are led tethered behind the camels, which are ridden. Note, too, that water is precious on campaign and it is offered to the horses first, showing the value placed by the Arabs on a good horse. The raid is carried out in the morning. The heat of the desert day often made traveling during daylight hours impossible. Arab raiders usually traveled by night, moving into position close to the enemy camp under cover of darkness and attacking just before sunrise. The raiders move into position along a wadi, a depressed dry streambed bordered by acacia trees, to hide their approach from the enemy. The bows come from Yathrib, the original name of Medina, famous for the manufacture of bows and arrows. The arrow fire is launched from a distance and in volleys in the hope that it will be sufficient to get the enemy to flee. Only when the "quivers were exhausted" did an attack with swords begin. In typical Arab fashion, the raid is about obtaining flocks or loot left behind by the fleeing enemy rather than about killing. Finally, camel hide was cheap and the raiders carried leather shields made from camel hide, indicating they were not wealthy. The claim that the leather shields were made from "the hides of well-bred camels" may be the poet's attempt to conceal the low status of the raiders.

MILITARY TRANSPORT

Camel

The camel and the horse were the two major means of military transport in Arabia, the camel being by far the more important. The camel was probably introduced from Arabia into the Middle East sometime around the second millennium B.C.E. There it was caught in the wild, domesticated into herds, and used primarily for food. By 1000 B.C.E. it was trained for use as a transport animal and beast of burden.[32] The animal was probably introduced to Palestine and Syria around the same time during the Midianite invasions of 1200–1100 B.C.E. The first recorded instance of the camel being used in war dates from this time. The Old Testament tells of Joshua's battle with the Amalekites at Rephidim. The Amalekites were nomads who rode the camel and attacked from camelback with bows and arrows. The biblical story of Gideon also tells of his battles against the Midianites and their camels when they invaded Israel during the Period of the Judges (1150–1050 B.C.E.).[33] The first instance of camels used in war recorded in an official document was in 825 B.C.E. when Gingibu the Arab is described in Assyrian records as providing one thousand camels and riders to the Assyrian army at the Battle of Karkar.[34]

Without the camel life in the desert would be impossible, for the camel nourishes the Arab in many ways. It is his primary means of transport, often where the horse and donkey cannot go, and his medium of exchange; wives and blood-wits are calculated in camels. The milk of the camel is the staple liquid food of the bedouin; the meat of the animal is consumed as well. One camel can provide meat for ninety to one hundred people.[35] Arab clothes were often made of camel hair, as were blankets and the all-important tents to shelter the bedouin from the heat and cold of the desert. The dung of the camel was a common fuel in a land where wood is scarce, and even its urine was used for medicine.[36] Little wonder that the Arabs came to call the camel "the gift from Allah."

The Arabian camel is a one-humped dromedary, not to be confused with the two humped Bactrian camel native to the Central Asian steppes. A camel can consume 106 quarts of water in ten minutes and stores the water in its stomach, not its hump as is sometimes believed.[37] The camel's hump is made of stored fat, on which the animal draws for nourishment during times when food is scarce. Relative to other animals the camel loses comparatively little water through skin evaporation, perspiration, and urination, permitting it to travel long distances between waterings.[38] Its short hair, padded feet, and high ratio of skin surface to body mass contribute to the animal's ability to function in the high-temperature, low-humidity environment of the Arabian desert. The camel can travel twenty days without water in 120°F. temperatures before being exhausted.[39] The animal can eat and digest almost anything, including thorny plants like the acacia and dry grasses that other animals, especially horses and mules, cannot digest. Bedouin camels were rarely fed, relying almost completely on natural grazing for food. In years of drought when fodder was scarce, camels and horses often became useless for military purposes because they were not strong enough to undertake rigorous journeys.[40] In towns and oases camels were sometimes fed on grain during harsh times. In oases where the date palm was cultivated, the pits of the dates were crushed to make food for the camels. A bedouin could tell if a camel belonged to a bedouin or an oasis dweller by examining the animal's dung to determine if it contained date pits.

The Arabic language is said to include some one thousand names for the camel, its breeds, functions, and stages of growth, a number rivaled only by the number of synonyms for the sword.[41] The general word for camel is *ba'ir* (a noun of feminine gender). Other descriptions include those for a transport camel (*rikab*), a camel used to draw water (*nadih*), and a riding camel (*dhalul*).[42] The camel's importance to Arab life is evident in the fact that distances among the Arabs are reckoned in camel travel days, not travel by foot, which, in any case, would be impossible. The range and speed of a camel depends on how the animal is encumbered. A transport camel, for example, can carry between four hundred and six hundred pounds packed in panniers. More baggage could be placed between the panniers if necessary.[43] If well fed and watered, a camel carrying this load could still make sixty miles a day.[44]

The terrain also influences range. Camels have soft feet and do not travel well over rocky ground; they are almost useless in mountains. The lava plains characteristic of the Hejaz serve as effective barriers to camel travel.

Camels ridden by Arab couriers carrying messages could make seventy miles a day for a short journey. Over a week they could travel sixty miles a day, and average fifty miles a day over two weeks, providing the animal was fed and watered reasonably.[45] The camel is also an emergency water reservoir. The animal carries water in its stomach. In an emergency an old camel that has been watered within the last three days can be killed, its stomach slit open, and the water used for human consumption or to water the horses. Another technique is to thrust a stick down the camel's throat to force it to vomit the water in its stomach. One source says, "if the camel has been watered within a day or two, the liquid is tolerably drinkable."[46] It is important to remember, however, that practical rates of movement by camel were far slower than those noted above. Arab clans and armies often moved with their possessions, wives, children, flocks, and horses. Any advance over a long distance had to be made in stages in order to sufficiently feed and water the animals as well as the humans. The major logistics problem was keeping the animals alive, not feeding the soldiers. The horse in particular was a considerable drag on military movement in Arabia. It did not have the speed, range, endurance, or the ability to feed on fodder possessed by the camel. Fodder for the horses had to be carried by the camels. Rates of movement were reduced accordingly.

The camel's use as an animal of war was primarily as a transporter of troops and supplies. While it is recorded that the standard bearer of the Hawazin tribe at the Battle of Hunayn fought with a lance from camelback, this was probably a rare occurrence. The lack of a proper high-backed saddle and stirrups and the height of the animal from ground would have made the effective use of the long lance impossible. Had the rider managed to strike his target, the momentum of the strike would likely have unseated him. So, too, the bow, which could only be fired effectively while standing in stirrups and holding the body above the moving animal. The camel's primary value was to move mounted infantry quickly into position permitting warriors to occupy favorable terrain and go into the defense before the enemy could react. This permitted the Arab armies of the conquest period to establish positions with narrow fronts and strong natural obstacles on both sides protecting the flanks, forcing the enemy to attack the strongest defense and with only those troops that the terrain and narrow front could accommodate. It also permitted Arab commanders to choose battlefields close to the desert frontier into which their troops could flee on camelback unpursued by enemy infantry and cavalry, neither of which could endure the desert heat for very long. The ability to move mounted infantry quickly over long distances permitted Arab armies to ambush the enemy almost anywhere in its area of operations. The camel made possible lightning strikes against towns and supply depots deep in the enemy's interior.

The camel's ability to carry much heavier loads than a donkey, mule, or horse and to do so rapidly and for long distances made it an excellent logistics animal. The simple Arab diet of dates, water, and camel milk could be easily transported in quantities that could sustain armies on the march for months. The camel itself could be eaten. The water carried in the camel's stomach could be used to water the horses whose inability to withstand the desert heat and thirst often made them a military liability. Used properly, the camel was a mobile logistics depot that provided Arab armies with a rapid and flexible line of communication and supply that permitted the armies to move quickly over long distances across hostile terrain where neither Persian nor Byzantine armies could follow.

Horse

The horse was probably introduced to Arabia from Syria sometime during the first century C.E. As an instrument of war the horse had been associated with the chariot in Egypt, Syria, Anatolia, and Mesopotamia since at least 1700 B.C.E. It did not become a cavalry mount, however, until the Assyrians first used it in this manner in the seventh century B.C.E.[47] The lack of sufficient pasture due to desert climate, the cost of feeding the horse on domestic grains, and the general expense of the animal within Arabia served to limit the horse's role in war until the Arab conquests. Only the wealthiest town dwellers, merchants, or bedouin chiefs could afford to maintain these animals, and their primary military use was in carrying out small-scale raids. Mecca, one of the largest and wealthiest towns in Arabia, could put only two hundred mounted men in the field in its battles with Muhammad.[48]

The horse was not ridden to the battlefield, but led by a tether tied to the camel carrying its owner. This practice was probably adopted from the Nabataeans, who, as allies of Rome, are recorded as having led their horses into battle when they attacked Jerusalem in 67 C.E.[49] The natural fragility of the animal and the desert heat considerably reduced the horse's endurance, and every effort was made to save its energy for the battle itself. The water and food requirements of the horse were much more demanding than those of the camel, and the horse's poor endurance slowed the rate of military movement considerably. A horse requires twelve to sixteen pounds of green fodder (grass or other natural pasturage) and another fourteen to sixteen pounds of hard fodder (grain) a day. Horses quickly become adapted to certain kinds of green fodder and fall ill if their diet is changed. Under normal climatic conditions a horse will consume fifteen to thirty liters of water each day, more in hot and dry conditions.[50] Feeding horses on grass only would require 2.47 acres of grassland per day to feed 130 horses.[51] Unlike camels, horses have no stored nutritional reserve. Failure to feed and water the animal adequately will quickly result in its death or debilitation.

As an instrument of war the horse was always a poor choice. It would have been far more efficient for armies of antiquity to outfit themselves with the hardier and more intelligent mule.[52] Despite its limitations the horse remained a primary instrument of warfare from at least 1800 B.C.E. until World War I. Why was this the case? The horse was probably introduced to the Middle East around 2000 B.C.E. (and possibly earlier) as part of the Indo-European dispersion that brought these people into the region at about that time. From that time forward the horse became identified with military status and conquest. The Assyrians were the first to use horse cavalry in their campaigns, followed by the Persians and Alexander the Great. The infantry armies of Rome were overrun by barbarian horsemen, leading the Byzantines to develop and use heavy cavalry on a large scale. The Sassanid Persians were also horse warriors, as were the Franks, medieval knights and Crusaders, and Turks. The mounted knight dominated European battlefields for almost a millennium until brought down by the resurrection of disciplined infantry by the Swiss. And so it continued with even modern nation-states equipping their armies with large contingents of cavalry in the face of gunpowder weapons.[53] It was culture, the association of the horse with military power and conquest over more than two thousand years, rather than the military capabilities of the animal itself that prompted armies to continue using the horse when their own experience with it should have prompted its replacement by the mule.

The horse came into its own in Arab armies once the lands beyond Arabia itself had been conquered. Some of the conquered lands raised horses in large numbers, something not possible in Arabia, so that large contingents of Arab soldiers could be provided with mounts for the first time. The conquered lands possessed large tracts of natural foliage and were agriculturally cultivated on a large scale so as to be able to produce sufficient feed for the animals. The climate in these newly acquired lands was less harsh than in Arabia, allowing the animal more endurance than in the desert, thereby increasing its military usefulness. During the period of the conquests Arab cavalry had been divided into armored and unarmored, or heavy and light, with heavy cavalry comprising only a small number of units used as shock troops, a lesson learned from the Byzantines. Light cavalry, when not used to skirmish and reconnoiter, was used mostly to complete the destruction of already disorganized or broken units. During the Umayyad period (661–750 C.E.) the bulk of Arab cavalry became armored in a transition toward the Byzantine model in mounts, armor, and weapons. Arab cavalry was trained in the old Arabic tradition of fighting first from horseback and then dismounting to fight on foot.[54] Cavalry did not become the decisive arm in Arab armies until much later, the heavy infantry long remaining the most important combat arm. Arab cavalry deployed safely behind the infantry, sallying forth as opportunity permitted to attack the enemy and then retreat behind its own infantry for protection. The use of cavalry against cavalry in open combat was unknown to Arab commanders.

In Muhammad's day the horse was not a decisive presence on the field of battle. As Muhammad's insurgency succeeded, the number of horse warriors he was able to put in the field increased dramatically. While the infantry remained the decisive arm, the increased visibility of the horse in Muhammad's armies lent his forces prestige and accustomed the town and oasis dwellers to the animal on the battlefield, preparing the way for the emergence of large horse cavalry contingents in the armies of conquest that followed Muhammad's death. Although camels greatly outnumbered horses in the experience of most Arabs, so revered was the horse in Arab thinking that there are more references to horses in Arabic texts than to camels.[55] In Arabic a horse is called *faras* (a noun of female gender) and the rider *faris*.[56]

The organization of Muhammad's cavalry is reflected in the Arabic terms in use at that time. The general name for cavalry in Arabic is *khayl*, generally used to describe horse combat formations. *Katiba* is a cavalry squadron that was subdivided into *kurdus*, perhaps equivalent to a platoon. A *tali'a* was a small mounted reconnaissance patrol comprising one to ten men; it is also associated with a raiding party. The *sariya* was a small unit sent out for forage. A *jarida* was a horse troop of moderate size operating independently of the main body perhaps for long-range reconnaissance or raiding. Cavalry could also be used as a *rabita*, a mounted garrison employed as a mobile guard force before an enemy fortification or town to keep the enemy penned within it and unable to mount forays.[57] It was probably used in conjunction with siege operations. It is probable that Muhammad's cavalry units were organized along similar lines and performed similar roles, even though cavalry never became a decisive combat arm of Muhammad's armies.

The tactical and strategic mobility of both horse and camel were limited by the terrain in which they were expected to operate. When the Arab armies moved beyond the Persian borders during the conquest period, they were required to abandon the horse and replace it with the mule because of the mountainous terrain. The vast open deserts of rolling hills and stony steppes in which Muhammad's army usually operated were more like the deserts of Arizona and New Mexico than the Sahara and its sand dunes and presented serious obstacles to military movement. The great lava fields (*harrah*) of fissured stone could easily make a horse or camel lose its footing and break a leg. The desert has many ravines (*shi'b*) and ditches, and the wadis, often used as highways around difficult terrain, can become impassable after rain has softened the ground. Wadis are also subject to flash floods. The desert itself is a fierce environment of heat and cold that can sap the strength of even the strongest animal or soldier. Finally, human-made obstacles in the form of fortified compounds, walled gardens, towers, and irrigation canals frequently served to hinder the ability of an army to maneuver.

Muhammad's Military Revolution

Muhammad brought about a revolution in the manner in which Arabs for generations had fought wars, transforming their armies into genuine instruments of large-scale combat operations capable of achieving strategic objectives instead of small-scale, clan, tribe, or personal objectives. In doing so he created both the means and historical circumstances that transformed the fragmented Arab clans into a genuine national entity conscious of its own unique identity. Under these conditions Arab military brilliance thrived, with the result that the greatest commanders of the early Arab conquests were identified and developed by Muhammad. Had Muhammad not brought about a military revolution in Arab warfare, it is possible that Islam might not have survived in Arabia. Within a year of Muhammad's death many of the clans that had sworn allegiance to Islam recanted, resulting in the War of the Apostates. It was the military brilliance of Muhammad's generals and the superior combat capabilities of his new army that made it possible for Islam to defeat the apostates and force them back into the religious fold. It was these same generals commanding the new Arab armies that made possible the Arab conquests of the Persian and Byzantine Empires. The old Arab way of war would have had no chance to win against the armies of either of these powers. In this sense, Muhammad's military revolution was an event that shook the ancient world and changed its history by creating the means that made the Arab conquests possible.

Muhammad's successful transformation of Arab warfare marks him as one of the great military reformers of the ancient world. Muhammad stands in good company with those whose military reforms made possible the creation of empires by their successors. Kamose of Egypt led the fight against the Hyksos occupiers reforming in the process the Egyptian army and making it possible for Thutmose III, the Napoléon of Egypt, to create the Egyptian empire of the New Kingdom. Philip II of Macedon completely changed the manner of classical Greek warfare forging a military instrument with which he united all Greece and which his son, Alexander the Great, used to create the empire of the Hellenes. The reforms of Augustus Caesar created the professional Roman army making possible the expansion of the Roman Empire to its greatest geographic extent. And it was Muhammad who reformed Arab warfare and fashioned the military instrument his successors used to establish the great Empire of Islam.

Social Composition

Muhammad changed the social composition of Arab armies from a collection of clans, tribes, and blood kin loyal only to themselves into a national army loyal to a national social entity called the ummah, or community of believers in God. The ummah was not a nation or a state in the modern sense, but a body of religious believers under the unified command and governance of Muhammad. It was a locus of loyalty that transcended the clans and tribes and permitted Muhammad to forge a common identity, national in scope, among the Arabs for the first time. It was leadership of this national entity that Muhammad claimed, not of any clan or tribe. Loyalty to the ummah permitted the national army to unify the two traditional combat arms of infantry and cavalry into a genuine combined military force. Historically, bedouin and town dweller had viewed one another with considerable suspicion, each living a very different way of life and fighting very different types of battles. Arab infantry had traditionally been drawn from the people living in the towns, settlements, and oases of Arabia. While the larger towns often had a sufficient number of wealthy men who could afford horses, these cavalry units were generally small and ineffective. Arab cavalry was traditionally drawn from bedouin clans whose nomadic warriors excelled at speed, surprise attack, and elusive retreat, skills honed to a fine edge over generations of raiding.[58]

These two different kinds of soldiers came from different socio-economic backgrounds and each possessed only limited experience in fighting alongside the other. Bound by clan loyalties and living in settlements, Arab infantry was steadfast and cohesive and could usually be relied on to hold its ground, especially in the defense. The infantry constituted the core of Muhammad's army throughout his life and remained so in the armies of the Arab conquest. Arab cavalry was unreliable in a fight against infantry, often breaking off the fight to escape damage to their precious mounts or make off with whatever booty they had seized. Bedouin cavalry was, however, proficient at the surprise attack, protecting the flanks, and pursuing ill-disciplined infantry. Each arm lacked the strengths of the other. Muhammad was the first commander of an Arab army to join successfully both combat arms into a national Arab army and to use them in concert in battle. This was more than a mere technical reform. The ability to combine both combat arms was the result of Muhammad's creation of a new type of community that made it possible to submerge the clan and blood loyalties of traditional Arab society into the larger religious community of believers, the ummah, and combine the two primary elements of traditional Arab society, town dwellers and bedouin tribes, into a single Arab national identity. The change in the social composition of Arab armies under Muhammad was preceded by a change in the social composition of Arab society.

Unity of Command

Before Muhammad Arab military contingents fought under the command of their own clan or tribal leaders, sometimes assembled in coalition with other clans or tribes. While the authority of these clan chiefs was recognized by their own clan, every clan chief considered himself the equal of any other with the result that there was no overall commander whose authority could compel the obedience or tactical direction of the army as a whole. Clan warriors fought for their own interests, often only for loot, and did not feel obligated to pursue the larger objectives of the army as a whole. They often failed to report to the battlefield, arrived late, or simply left the fight once they had captured sufficient loot. Warriors and horses were precious, and clan leaders often resisted any higher tactical direction that might place their men and animals in danger. Under these conditions Arab battles often resembled little more than disorganized brawls lasting but a short time and producing no decisive outcome.

To correct these deficiencies Muhammad established a unified command for his armies: Command was centered in his hands alone. Within the *ummah* there was no distinction between the citizen and the soldier, at least if the battle was considered defensive. All members of the community had an obligation to defend the clan and participate in its battles. The community of believers was truly a nation at arms, and all believers followed the commands of Muhammad, God's Messenger. As commander in chief Muhammad established the principle of unified command by appointing a single commander with overall authority to carry out military operations. Sometimes a second in command was appointed as well. Muhammad often commanded his troops in the field himself. All other commanders were appointed by him and operated under his authority. As Muslims all members of the army were equally bound by the same laws, and all clan members and their chiefs were subject to the same discipline and punishments as all Muslims. When operating with clans who were not Muslims, Muhammad always extracted an honor oath from their chiefs to obey his orders during the battle. The establishment of a unified military command gave Muhammad's armies greater reliability in planning and in battle. Unified command also permitted a greater degree of coordination among the various combat elements of the army and the use of more sophisticated tactical designs that could be implemented with more certainty, thereby greatly increasing the army's combat power. For the first time Arab forces became an instrument of their commander's tactical will.

After Muhammad's death and during the *Riddah* (civil war), Muhammad's successor, Abu Bakr, replaced many of the old generals who had fought under Muhammad with new officers selected mostly from among the generals of Mecca. Unity of command extends not only to the strategic level, but to the operational and tactical levels as well. The fact that the old commanders could be replaced and the troops, tribes, and clans under them would obey Meccan commanders who, after all, had been their former enemies, is testimony to Muhammad's success in establishing unity of command as a major institutional reform in Arab armies.

Combat Unit Cohesion

The moral basis of traditional Arab warfare placed an emphasis on the courageous performance of individual warriors in battle. While every warrior recognized that he was part of a larger kin group, Arab warfare placed no emphasis on the ability of the clan to fight as a unit. The Arab warrior fought for his *own* honor and social prestige within the kin group, not for the clan per se. One consequence was that Arab armies and the clan units within them did not usually reflect a high degree of combat unit cohesion, the ability of the group to remain intact and fight together under the stress of battle. Muhammad's armies, by contrast, were highly cohesive. These armies usually held together even when they fought outnumbered or were overrun. Muhammad did not just strengthen the blood and kin ties of the traditional Arab clan. He went far beyond that in creating the ummah as a higher locus of the soldier's loyalty that transcended the clan. It is important to remember that many of Muhammad's early converts had left their families and clans to follow the Prophet. It was a common occurrence to find members of the same clan and family, and even fathers and sons, fighting on opposite sides during Muhammad's early battles. Religion turned out to be a greater source of unit cohesion than blood and clan ties, the obligations of faith replacing and overriding the obligations of tradition and even family. Muhammad's soldiers quickly gained a reputation for their discipline and ferocity in battle, soldiers who cared for each other as brothers, which under the precepts of Islam they were.

Motivation

Muhammad's armies demonstrated a higher degree of military motivation than traditional Arab armies. Being a good warrior had always been the central core of Arab military values. Muhammad raised the status of the warrior to an even greater degree. It was a common saying among Muslims that "the soldier is not only the noblest and most pleasing profession in the sight of Allah, but also the most profitable."[59] Muhammad's soldiers were always guaranteed a share in the booty. Instead of the usual one-fourth, Muhammad himself took one-fifth of the booty in the name of the ummah, leaving more booty to be distributed to the soldiers. Under these arrangements Muhammad's soldiers were actually paid better than Persian or Byzantine soldiers.[60]

But better pay was only a small part of the motivation of the soldiers of Islam. The idea of a soldier motivated by religion in the certainty that he was doing God's work on earth seems to have been one of Muhammad's most important military innovations. There were, of course, Christian soldiers who must have felt that they were doing their religious duty even when they attacked their fellow Christians denounced as heretics. But no army before Muhammad ever placed religion at the center of military motivation and defined the soldier primarily as an instrument of God's will on earth. The soldiers of Islam were usually extremely religious and saw themselves as fighting under God's instructions. The result, often still seen in Islamic societies, was a soldier who enjoyed much higher social status and respect than soldiers in armies of the West.

A central part of the motivation of the Islamic soldier was the teaching of his faith that death was not something to be feared, but to be sought. Muhammad's pronouncement that those killed in battle would be welcomed immediately into a paradise of pleasure and eternal life because they died fulfilling the command of God was a powerful inducement to perform well on the field of battle. To die fighting in defense of the faith (jihad) was to become a martyr. Life itself was subordinate to the needs of the faith; to die a martyr was to fulfill God's will. Muslim soldiers killed in battle were accorded the highest respect on the Arab scale of values. While those who died in battle had been traditionally celebrated as examples of courage and selflessness, it was never suggested that death was to be welcomed or even required to be a good soldier. Muhammad's religious pronouncements changed the traditional Arab view of military sacrifice and produced a far more dedicated soldier than Arab armies had ever witnessed before.

Strategic War

Arab warfare prior to Muhammad's reforms involved clans and tribes fighting for honor or loot. No commander aimed at the enslavement or extermination of the enemy, nor the occupation of its lands. Arab warfare was tactical warfare, nothing more. There was no sense of strategic war in which long-term, grand-scale strategic objectives were sought and toward which the tactical application of force was directed. Muhammad was the first to introduce the notion of war for strategic goals to the Arabs. Muhammad's ultimate goal, the transformation of Arab society through the spread of a new religion, was strategic in concept. His application of force and violence, whether unconventional or conventional, was always directed at the strategic goal. Although Muhammad began as an insurgent, he was always Clausewitzian in his thinking in that the use of force was seen not as an end in itself but as a tactical means to the achievement of strategic objectives. Muhammad was the first Arab commander to use military force within a strategic context. Had he not introduced this new way of thinking to Arab warfare, the use of later Arab armies to forge a world empire would have been not only impossible, but unthinkable.

Once war was harnessed to strategic objectives, it became possible to expand its application to introduce tactical dimensions that were completely new to traditional Arab warfare. Muhammad used his armies in completely new ways: He attacked tribes, towns, and garrisons before they could form hostile coalitions; he isolated his enemy by severing their economic lifelines and disrupting their lines of communication. He was a master at political negotiation, forming alliances with pagan tribes when it served his interests. He laid siege to cities and towns. Muhammad also introduced the new dimension of psychological warfare, employing terror and even massacre as means to weaken the will of his enemies. Various texts mention Muhammad's use of the catapult (*manjaniq*) and movable covered car (*dabbabah*) in siege warfare.[61] Most likely these siege devices were acquired in Yemen where Persian garrisons had been located on and off over the centuries. Muhammad seems to have been the first Arab commander to use them in the north. Where once Arab warfare had been a completely tactical affair, Muhammad's introduction of strategic war permitted the use of tactics in the proper manner, as means to greater strategic ends. War, after all, is never an end in itself. It is, as Clausewitz reminds us, always a method, never a goal.

Experienced Combat Officer Corps

As an orphan Muhammad lacked even the most rudimentary military training provided by an Arab father. Perhaps to compensate for this deficiency, he surrounded himself with other men who were experienced warriors. He constantly asked questions of these more experienced soldiers and frequently took their advice. He frequently appointed the best warriors of his former enemies to positions of command once they had converted to Islam. As commander in chief Muhammad sought to identify and develop good officers wherever he found them. Young men were appointed to carry out small-scale raids in order to give them combat experience. He sometimes selected an officer from a town to command a bedouin raid in order to broaden his experience in the use of cavalry.[62] Muhammad always selected his military commanders on the basis of their proven experience and ability, and never for their asceticism or religious devotion.[63] He was the first to institutionalize military excellence in the development of an Arab officer corps of professional quality. It was from Muhammad's corps of trained and experienced field commanders that the generals who commanded the armies of the conquests were drawn. Khalid al-Walid (The Sword of Allah) and Amr ibn al-A'as were both former Meccan enemy commanders who converted to Islam and served as field commanders in Muhammad's armies. Both became great generals during the Arab conquests.

Training and Discipline

We have only scant references to how Muhammad trained his soldiers; that he did so is almost a certainty. There are clear references to required training in swimming, running, and wrestling. The early soldiers of Islam had left their clan and family loyalties behind in order to join the ummah. The clan-based military units typical of Arab warfare would have been impossible to re-create within the ummah-based armies. Muhammad's converts had to be socialized to a new basis of military loyalty, the faith, and new military units would have had to be created that contained soldiers from many clans. References in various texts suggest that Muhammad trained these units in rank and drill, sometimes personally formed them up and addressed them before a battle, and deployed them to fight in disciplined units, not as individuals as was the common practice. These disciplined "artificial clan" units could then be trained to use a wider array of tactical designs than was heretofore possible. Muhammad's use of cavalry and archers in concert with his infantry was one result. While Arab fathers continued to train their sons in warfare long after Muhammad's death, the armies of the Arab conquests and later those of the Muslim Empire, instituted formal military training for recruits.

Logistics and Force Projection

Muhammad seems to have had the caravanner's concern for logistics and planning, an expertise that permitted him to project force and carry out operations over long distances across inhospitable terrain. Muhammad had been an organizer of caravans for twenty-five years before he began his insurgency. During that time he made several trips to the north along the spice road. He gained a reputation for honesty and as an excellent administrator and organizer of caravans. Planning a caravan required extensive attention to detail and knowledge of routes, rates of march, distances between stops, water and feeding of animals, location of wells, weather, places of ambush, and so on, knowledge that served him well as a military commander. Unlike some other armies that he fought, Muhammad never seems to have had to change or abandon his plans due to logistical difficulties. Muhammad's armies could project force over hundreds of miles. In 630 he led an army of twenty thousand to thirty thousand men (the sources disagree) over a 250-mile march from Medina to Tabuk lasting eighteen to twenty days across the desert during the hottest season of the year. By traditional Arab standards Muhammad's ability to project forces of such size over these distances was nothing short of astounding. Without this capability the Arab conquests that followed Muhammad's death would have been impossible.

Muhammad's concern for logistics extended to making certain his soldiers were adequately supplied with the best weapons, horses, camels, and armor that he could obtain by purchase, seizure as loot or tribute, or manufacture. In the early years Muhammad's troops were frequently short of everything from weapons to transport. At the Battle of Badr he had only seventy camels and two horses to transport 314 men more than eighty miles to the battlefield. The men took turns riding the camels and arrived at Badr exhausted from the trek. Often his soldiers had no armor or helmets and were sometimes short of weapons. Muhammad placed great emphasis on having enough camels, for they were the key to the mobility and endurance of his army. All distances in the desert are reckoned by the time it takes a camel to cover it. Movement on foot is simply not possible for any distance. According to the textual accounts, when Muhammad moved against Mecca every man in his army was fully equipped with weapons, armor, helmets, shields, and either a horse or a camel. For an army of ten thousand men this was no small achievement by a leader who a decade earlier had had only four disciples. It was Muhammad who taught the Arab armies how to supply themselves for long periods in the field and to ensure themselves of adequate weapons and equipment. Once again, had he not accomplished this, Arab armies would have remained militarily incapable of forging an empire.

Conclusion

What emerges from the analysis presented here is that Muhammad revolutionized the conduct of Arab warfare in ways that made possible the transformation of Arab armies from entities fit only for tactical engagements to forces capable of waging war on a strategic level where they could engage and defeat the major armies of their day. This military transformation was preceded by a revolution in the manner in which Arabs thought about war, what I have called the moral basis of war. The old chivalric code that limited the bloodletting was abandoned by Muhammad and replaced with an ethos less conducive to restraint in war, the blood feud. Extending the ethos of the blood feud beyond the ties of kin and blood to include members of the new community of Muslim believers inevitably worked to make Arab warfare more encompassing and bloody than it had been.

Supporting all these changes was a change in the psychology of war introduced by Muhammad's teaching that soldiers fighting in defense of Islam were doing no less than God's work on earth, and that to die in carrying out His will earned the soldier eternal life in paradise. The usual sense of risk to one's life that tempers the violence of the battlefield was abandoned, replaced by a psychological doctrine that "war to the knife," or fighting until one kills the enemy or is slain oneself, became the ideal in the conduct of war. In every respect Muhammad's military revolution increased the scale and violence of the military engagements that Arab armies were now capable of fighting.

4

MUHAMMAD

Muhammad was born on August 20, 570 C.E., in the town of Mecca. The original inhabitants of Mecca were the Jerhum tribe, who, according to legend, were related to the Amalekites of the Old Testament. At some point the Khuza'a tribe migrating north from Yemen drove the original occupants from the town and took up residence there. About a century before Muhammad's birth the Quraish tribe, led by one Qusai, drove the Khuza'a from Mecca and settled his people there. The Khuza'a had not lived in houses, but in tents surrounded by shallow walls to break the wind and driven sand. Qusai is said to have convinced his people to give up their previous bedouin ways and to build houses. These houses were little more than hovels made from rough stones held in place with mud mortar and roofed with palm logs or brushwood that offered some protection from the sun. Some of the tribe lived in the town while other clans, the Quraish of the Hollow, lived outside its confines. Muhammad was a member of the Quraish residing in Mecca. By the time of Muhammad's birth, Mecca's strategic location as a key stopping and transfer point for the north–south trade route between Marib and Gaza had led to the growth of a merchant class. Mecca became an urban society consisting of many groups of traders and artisans. While the Quraish dominated Mecca's affairs, they were not the only ones whose interests had to be considered.

Mecca lay forty-eight miles inland from the Red Sea in a barren rock valley six hundred yards wide and a mile and one-half long squeezed among stony mountains. It is described in the Quran as "unfit for cultivation."[1] The name of the town in Arabic was originally *Makkah*, derived from the ancient Sabean word *mukuraba*, which means "sanctuary."[2] From time immemorial Mecca had possessed a shrine (*ka'ba*) where Arabs had come to worship idols kept there. It is not known which idol had first been worshipped there, but for at least a century before Muhammad's birth the main idol worshipped in Mecca was Hubal. Although Christianity and Judaism had made some small inroads in Arabia, most Arabs remained idol worshippers until their conversion to Islam. Other towns and settlements had their own shrines and idols. Tradition credits Qusai, the chief of the Quraish, with organizing the first annual pilgrimage to worship Hubal at the Kaaba.[3]

Once a year Arabs came from all over Arabia to worship at the Kaaba in Mecca. Providing services to these pilgrims was a lucrative business, and the Quraish profited handsomely. The pilgrimage itself lasted only three days. In the weeks before the pilgrimage, however, a number of trading fairs grew up around Mecca that offered rich commercial opportunities for trade to the Meccan merchants. All violence was banned during these fairs. There was a large sacred territory, the *haram*, that surrounded the Kaaba and within which fighting and the carrying of arms was prohibited. Peace was good business. By Muhammad's time Mecca had established itself as the most important commercial and religious center in Arabia, and the Quraish controlled the Kaaba and much of the city's commerce.

One of Qusai's great-grandsons, Abdul Muttalib (b. ca. 497), was the grandfather of Muhammad. He was the head of the Hashim clan and in charge of the wells around the Kaaba that provided water to the pilgrims. As a clan chief he was a man of considerable influence. Abdul Muttalib had five sons, one of which, Abdullah, was Muhammad's father. Abdullah died in 570 leaving his wife pregnant. The child she was carrying was Muhammad, who was born in August 570 C.E. It was the custom among Arab town dwellers to place their new babies in the care of a wet nurse of a bedouin tribe to care for the child as its foster mother. The child mortality rate from disease and malnutrition in Arab settlements was horrendously high, and it was believed that sending the child into the healthier environment of the desert increased the child's chances of survival.[4] Because Muhammad had no father, it was difficult to find a wet nurse willing to take him. A poor orphan with no family offered few opportunities to the woman for favors or money. Eventually, however, Muhammad was accepted by a woman of the Beni Saad tribe living outside Mecca. Muhammad spent two years with his foster mother before being returned to his mother in Mecca, where he lived with her for four years until she died. Muhammad was six when he was orphaned. His grandfather took him, and he was looked after by a slave girl in his grandfather's household. Two years later, when Muhammad was eight, his grandfather died, and he was placed in the charge of his uncle Abu Talib, the new head of the Hashim clan.

At the age of twelve Muhammad accompanied his uncle on a caravan journey to Damascus. The fortunes of the Hashim clan were in decline, and Muhammad continued to live in poverty. As an orphan he had no one to protect him, educate him, or supply him with money and contacts to make his way in business. Muhammad sometimes worked as a shepherd and spent considerable time alone. He became a fixture around the Kaaba, where he sometimes helped provide water to the pilgrims and other worshippers. When Muhammad was about fourteen a tribal war broke out between the Quraish and the Hawazin that lasted for five years. In one of the earliest battles of this war Muhammad went along with his uncles to retrieve arrows so they could be shot back at the enemy. As far as the texts tell us, this was Muhammad's only military experience prior to commanding his own troops in the later war with the Quraish. Military training was provided to Arab males by their fathers or uncles as a matter of course, and the fact that Muhammad received no military training is curious. All the more so since one of his uncles, Hamza, was already a renowned warrior when Muhammad was a boy. Perhaps because Muhammad was a quiet boy who kept to himself spending long hours tending flocks or at the Kaaba, his uncles may have concluded that he lacked the necessary aptitude for fighting. If so, they could hardly have been more mistaken.

Over the next decade Muhammad tried his hand at commerce with no noticeable success. Lacking money and social contacts, it would have been a surprise if he had succeeded. He did, however, acquire a reputation for honesty and may have acquired the nickname "the trustworthy," but we cannot be certain of this.[5] When he was twenty-five his uncle secured a place for him in another caravan to Syria. His reputation for honesty served him well, and he was made responsible for the sale of some of the goods as well as the purchase of some return goods. The caravan belonged to a rich widow of the Quraish tribe named Khadijah. The death rate among Arab men from disease, injury, and blood feuds left Mecca with a considerable number of widows, among whom a few, like Khadijah, had property and considerable wealth. Khadijah's assignment of her caravan to Muhammad was apparently a testament to his merchant skill and honesty.

Upon Muhammad's return to Mecca, Khadijah proposed marriage. Muhammad was twenty-five. Khadijah was already twice widowed and said to have been about forty years old, but may have been somewhat younger since she bore him several children, four girls and two boys, although some sources (Seyyid Hossein Nasr) say Muhammad had only one son.[6] The marriage provided Muhammad with considerable commercial opportunities, and he succeeded very well. More important was his relationship with Khadijah. She became his true love and confidante. He trusted her in all things, and she supported him when he began to have his revelations. It was Khadijah's cousin, Waraqah, a Christian, who also supported Muhammad on Khadijah's word that his revelatory experiences were the signs of genuine prophethood. Muhammad loved Khadijah until the day she died, and while she lived Muhammad never loved another woman.

The next fifteen years, 595 to 610, are the "hidden years" in which the texts are mostly silent about Muhammad's life. He seems to have had a modestly successful business career, and as an organizer of large caravans he gained experience as both an administrator and logistician. For some reason, however, perhaps because he began life as an orphan, he was excluded from the inner circle of the more powerful Meccan merchants. Muhammad must have traveled with the caravans several times, and the texts tell us of his encounters with Christian monks living in caves along the caravan route. We may disregard the accounts of the miraculous happenings and prophecies of the monks as non-historical; nor can we discern what effect, if any, the religion of these monks may have had on Muhammad's thinking. It was during this period that Muhammad's infant son or sons died. He adopted his cousin, Ali, the son of his uncle Abu Talib, who had looked after him. Abu Talib was growing old and falling on harsh economic times. Muhammad also took in Zayd, a Christian slave boy given to him by his wife's nephew while on a trip to Syria. Both Ali and Zayd looked on Muhammad as their father and were among his earliest converts.

Sometime during this period Muhammad developed the habit of going off by himself, often taking refuge in a cave for days at a time to meditate. Certainly his financial condition was such that he would have been able to make time for meditation and thinking. It is noteworthy that other Arabs would not have found Muhammad's habit an unusual occurrence. Even the idolaters of Mecca sometimes turned to this form of desert asceticism. In Arabic the practice is known as *tahannuth* and was something like a modern retreat, a temporary withdrawal from worldly affairs for the purpose of religious meditation.[7] Tradition holds that Muhammad's grandfather, Abdul Muttalib, was in the habit of spending the entire month of Ramadan each year in a cave in the mountains around Mecca.[8] It is not unreasonable to suppose that the old man may have introduced the young Muhammad to the practice. It may have been no more than coincidence, however, that Muhammad experienced his first revelation while living in a cave during the month of Ramadan.

Muhammad continued his practice of retreating into the desert throughout his life. Aisha, whom he married after the death of his beloved Khadijah in 619, recalled that "solitude became dear to him and he would go to a cave on Mount Hira to engage in meditation there for a number of nights, before returning home for a short time to procure provisions for another stay."[9] It was during one of these retreats, during Ramadan in 610, that Muhammad experienced his first revelation. Muhammad interpreted these revelatory experiences as instructions from God, and they continued for the rest of his life. He would repeat the instructions to his followers, who memorized them and/or wrote them down. Sometime later they were collected in what became known as the Quran. The Quran and its moral instructions became the foundation for the new religion of Islam. There is no need to dwell on the instructions contained in the Quran since only a few are relevant to Muhammad's military life and they will be dealt with later. It is interesting, however, to examine the physical circumstances that Muhammad himself described as accompanying the onset and duration of his revelations insofar as they possibly indicate an identifiable medical condition that may have accompanied the revelations.

Muhammad's revelations are interesting. Only two of them, his first call to God's service and the revelation in which he recounted journeying from Mecca to Jerusalem in a single night where he met Moses and Jesus, seem to have been *visual* experiences. This is at least a reasonable conclusion judging from the specific details that Muhammad's own descriptions of the events include. All other revelations that came to him throughout his life seem to have been completely *auditory* in nature and not to have included any visual component.[10] When Muhammad was asked to describe his revelatory experience, he said, "Sometimes it cometh unto me like the reverberations of a bell, and that is the hardest upon me; the reverberations abate when I am aware of their message. And sometimes the Angel taketh the form of a man and speaketh unto me, and I am aware of what he saith."[11] Whenever a revelation was imminent, Muhammad was gripped by a feeling of pain. Even on cold days he would sweat profusely.[12] Ibn Ishaq records that the prophet knew when a revelation was about to occur. He would lie down and be covered with a cloak or blanket. He would perspire profusely. At the end of the event Muhammad sat up and repeated the message he had been given. In only a few instances did the revelation come upon him when he was riding or at a public gathering.[13]

The symptoms recorded as accompanying Muhammad's revelations seem strongly similar to those associated with recurrent malaria, a disease whose episodes are often accompanied by vivid visual and auditory hallucinations. Often the first onset of the disease is "acute"; that is, its symptoms are greatly exaggerated and the fever is very high. Ibn Ishaq, in describing the first attacks of "the fever" that afflicted Muhammad's followers when they arrived in Medina, seems to describe an acute onset. He tells us that "[w]hen the Apostle came to Medina it was the most fever infested land on earth, and his companions suffered severely from it . . . they were delirious and out of their minds with a high temperature."[14] Malarial infection does not confer "immunity" from further outbreaks but confers only a "resistance" to the disease so that follow-on episodes are usually not as severe as the initial bout. And so it was that while Muhammad's followers arrived in Medina from Mecca and immediately contracted malaria, Ibn Ishaq tells us, "God kept it from his Apostle."[15] This suggests strongly that Muhammad may have already contracted the disease and was "resistant" though not "immune."

Mecca is a hot and dry place where malaria was not endemic, so that if Muhammad had malaria, it is unlikely that he first contracted the disease there. Malaria thrived in places like Medina and other swampy, humid, and hot oases throughout Arabia. Medina itself had a reputation among caravanners as a place where fever was endemic, and they sometimes bypassed the town to avoid contracting it. Four days travel south of Medina is the village of Mahya'a, where caravans wishing to bypass Medina often stopped, whenever there was an outbreak of the disease, thereby depriving Medina of the money to be made supplying and entertaining the caravanners. During a severe outbreak of fever in Medina Muhammad is said to have prayed to God to take the fever out of Medina and "carry it to Mahya'a," probably as a curse upon the village for its economic competition to Medina.[16] As a caravan organizer Muhammad would likely have stopped at any number of oases during his journeys where he might have been exposed to and contracted malaria. Moreover, the symptoms that accompanied Muhammad's later revelations are not those of an acute onset, but of an episodic recurrence. None of this, of course, is meant to bring into question the legitimacy of Muhammad's claim that his revelations were of divine origin, a question best left to theologians in any case. It is only to say that Muhammad's own descriptions of his revelations suggest they were accompanied by symptoms usually associated with malaria.[17]

After his first revelation Muhammad had no further revelations for three years. Then a second revelation commanded him to preach the message of Allah. Muhammad's ministry lasted from 610 to his death in 632, with the public phase beginning in 613. Although some Meccans first thought Muhammad mad, most had no difficulty with his preaching or behavior until he began to denounce their worship of idols. This denunciation of idol worship at the Kaaba generated much ill will since the Kaaba was the object of the annual pilgrimage to Mecca and the trade fairs that brought considerable income to the city. The most objectionable of all Muhammad's pronouncements, however, was his claim that all those who had not become Muslims before their deaths were suffering in hell. To claim that non-Muslims were in hell was a direct attack on the memory and reputation of one's ancestors who, after all, had no opportunity to save themselves before Muhammad's ministry. In a society that revered ancestors whose exploits preserved in oral accounts established the ideals of virtuous behavior, Muhammad's condemnation was a grievous insult to Arab honor, one that could result in a blood feud. Muhammad was treading on dangerous ground, and the opposition to him in Mecca grew stronger.

For the next six years Muhammad and his few followers were the objects of ridicule and persecution. Conversions to Islam cut across tribal and familial lines with the result that Muslim converts were sometimes

A Prophet is always followed by wrong way. Moses & Jesus & Muhammad. On a lighter note, Bush is followed by Rich. Poor

60   MUHAMMAD

persecuted by their own kin. The most severe persecutions were suffered by the converts who came from the lower social classes—slaves, widows, orphans, and the poor who had no families or clans to protect them. Ibn Ishaq tells us that "[t]he Quraish showed their enmity to all those who followed the Apostle; every clan which contained Muslims attacked them, imprisoning them, and beating them, allowing them no food or drink, and exposing them to the burning heat of Mecca, so as to seduce them from their religion."[18] Muhammad never forgot the persecution inflicted on his early followers, and when the time came he took his revenge in blood.

In 619 Muhammad's beloved Khadijah died. Abu Talib, Muhammad's uncle, clan chief, and Muhammad's protector in Mecca, died shortly afterward. Muhammad was now alone with no clan relatives to protect him from violence. The Meccans continued their ridicule and harassment, but stopped short of any violence directed against Muhammad himself. It was becoming clear, however, that life in Mecca was becoming dangerous and that sooner or later someone would try to kill him. To avert this fate, he journeyed to Ta'if, a small trading town fifty miles east of Mecca, to see if their chiefs might permit him and his followers to emigrate to the town. He was met with ridicule and rejection, and Muhammad returned to Mecca even more afraid for his life. Desperate for someone to protect him, he approached three clan chiefs in Mecca to ask for their protection. Two refused, but one, al-Mut'im bin 'Adiy, chief of the Nofal clan of the Quraish, agreed to take Muhammad under his protection for reasons that are not entirely clear.[19] The next day, he and his sons appeared under arms in the public square of the Kaaba to announce that Muhammad was under their protection.[20] Now at least Muhammad could not be slain without consequences.

Even with al-Mut'im's protection, Muhammad was still in danger if he continued to preach among the Meccans who regarded his preaching as both insulting to their family lineages and dangerous to their commercial interests. Muhammad ceased his efforts in Mecca itself and began to preach to the pilgrims and traders who came to the trade fairs and encamped on the outskirts of Mecca. In 620 Muhammad preached to a group of seven pilgrims from the oasis of Yathrib (Medina). The next year these seven returned bringing with them five more to hear his message. Muhammad met with the group in a little valley in the mountains outside Mecca at a place known to the locals as Aqaba.

Here the pilgrims from Yathrib were converted to Islam. Along with a number of moral maxims that they agreed to obey, the new converts pledged to obey Muhammad and recognized him as the Messenger of God. In the history of Islam this pledge is called the First Pledge of Aqaba. It is also called the Pledge of Women because the pilgrims did not undertake any obligation to take up arms in defense of Islam or to use force to protect Muhammad himself.

The following year, 621, a larger group of seventy-three men and two women pilgrims from Medina arrived and met with Muhammad at Aqaba and converted to Islam. This is called the Second Pledge of Aqaba, and it is a very important event in the history of Islam. Unlike the First Pledge, the converts swore an oath to protect Muhammad as they would their own family members by force if necessary. The leader of the group, Al-Bara, swore that "we will protect you as we protect our women. We give our allegiance and we are men of war possessing arms which have been passed from father to son."[21] Muhammad replied, "I am of you and you are of me. I will war against them that war against you and be at peace with those at peace with you."[22] The pledge at Aqaba was a traditional Arab oath of mutual obligation requiring mutual armed assistance. But Muhammad promised the new converts, known now as the *ansar*, or Helpers, something that no traditional clan chief could ever have offered: everlasting life in paradise.

The group of pilgrims seems to have come from the Kazrai clan of Medina. By these pledges Muhammad gained two things. First, he expanded his influence to a clan beyond Mecca and his own Quraish tribe. Here was the embryonic beginning of what became the ummah, the new community of believers whose loyalties transcended the old clan and kin loyalties but retained the moral exclusiveness of the blood feud. Second, Muhammad gained the protection of a clan living in Medina. Their guarantee of protection made it possible for Muhammad and his followers to leave Mecca and emigrate to a less hostile place where they would be safe from persecution.

Before the Second Pledge of Aqaba Muhammad's instructions received through his revelations had commanded him only to call men to God. Shortly after the Second Pledge, Muhammad received another revelation that granted permission for him and his followers to fight and shed blood. Ibn Ishaq tells us that the first permission for Muslims to fight appears in sura 22, verses 39–42, of the Quran, which says, "Permission to fight is given to those who are being killed unjustly and God is well able to give victory. Also to those who have been unjustly turned out of their country, merely because they said, 'God is our Lord.' Had God not used some men to resist others, the wicked would before now have demolished the cloisters, the churches, and the places of prayer and worship where the name of God is constantly remembered would have been destroyed. Assuredly God will help those who help Him. God is Almighty."[23] The passage seems to justify violence only in self-defense. According to Ibn Ishaq, the resort to violence was expanded by a later revelation: "Then God sent down to him [Muhammad]: 'Fight them so that there be no more seduction,' that is, until no believer is seduced from his religion. 'And the religion is God's,' that is, 'until God alone is worshipped.'"[24] The second and later revelation seems to justify violence beyond self-defense to include preemptory force to prevent someone from being "seduced" from God's correct path. The significance of these passages for the military historian is that Muhammad seems to have anticipated the need for violence in order for his ministry to survive.

Muhammad must have been a man of some physical strength, which he demonstrated through his enjoyment of wrestling and swimming and, on more than one occasion, by throwing his opponents to the ground when they angered him. He seems to have exuded physical energy: "He always walked as if he were rushing downhill, and others had difficulty keeping up with him. When he turned in any direction, he did so with his whole body."[25] Martin Lings has put together a convincing physical description of the man from the extant original sources.

He was of medium stature, inclined to slimness, with a large head, broad shoulders, and the rest of his body perfectly proportioned. His hair and beard were thick and black, not altogether straight but slightly curled. His hair reached midway between the lobes of his ears and his shoulders, and his beard was of a length to match. He had a noble breadth of forehead and the ovals of his large eyes were wide, with exceptionally long lashes and extensive brows, slightly arched but not joined. In most of the early descriptions his eyes are said to have been black, but according to one or two of these earliest sources they were brown or even light brown. His nose was aquiline and his mouth was wide and finely shaped, a comeliness always visible for although he let his beard grow, he never allowed the hair of his moustache to protrude over his upper lip. His skin was white, but tanned by the sun.[26]

Muhammad was handsome by any Arab standard of manliness and beauty, and women found him very attractive. He once said, "I like women and perfume better than anything else, but the apple of my eye is prayer."[27] Until he was fifty Muhammad had only one wife, his beloved Khadijah. After her death at sixty-two he had twelve others. He had six children by his first wife, but no children by the twelve who followed although all were still of child-bearing age. He did, however, father a son with Mariya, an Egyptian Coptic Christian concubine given him as a gift, but who never became his wife.[28] Nearly all of Muhammad's later wives were widows. Perhaps he preferred the company of mature women to young girls; perhaps these older women reminded him of Khadijah or of his own mother, who died when he was six.

Muhammad must have been a very psychologically complex person. Whatever glimpses into his psychology that may be gained from historical accounts must be regarded as incomplete and, perhaps, fraught with error. The preeminent scholar W. Montgomery Watt, drawing on Ibn Ishaq's notes, offers the following description of Muhammad's general psychological disposition.

> He was given to sadness, and there were long periods of silence when he was deep in thought; yet he never rested but was always busy with something. . . . He never spoke unnecessarily. What he said was always to the point, and sufficient to make his meaning clear. He spoke rapidly. Over his feelings he had firm control. . . . His time was carefully apportioned according to the various demands on him. In his dealings with people he was above all tactful. He could be severe at times.[29]

Although capable of ferocious anger, Muhammad seems to have generally been a calm man open to suggestions who regularly sought the advice of others and he often accepted it. There is no evidence that his followers were afraid to approach him and offer advice. Although he seems to have possessed an innate gift for things military, he often sought the advice of his more experienced officers before a military operation. He was democratic in the typical manner of Arab clan chiefs, and remained accessible to his followers to the end. He was kind to the poor, widows, and orphans, and greatly loved by his followers and, later, by even some of his former enemies.

There is no doubt that Muhammad believed sincerely and deeply in his having been called by God and in his mission to spread the new faith. Yet, he remained psychologically balanced. He always knew the difference between his own thoughts and those he had received from his revelations. When, for example, he was arranging his troops before the Battle of Badr, one of his officers thought the disposition a mistake. He asked Muhammad if he was giving his men instructions he had received from God or were they just his own ideas. Muhammad replied that the instructions were only his ideas. The officer suggested that the dispositions be changed for sound military reasons, and Muhammad agreed. Although the hadith and oral traditions of Islam are full of accounts of Muhammad performing miracles, Muhammad himself never claimed to be able to do so, and was well aware of his own mortality. This sense of balance was also reflected in his condemnation of religious asceticism that he had once witnessed among Christian monks living in the desert. In this regard, he remarked, "God has not ordered us to destroy ourselves."[30] He was scrupulously clean, perhaps even compulsively so, and often remarked how the presence of food adhering to a man's moustache disgusted him. He disliked strong smells, and would not eat anything flavored with onions or garlic.[31]

None of these dispositions completely overcame Muhammad's fierce sense of rectitude, anger, and violence, which he could display when he thought it necessary. Like Moses, Christ, and Akhenaton of Egypt, Muhammad was "a god-intoxicated man."[32] He was also a man of physical courage and never seems to have feared death. Ibn Ishaq records an incident in which one Umar bin al-Khattab, one of the chief persecutors of the Muslims in Mecca, came to see Muhammad. He was armed with his sword, and the Apostle's bodyguards feared that Umar might attempt to kill Muhammad. Muhammad ordered his bodyguards to stand aside and let Umar enter the house. "The Apostle gave the word and he was let in. The Apostle rose and met him in the room, seized him round the girdle or by the middle of his cloak, and dragged him along violently, saying, 'What has brought you, son of Khattab, for by God I do not think you will cease your persecution until God brings calamity upon you.'"[33] To attack an armed man who is openly your enemy with your bare hands requires a degree of fearlessness that most do not possess. But Muhammad was an Arab chief and courage was a required trait, especially in a warrior of God.

Muhammad's sense of divine purpose led him to regard violence as an acceptable means to achieve God's ends. This tendency revealed itself early, during the period when his few followers were being persecuted by the Quraish in Mecca. One day Muhammad was spending some time at the Kaaba when he was approached by a small group of men who began to insult and harass him. After enduring their taunts and threats for some time, Muhammad turned to them and said, "Will you listen to me O Quraish? By Him who holds my life in his hands, I will bring you slaughter."[34] For a man of such rectitude, Muhammad seems to have possessed an acute sensitivity to personal ridicule. He hated poets and singers who were the primary spreaders of political propaganda and unkind portrayals of the enemies of the people who had hired them. In a society where honor meant as much as life, a man's reputation was sacred. Hiring a poet to travel about and ridicule a man was serious business indeed. At the same time, the poet was a respected member of Arab society and usually not subject to violence, although the person who hired the poet was. But Muhammad seems to have had a deep loathing for poets per se. Ibn Ishaq tells us that when Muhammad experienced his first revelation he was extremely frightened. Muhammad thought he might be possessed or worse, a poet! "Now none of God's creatures are more hateful to me than an ecstatic poet or a man possessed." Muhammad was so frightened by what was happening to him that the said, "I will go to the top of the mountain and throw myself down that I may kill myself and gain rest."[35] Muhammad's hatred of poets was almost irrational in its intensity. As a poor orphan Muhammad must have been regularly subject to insults and taunts by others when he was a child, and it is possible that his hatred of poets was rooted in this early childhood experience. Whatever the case, several poets and singers who had ridiculed him were later murdered on Muhammad's orders.

Muhammad gave permission for his Meccan followers, the *muhajirun*, or Emigrants, to emigrate to Medina shortly after the Second Pledge of Aqaba. Muhammad and a few of his closest followers remained in Mecca waiting for their opportunity to leave. Some Meccan hotheads gathered and formulated a plot to kill him in his bed. Legend has it that Muhammad was warned by the angel Gabriel not to sleep in his bed that night and escaped harm. Muhammad and one of his followers hid in a cave near Mecca for three days while the Meccans searched for them. The Meccans soon lost interest, and Muhammad left Mecca and made his way safely to Medina. Ibn Ishaq tells us that "the Apostle on that day (when he arrived in Medina) was fifty-three years of age, that being thirteen years after God called him."[36] Muhammad's journey to Medina is known to the Arabs as the *Hijra* (Hegira), and marks the Year 1 on the Arab calendar from which all subsequent historical events have since been measured.

5

INSURGENCY

Medina was a very different place than Mecca. The city was located 240 miles north of Mecca, about 100 miles inland from the Red Sea and 80 or so miles distant from the main caravan route linking Mecca with Gaza. A caravan traveling between the two cities took between ten and twelve days to cover the distance; Muhammad made the journey in nine days when he emigrated from Mecca. Like most Arab "cities" Medina had no walls. It was mostly an open plain comprising some thirty-seven square miles.[1] Unlike Mecca with its hot and dry climate, Medina was a well-watered oasis with a swampy atmosphere in which malaria and other climate and waterborne diseases flourished. Medina was home to two large Arab tribes, the Aws and Kazrai, eight Arab clans, and three Jewish tribes—the an-Nadir, Qurayzah, and Qaynuqa. The town was somewhat haphazardly divided into districts in which individual clans resided. Each district consisted of houses, clan compounds, farming plots, date palm groves, walled gardens, pastures, wells, and plots of swampy wasteland. The population of Medina at the time of Muhammad's arrival was probably close to ten thousand souls.[2]

An agricultural oasis, Medina was noted for its date palms as well as camel herding and grain cultivation, enterprises that made its inhabitants relatively wealthy by Arab standards of the day. The place was probably first settled by Jews fleeing the Roman suppression during

either the Jewish War or the Bar Kokhba Revolt in the first and second
centuries C.E. It was probably these Jews who introduced agriculture to
the oasis.[3] The oasis had been called Yathrib since Sabean times. The
Jewish refugees spoke Aramaic and changed the name to the Aramaic
Medinta, or simply "the town." It is uncertain when the name was
changed to the Arabic *al-Medina*, or "the town of the Prophet," but it
was somewhat later, perhaps even after Muhammad's death.[4] The Jews
were well established in the oasis long before the arrival of the Kazrai
and Aws tribes, both of which probably emigrated from Yemen sometime after the destruction of the Marib dam. At first the Arab tribes
were clients of the Jewish tribes. By Muhammad's day, however, the roles
had been reversed and the Arab tribes were in the dominant position
with the Jews taking sides in the various clan wars as clients of the
Arabs. Except for their adherence to the Jewish faith, the Jewish tribes
of Medina were indistinguishable in every way from the Arab tribes.
The Beni an-Nadir and Beni Qurayzah tribes were agriculturalists, while
the Beni Qaynuqa were traders, goldsmiths, and armorers.

The inhabitants of Medina lived in houses constructed of mud
bricks and placed close together and surrounded by a wall of mud-
brick and stone. These *qasr*, or residential compounds, were still in
use in 1900. The following description of a qasr dates from that later
time though it had remained unchanged in its essentials since the
time of Muhammad.

> The high walled *qasr* . . . was a four-square building in clay, sixty
> paces upon a side, with a low corner tower. In the midst is the
> well . . . steyned (stuccoed) with dry masonry, a double camel-
> yard, and stalling for kine and asses; rooms for a slave-woman
> caretaker and her son, rude store houses in the towers. . . . An
> only gateway into it is closed and barred at nightfall. Such
> redoubts are thought to be impregnable in Arabian warfare.[5]

A strong tower house, the *utum*, built into the wall served as a keep
in which women and children could take refuge and which served as
a strong defensive position during an attack. A compound usually had
more than one well, and at least one was always located within the
utum itself. Several families might live in a single compound, and
several compounds would house a clan. The compounds were often
clustered near one another and joined by low walls that protected the
paths between the compounds. Nearby, often arranged in a zigzag

pattern, were the gardens whose walls kept out the wind and blowing sand. This combination of compound walls, path walls, and walled gardens interspersed with date palm groves and patches of swampy ground formed a complex maze that created difficulties for the movement of troops in any formation but a single file that could be easily ambushed by defenders. These mazes "canalized" the movement of the attackers so that superior numbers could not be brought to bear effectively within the city, permitting small numbers of defenders to hold out against much greater numbers of attackers. Until Muhammad's time Arab armies lacked siege machinery so that even the flimsiest walls provided the defenders with a considerable advantage. An attacker might hope to starve the defenders into submission and ravage the crops, but little more. Destroying the date palms, however, was considered an atrocity and rarely done. Muhammad ordered date palms destroyed on more than one occasion, more to make a political than a military point.

Muhammad and his four traveling companions left Mecca in the heat of the summer for Medina, arriving nine days later on September 24, 622. The political situation in Medina was tense. The two Arab tribes had been engaged in a continuing blood feud that had begun in 616. Two of the Jewish tribes had fought with the Aws; the other Jewish tribe sided with the Kazrai. Two years earlier, the rival coalitions had met in battle at what came to be known as the Day of Bu'ath. Both forces were badly mauled, each side losing scores of fighters. The result was an uneasy truce. It is likely that the pilgrims that had met with Muhammad at Aqaba were drawn mostly from the lesser clans who had the most to lose from a continuing war. They may have been interested in more than Muhammad's new religion. Muhammad had earned a reputation for honesty and fairness in his business dealings, and it is probable that the members of the lesser clans were interested in sounding out Muhammad's willingness to come to Medina to serve as an arbiter in the clan wars. As an outsider he was neutral, had no blood debts, and could serve as an impartial judge to bring the conflict to an end.[6]

To emigrate to Medina with only a handful of followers while the town was simmering from a blood feud was risky business indeed. Muhammad was no fool, and must have surely understood that any attempt to lay claim to being a judge in a clan war would put him at considerable risk. That is why he insisted on the pledge of protection from the Medina pilgrims when he met with them at Second Aqaba. Without that pledge it would have been suicide for a foreigner to interfere in a blood feud. In this sense, then, the converts at Aqaba who pledged to protect Muhammad were acting as his bodyguard. Ibn Ishaq recalls an incident soon after Muhammad's arrival in Medina in which a man attempted to approach Muhammad with a message only to encounter his bodyguard of ansar cavalry, who beat the man with their spears.[7] Muhammad was concerned for his safety from the first day of his arrival. He entered Medina from the south on the edge of the oasis in a district called Quba. At first he thought he might settle there. But it was too close to the strongholds of the Jewish tribes as well as some strongholds of the Aws tribe, which had not been party to the agreement at Aqaba. Muhammad moved a mile or two to the north to select a less dangerous place to build a house.

It was probably only a few months after arriving when Muhammad drew up the Covenant that set out the rules for Muslims to follow in dealing with the Jewish tribes and other Medina Arabs who remained idolaters. Here was the first official formulation of the ummah, Muhammad's community of believers whose loyalties transcended all other traditional clan and family obligations. Central to membership in the ummah was the oath that there was only one God, Allah, and that Muhammad was his Prophet. Muhammad himself was to be obeyed because he was the Messenger of God. The ummah constituted the beginnings of a revolutionary cadre of believers whose task it was to spread the new religion. Their obligations to this cause excluded all other social relationships. The Covenant provides the first glimpse of the new social order, the community of religious believers and the rules by which it was to be governed, that Muhammad envisioned for the future.

Muhammad's dictates governing the relationship of members of the ummah to all others outside the community could not have been clearer. "They [the members of the ummah] are one community to the exclusion of all men."[8] In this instruction Muhammad appears to have divided the world between members of the community and all others in much the same way that traditional Arab culture divided the world between clan members and those outside the clan where individuals outside the clan or tribe have no moral standing. The difference, of course, is one of scope. "Believers are friends to one another to the exclusion of outsiders. No separate peace shall be made when believers are fighting in the way of God."[9] Muhammad replaced the traditional moral code that governed the conduct of war among Arab clans with the notion that war fought over religion was a new type of war, total war in which the old limits on violence no longer applied. Only membership in the community offers ethical limits to war; all those outside the community lack these protections. Thus, "[a] believer shall not slay a believer for the sake of an unbeliever, nor shall he aid an unbeliever against a believer."[10] The role of revenge against outsiders is clearly that required by the blood feud, not the traditional code of war: "The believers must avenge the blood of another shed in the way of God."[11] The code of the blood feud is also evident in the practice of paying a blood-wit as compensation. "Whoever is convicted of killing a believer without good reasons shall be subject to retaliation unless the next of kin is satisfied with blood money."[12] Finally, the Covenant makes clear that loyalty to the ummah, even among believers themselves, takes precedence over any loyalty to clan or even family. Muhammad instructs that the believers shall "be against the rebellious or him who seeks to spread injustice or enmity or corruption among believers; the hand of every man shall be against him even if he be a son of one of them."[13] This harsh doctrine applied to the believers themselves. The limits that Arab traditions had once placed upon the treatment of one's own family or clan were now gone. Even a father was required to turn against his son and a son against his father in defense of the faith.

The Covenant at Medina created a revolutionary religious community of insiders versus outsiders in which membership was total and irrevocable. The individual was completely submersed in the community, even to the degree that blood kin and family were subordinated to the precepts of the community. As the Messenger of God Muhammad himself was to be obeyed unconditionally. The traditional democratic aspects of Arab clan and tribal leadership were completely eliminated, replaced by a sacerdotal authoritarianism that was beyond disobedience, refusal, or reproach. Whereas previously Arab life had been lived mostly according to moral codes that had, even in war, placed strict limits on violence and revenge, those codes and limits were now abrogated and replaced by the higher morality of religious sanction. Where once the harsh rules of the blood feud had been only *part* of Arab life and a relatively rare occurrence, the norms of the blood feud were now placed *at the center* of social life within the ummah. The result was the elimination of the practical and ethical limits to warfare and violence when undertaken against unbelievers in the service of the faith. Muhammad had invented a new kind of Arab community, one in which a revolutionary religious ideology that permitted an expanded scope of military and social violence in service to the faith was at the center.

As the leader of this new community Muhammad was responsible for ensuring that it survived. He and his people were on the brink of starvation and living in poverty. During the early days in Medina they survived on dates and water, having no money to purchase much else. Muhammad's Meccan émigrés were urban people, familiar with trading and commerce, not farmers. There was, in any case, little new land to be cultivated by the newcomers in the already developed agricultural community of Medina. The Jewish tribes dominated local commerce, closing off any new business opportunities for the émigrés. To keep his people alive Muhammad divided his followers into the muhajirun, or those émigrés who had followed him from Mecca, and the ansar, allied converts from Medina. Each ansar was required to adopt a muhajirun as his "brother," and to do what he could to feed and find work for him. The single virtue of these difficult times is that the common suffering helped bond the new community together and encouraged it to believe even more strongly in Muhammad's claim to be God's Prophet.

It is unclear how large the Muslim community in Medina was at this time. A tradition from Bukhari suggests that six months after Muhammad's arrival the Muslim community numbered around fifteen hundred people.[14] Some of these followers, the famous "Hypocrites," had taken the oath of conversion but supported Muhammad mostly for the opportunity to obtain loot. Nonetheless, they were technically members of the Muslim community at the time and counted as such. At the Battle of Badr which took place in March 624, Muhammad put 314 men in the field. Of these, 83 were emigrants and 231 were Medina ansar. A community that could raise three hundred males of military age for a battle might easily number fifteen hundred souls if one counts wives, children, and elderly relatives of the families of the soldiers. The number of ansar warriors suggests that Muhammad was having some success in converting the members of some Arab clans in Medina.

Seven months after arriving in Medina, Muhammad undertook his first military operation by attacking the Meccan caravans. One must ask why he did this. Muhammad and his followers were free from persecution and danger from the Quraish in Medina. Occasionally a father or uncle of a Muslim convert would arrive from Mecca and attempt to convince the convert to return to his family, usually without success. But this was hardly a danger. With his own people destitute, perhaps

Muhammad turned to the old Arab practice of raiding to solve the problem. Although raiding might have been a short-term solution to Muslim poverty, it seems an unlikely solution to the long-term problem for a number of reasons. First, most Muslims were urban or agricultural folk, not bedouins, and knew very little about how to undertake a successful caravan raid. Second, raiding a Meccan caravan was a risky proposition. Caravans were always accompanied by an armed guard, often experienced bedouin warriors hired for the purpose. Third, many bedouin chiefs made a living providing the caravans with protection, water, camp sites, and other services. The disruption of the Meccan caravans by a religious upstart recently arrived in Medina could hardly have been welcomed by these chiefs. The bedouin chiefs commanded retinues of experienced warriors who might easily have been turned against Muhammad and his followers if circumstances warranted. By any strategic calculation, then, Muhammad's attacks on Meccan caravans, if undertaken to alleviate the problem of Muslim poverty, were unwise and dangerous. When Muhammad decided to take up arms against the Meccans, it must have been for larger strategic objectives.

Muhammad must have known that any attack on the Meccan caravans would have been but the opening skirmish in a long campaign in which the Meccans would try to exterminate him and his followers. In the first place, the decision to raid his own kinsmen was something that would have been unthinkable in pre-Islamic times as an atrocity of the worst kind. There was no greater sin among Arabs than to abandon or abuse one's own kin. In attacking the Meccans, Muhammad was turning his back on Arab tradition. It is no wonder, then, that Muhammad claimed a divine imperative (sura 22:39-40) to justify his actions. Second, the caravan trade was the major source of wealth for the Meccan merchants, and they could be expected to protect it with every resource they possessed. If Muhammad succeeded, the larger strategic threat to the merchants was that Medina would displace Mecca as the primary commercial center in the Hejaz. Muhammad's success in attracting converts at Medina cannot have gone unnoticed either. Any military success by Muhammad would only increase his prestige and following. In the long run this threatened Mecca's position as the preeminent religious center in the region and along with it the rich commercial opportunities provided by the pilgrimage and trading fairs. Finally, the Meccan chiefs could raise significant military forces on their own, including cavalry, and had the money to hire mercenaries and bedouin warriors. Muhammad's forces in Medina were small by comparison and certainly no match for the Meccans.

Muhammad was too good a strategic thinker not to have been aware of these realities. And yet, he went ahead with his plans to challenge the Meccans. There may be two reasons why Muhammad did so. First and foremost, Muhammad was a "god-intoxicated man," a true believer in himself as God's Messenger tasked by Allah to spread the doctrine of Islam to the unbelievers. Muhammad's revelations had condoned the use of violence to accomplish the task that God had set for him. If the struggle was ordained by God, then its successful outcome must also be ordained. Like later revolutionaries who believed in the "inevitable forces of history" to guide their actions, Muhammad relied on his personal relationship with God to guide his. He declared war on the Meccan idolaters because it was God's wish that he do so. The attacks on the Meccan caravans were but the first strike in a larger strategy of conquest and destruction of his enemies. Second, the rectitude and certainty that often accompany such thinking sometimes have more worldly roots. In this case the insults and taunts Muhammad had suffered as an orphaned child in Mecca and the cruel, sometimes fatal, persecution laid upon his early followers by the Meccans, as well as his own ridicule at their hands, might easily have permitted a psychology of personal revenge to influence Muhammad's thinking. Both influences, a deep belief in God's will and a searing hatred for his tormenters, may have combined and led Muhammad to believe he was capable of overcoming the strategic realities that would obviously attend a war with the Meccans. Only someone who believed that victory was inevitable would have begun such a war.

If the strategic realities were against Muhammad, it was nevertheless true that his tactical position conferred a number of advantages. Ensconced in Medina, he had a base of operations from which he could attack the Meccan caravans. Medina itself was no easy position to subdue if the Meccans responded with a direct attack upon the oasis. Surrounded by lava fields and ravines, Medina allowed of only one axis of advance, from the north. The compounds, walled gardens, agricultural groves, swamps, and fields provided excellent defensive positions should they be needed to resist a Meccan assault. By striking at the Meccan caravans Muhammad was striking at the root of Meccan economic and military power, the commercial lifeline that sustained Quraish control of Meccan politics. In the manner of a true insurgency,

Muhammad intended to isolate and weaken his enemy's social and economic base of power.

Muhammad had already established a revolutionary ideology attractive to that segment of the Arab population that lacked status, wealth, and protection from the harsh life of the poor and weak. The ideology of Islam served as a means to recruit the manpower and committed followers that formed the core of the insurgency's military arm. Muhammad's recruitment efforts were already moderately successful in Medina, attracting several subclans of the Kazrai to his cause. Muhammad had already begun to surround himself with a small group of dedicated advisers and trusted men on whom he could rely to carry out his every order without question. Within a few months he had established the *suffah*, a center of religious study in the mosque, from which he selected a group of highly dedicated, ascetic, true believers who could be used to discipline those within the ummah who might begin to lose faith in the cause. It was from here that the seeds of a kind of secret police and terror arm took root that Muhammad used to terrorize and assassinate some of his opponents. From the beginning Muhammad had surrounded himself with a personal guard who were drawn from the ansar clans in Medina and who had sworn an oath to protect him at Aqaba. All these mechanisms characteristic of an insurgent movement were in place to some extent even before Muhammad carried out his first raid on the Meccans.

Like insurgencies in the modern period, the strength of the movement lay mostly in the dedication of its followers and the genius of its leader. Muhammad's accomplishments so far were important advances but would not in themselves be decisive in any conflict with the Meccans. Still, in the hands of a talented revolutionary like Muhammad, it was a very auspicious beginning indeed. Muhammad realized that his insurgency depended ultimately on a secure base from which to operate, and he immediately took steps to protect his back by neutralizing the potential opposition within Medina itself. The chiefs of the two major Arab tribes still regarded Muhammad and his movement with suspicion. The Jewish tribes regarded him as a direct threat and regarded his teachings and claims to be insulting to their own religion. When Muhammad drew up the Covenant to establish the rules governing the ummah, he had also concluded an agreement of mutual assistance with the Jewish tribes that set out rules for their respective treatment at the hands of the other. The pact was a traditional Arab pact among tribal chiefs save for the caveat that the obligations of the Muslims toward the Jews "must be carried out except in the case of holy war."[15] It is unlikely that either party regarded the pact as more than a temporary arrangement pending future developments. For the time being, however, Muhammad was free to operate against the Meccans without having to worry about being attacked by the significant military forces of the non-Muslim tribes within Medina.

Seven months after he arrived in Medina, Muhammad opened hostilities against Mecca by undertaking a series of raids against the Meccan caravans plying the road between Mecca and Gaza. The caravan route passed about 80 miles to the west of Medina, a relatively short distance for Muhammad's raiders to travel and wait in ambush. The distance to Mecca was almost 160 miles, too far for the Meccans to respond in time with a rescue force. To mount any military operation against Muhammad would require the Meccans to travel ten to twelve days before being in a position to bring force to bear, assuming they could find him. The tactical advantage lay with Muhammad.

The caravans usually traveled with an armed guard. Sometimes the guards stayed with the caravan from Mecca to Gaza and back; other times, only a token guard stayed with the caravan for the complete journey, augmented by bedouins hired along the way who escorted the caravan for short distances. From his experience as a caravanner Muhammad knew that the caravan guard contingents were usually small. This meant that Muhammad's raiders could usually outnumber the caravan guard even with their own small numbers. Taking the caravan by surprise attack at the first light of dawn gave Muhammad another tactical advantage. If Muhammad could raid the caravans successfully, he could provide his followers with a livelihood of sorts and strangle Mecca's merchant trade.

In Arab society a man's reputation and honor were one. Having been hounded out of Mecca, Muhammad needed to improve his reputation among friend and foe alike if he was to have any chance of success. In this regard a display of military power would likely impress the pagan tribes whom he hoped eventually to convert and who were critical to his strategy of isolating Mecca. To traverse the hostile landscape of Arabia required caravanners to secure the aid of the numerous bedouin clans who lived along the route. Caravans required water, food, lodging, forage for their animals, and other support services that the bedouins and oasis dwellers provided for a fee disguised in the form of tolls and taxes. Without these en route services, no caravan could realistically hope to complete the journey on its own. It was imperative, then, that the Meccan merchants maintain good relations with the bedouin clans who were in a position to bring the caravans to a stop by simply refusing to provide them with the services they required to complete their journeys. Muhammad knew that he could not stop the Meccan caravans with raids alone. The key to his success was to befriend the bedouins and entice them to change loyalties with promises of loot, the spiritual enticements of the new religion, and displays of military force and prestige to win their respect. From the very beginning Muhammad's raids were intended to achieve the political objective of winning the "hearts and minds" of the bedouins. The military value of the raids was only a means to this end.

Muhammad probably could not muster more than two hundred or so men to participate in the raids. Most of the first raids were carried out entirely by the Emigrants and involved no more than fifty men at a time, often only ten or twenty. As events progressed Muhammad was able to convince some of the ansar to take part as well. This was an important achievement. The ansar had taken an oath to defend Muhammad, not to engage in any other kind of military action. Their willingness to participate in the raids greatly increased Muhammad's resources and probably reflects the fact that most ansar clans had already converted to Islam. From time to time, however, Muhammad recruited raiders from among the pagans of Medina with promises of a share in the loot. Still, the military force available to Muhammad at the beginning of the insurgency was quite small, perhaps not more than 300 to 350 men counting both Emigrants and ansar.

In January 623 Muhammad sent out his first raiding party under the command of his experienced warrior uncle, Hamza. The party was made up of thirty men, all Emigrants.[16] Hamza overtook a Meccan caravan near al Ais, which was south of Yanbu on the shore of the Red Sea. Hamza seems to have been taken by surprise by the size of the caravan guard. Ibn Ishaq tells us, "He [Hamza] met Abu Jahal [the caravan commander] with three hundred riders from Mecca on the shore."[17] Had Hamza chosen to engage, it is likely that he and the Muslim raiders would have been massacred. Fortunately for them, the local chieftain intervened and prevented a fight, "so they separated without fighting." The size of the caravan guard was unusually large and consisting entirely of Meccans. That the caravan was returning to

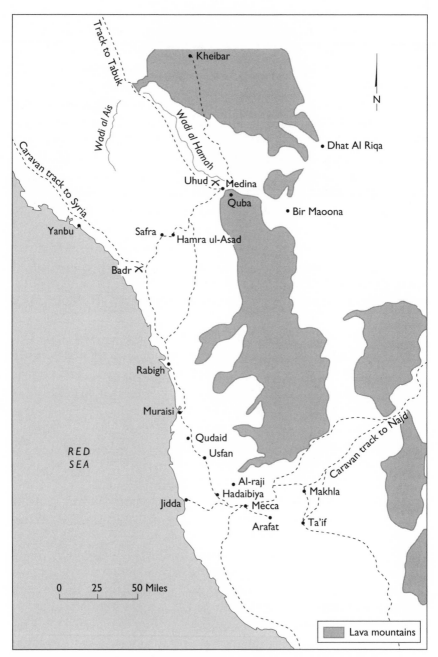

Map 5. Muhammad's Raids, 623 C.E.

Mecca when Hamza attempted to stop it suggests that the guards had traveled with the caravan from the start of the journey in Mecca. For a guard of this size to do that was unusual and strongly suggests that the Meccans had gotten wind of Muhammad's plan to begin raiding the caravans and prepared to protect them.

If the size of the caravan guard had impressed Hamza (as well it should have!), it did not impress Muhammad. A month later, in February 623, Muhammad sent another raiding party of sixty men to intercept a Meccan caravan outside the coastal town of Rabigh. Details of the raid are sketchy, but at the least there must have been a skirmish between Muhammad's men and the caravan guard for it is marked in the history of Islam that it was during this raid that one Sa'ad ibn Abi Waqqas, a convert, fired off an entire quiver of arrows at the Meccans.[18] There were no hits and no combat took place. But the event is remembered as the first use of war to defend Islam, although no blood was shed on either side.

Of greater interest, however, are the direction and distance over which the raid was carried out. The first raid had attempted to intercept a caravan returning to Mecca; the second raid attempted to attack a caravan that was leaving from Mecca. The distance covered in the second raid was twice that of the first, and the raiding party was twice as strong. The texts do not tell us why the second raid failed. Perhaps the attackers could not get into position to attack before sunrise (the traditional Arab time of attack), or the caravan guard was too strong, or the weather intervened. From a political perspective, however, the raid demonstrated to the bedouin tribes that Muhammad was becoming a force to be noticed. The first raid had sent this message to the tribes north of Medina; the second reached far to the south. Muhammad was demonstrating an ability to project force considerably beyond Medina.

It was also likely that these first raids served to train Muhammad's men in how to conduct operations in the desert environment and to gain familiarity with the terrain over which the raiders were required to maneuver. It must be remembered that Muhammad and his followers, both Emigrants and ansar, were townsfolk, not bedouins. They were mostly unfamiliar with the desert and how to move and survive within it. Even when Muhammad fled Mecca he had to hire a bedouin to guide him over the desert route to Medina. Beyond the need to get to know the desert, there was the issue of military expertise. Muhammad's followers would have received basic military training at the hands of their fathers, but this was not the same thing as knowing how to plan and conduct a raid on a caravan, especially if it was guarded by bedouins who were known for their skill and ferocity in battle. All these factors make it likely that Muhammad saw these initial raids as having more political and prestige value than military value.

In May 623 Muhammad sent a party of eight Emigrants to try to intercept a small caravan on the road from Mecca to Syria. They arrived a day after the caravan had passed. Several other raids launched in quick succession also came up empty. It was probably apparent to Muhammad by this time that his lack of an intelligence apparatus was making it almost impossible to determine the location and time of a caravan's passage. The Emigrant raiders consistently had difficulty navigating in the desert. It was becoming clear that unless Muhammad secured close relations with the bedouin tribes near the caravan route, all his efforts to strangle the Meccan lifeline would come to naught. The day would come, of course, where nothing moved in the Hejaz that went undetected by Muhammad's intelligence service. For the time being, however, he was operating mostly in the dark.

Probably to bolster morale after so many failed raids, Muhammad himself led a party of raiders out of Medina in June 623 and headed south. Muhammad had no greater expertise in navigating the desert or leading men in battle than any of the previous commanders who had led the Muslim raids. Like his followers, Muhammad had been a town dweller all his life. As a consequence of his experience in organizing caravans, he was an accomplished administrator and logistician. But he was not a field general or combat commander, at least not yet. For these reasons it is unlikely that Muhammad set out this time to raid the Meccan caravans. His journey took him and his party (we have no idea as to the size of the contingent, but it was probably relatively small) far to the south of Medina, indeed even south of Mecca, to the territory of the Beni Kinana tribe. The territory of the Beni Kinana was close to the caravan route that led from the southern ports to Mecca. These bedouins were perfectly positioned to observe the traffic on the road as well as to learn of all comings and goings around Mecca itself, the route to Ta'if, and the major caravan route that ran northeast from Mecca to Hira on the Euphrates. Muhammad's visit paid significant dividends when he negotiated a treaty of friendship with the Beni Dhamra clan of the Beni Kinana. The details of the pact are not recorded;

it is not unlikely, however, that the Beni Dhamra agreed to report any Meccan caravan movements to Muhammad.

Between June and October 623 four raids attempting to ambush Meccan caravans were undertaken without success. Muhammad's followers in Medina were still living in poverty, and his string of military failures was probably making it more difficult to attract converts; the ansar were also losing confidence and were less willing to participate in future raids. To add to his woes, Muhammad suffered the public insult of having a group of local bedouins make off with some of his camels. He formed a posse of sorts and chased the thieves for three days, but to no avail. Muhammad returned to Medina poorer than when he left. The prestige of Muhammad and the Muslims of Medina sank.

In September 623 Muhammad led another raiding party of 150 men in an attempt to intercept a large caravan traveling to Damascus. He chose a place near the town of Yanbu on the coast of the Red Sea, about eighty miles due west from Medina, to lay his ambush. Once more there was no caravan! The party spent several days and nights in the area, and Muhammad used the time to his advantage by negotiating a friendship pact with the Mudlij tribe living near Yanbu. Muhammad now had a source of intelligence north of Mecca as well as to the south. The pacts with the Beni Dhamra and Mudlij served him well, and the Meccan caravans became more vulnerable to successful attacks.

It must have been apparent to Muhammad by now that his failure to locate and attack the Meccan caravans was due to more than his own poor intelligence. Much of it could be attributed to the ability of the Meccans to learn of Muhammad's planned attacks well in advance. There was no shortage of enemies in Medina that would have willingly supplied Meccan agents with knowledge of Muhammad's movements. The Jewish tribes of the city thought him crazy, blasphemous, and dangerous. The chiefs of the Aws had begun to regard him as a potential competitor for power, and many of the Kazrai clans remained unconverted to the new faith. Muhammad himself seemed not to understand the concept of operational security. Whenever he planned a raid he would go to the mosque and gather any and all around him who might be interested in participating. He would answer questions and then select his raiding party from among the volunteers. It is likely that every time Muhammad set out to assemble a raiding party the information was passed to the Meccans by his enemies. A good riding camel could cover sixty-five to seventy miles a day for about a week's duration, sufficient time for the Meccans to dispatch a messenger to warn the caravans.[19]

In November 623 Muhammad gathered a small party of eight under the command of one Abdullah ibn Jahash to undertake a mission far to the south near Nakhla, a town that sat astride the eastern caravan route from Mecca to Hira. This time Muhammad greatly improved his operational security. The small number of raiders, all Emigrants, suggests that they were selected without the usual public gathering at the mosque. In addition, neither the raiders nor their commander was told the nature or the objective of the mission. The commander was given a sealed letter containing instructions to be opened two days after the group departed their base. To further conceal the party's purpose, Muhammad instructed ibn Jahash to march east for two days before opening his instructions. Having done this, he opened the letter which ordered him to turn due south over the open desert and make for Nakhla. Ibn Ishaq records ibn Jahash's instructions in the letter. "When you have read this letter of mine proceed until you reach Nakhla between Mecca and al Ta'if. Lie in wait there for Quraish and find out for us what they are doing."[20] Nakhla is fewer than fifty miles east of Mecca along the Hira road and more than two hundred miles from Medina. It is hardly likely that Muhammad would have taken such security precautions to send an eight-man team so great a distance only to observe the road for caravan traffic.

As luck would have it, though, a small local caravan traveling from Ta'if to Mecca carrying wine, raisins, and leather goods came down the road passing under the observation of the Muslim raiders. More luck. The caravan was escorted by only four men and otherwise unguarded. Ibn Ishaq tells us that the raiders followed the caravan until it made camp for the night. The raiders then moved into position for the traditional dawn attack. The difficulty was, however, that it was the last day of Rejeb, one of the sacred months of truce among the Arabs. Any act of violence or bloodshed committed during this time was a grave sin and an impiety. Worse, the caravan was now very close to Mecca's sacred zone, where no violence was permitted. Muhammad's letter, at least the version that history has preserved for us, made no mention of any attack on any caravan. It had instructed the raiders only to observe the traffic along the road. After some discussion among the raiders as to exactly what they were expected to do, the Muslims attacked the four caravan attendants. One of the attendants, Abdullah ibn al Hadhrami, was killed, two were taken prisoner, and one escaped to Mecca to spread the alarm. The raiders returned to Medina with their booty and reported to the Prophet.

Both Muslims and pagans in Medina were furious at the news of the killing of Hadhrami during the sacred month of Rejeb and at Muhammad, who most assumed had ordered it. There is no evidence that Muhammad cared particularly for having violated an old pagan law. Like Moses, who had to use violence on more than one occasion to keep his followers from deserting him,[21] Muhammad was probably most concerned about losing his hold over his followers. At first Muhammad denied having ordered the attack during the sacred month and refused to accept his share of the booty from the raid. There followed one of his revelations, which placed the matter in a larger religious perspective and contained a tacit admission of the order to attack. Ibn Ishaq tells us that the revelation is contained in sura 2, verse 214, of the Quran, which says, "God sent down to the Apostle. They will ask you about the sacred month, and war in it. Say, war is therein a serious matter, but keeping people from the way of God and disbelieving in Him and in the sacred mosque and driving out his people therefrom is more serious with God. And seduction [i.e., schism in this context] is worse than killing. And they will not cease to fight you until they turn you back from your religion if they can."[22]

The language of Muhammad's revelation suggests that he was not concerned with the violation of the old Arab code as much as he was concerned with keeping command over his followers. The Quranic verse admits to the violation of the idolaters' law, something that Muhammad intended to destroy in any case. Muhammad's leadership had accomplished little for his followers so far, a fact that made him vulnerable to a revolt by his own people. The caravan raids had failed one after another producing no income for his people, most of whom still lived in poverty without employment and sustained mostly by charity. Muhammad may have begun to fear that he would be rejected even by those who first believed most earnestly in him as God's Messenger. Why else, then, the instruction from God "that schism is more important than killing . . . and that any of you who recant will die a pagan,"[23] and suffer in hell for eternity. This command seems aimed at sustaining the support of the Muslims more than anything else.

If the analysis is correct, then we might speculate why Muhammad sent eight men more than two hundred miles to watch the

Mecca–Hira road in the first place. Surely it could not reasonably have been only to observe the caravan traffic, a mission of no political or military value whatsoever. It might have been that Muhammad had in fact instructed the commander of the raiders to attack a small caravan at the first opportunity and, if necessary, to shed blood during the sacred month.[24] Arab history has accepted God's instructions to Muhammad as sufficient justification and the raid on the caravan at Nakhla is remembered in Arab history as the first time when Muslims shed blood for their faith. Muhammad surely knew that it was the month of Rejeb and that killing was forbidden. Indeed, an intriguing loophole is provided in Muhammad's letter of instruction to the commander of the raiders that anyone who did not wish to continue with the mission could simply return to Medina.[25] It is clear from Ibn Ishaq's account that the raiders themselves knew they were violating the sacred month and had a long conversation among themselves about it.[26] But why the exception to take part unless the instructions directed the raiders to attack a caravan and, if necessary, shed blood during the sacred month in the first place permitting those who objected to the violation of Arab law to refuse to take part, if Muhammad did not intend all along deliberately to provoke a violation of the Arab sacred law?

If this was Muhammad's intention, what did he hope to gain by committing such an impiety? Muhammad's failures were catching up to him. Perhaps there had already been defections from the movement. Perhaps there had been overt challenges to Muhammad's claim to be the Messenger of God, perhaps rumors that he was a fraud as many non-Muslims openly thought. Muhammad may have cast about for a means to bind his followers more closely to him. One way to do that was to commit an atrocity in their name and require them to choose him over the outrage of the pagans or recant from Islam, die a pagan, and suffer in hell. Modern revolutionary movements—the Irugun, the Vietcong, the Mau Mau, Mao's followers, the insurgents in Iraq who behead their captives, and even the patriots of the American Revolution who tarred, feathered, hanged, and burned alive their Loyalist enemies—have all used atrocity as a means of strengthening revolutionary loyalty and fervor. Once bound in this way, it becomes very difficult for adherents to the cause to renounce their loyalties. Modern terrorists have committed atrocities in the name of history, race, and ideology. Muhammad justified the killings at Nakhla in the name of God.

This said, Muhammad may have given too little thought to the fierce reaction that the Meccans might have to the killings. The murder of Abdullah ibn al Hadhrami engaged the ancient rules of the blood feud. Hadhrami had been under the protection of Utba ibn Rabia, a powerful and respected member of the Meccan community who was now bound by the Arab code of honor to avenge the death of his client. If the Meccans had not understood before that Muhammad intended to destroy them, the incident at Nakhla and the revelation excusing the grave violation of Arab sacred law should have left few in doubt. The result was an open state of war between Muhammad and his former fellow tribesmen, the Quraish of Mecca.

6

THE BATTLE OF BADR
March 15, 624

A few weeks after the incident at Nakhla, in the autumn of 623, the annual Quraish caravan to Syria set out from Mecca. It took the usual route along the coast of the Red Sea passing some eighty miles east of Medina. There were two large Meccan caravans a year, one in the autumn to Syria and the other in the spring to Iraq. These were major commercial events that generated a large part of the annual income of the city. Almost everyone in Mecca had some share in the caravans. The caravan of autumn 623 comprised a thousand pack camels laden with expensive trading goods. If the Muslims could capture it, they would go from living in poverty to wealthy almost overnight. Muhammad's share of the booty would permit him to purchase the arms and weapons his men sorely lacked. Muhammad's previous attempts to seize smaller Meccan caravans had put the Meccans on their guard. The caravan was under the command of Abu Sufyan ibn Harb, an important merchant who was one of the leaders of the opposition against Muhammad and an experienced military officer who commanded the Meccan cavalry. The caravan was accompanied by a guard of forty men.

Muhammad did not attempt to attack the caravan on its outbound journey. This is curious for several reasons. First, the caravan was laden with valuable goods; it would also be transporting goods on its return journey, but probably not in such quantity or of such value. Second,

Muhammad had an excellent intelligence source in Mecca. Abbas, one of Muhammad's uncles, was an important banker in Mecca. He stayed in regular contact with Muhammad by letter.[1] Abbas's involvement in the commercial affairs of the city made him an excellent agent-in-place when it came to reporting important political and commercial information to Muhammad. Abbas was in a position to provide the route (not much of a secret in any case) and the exact date and time of departure, information that would have allowed Muhammad to move his forces into place in plenty of time to ambush the caravan. Instead, Muhammad chose to employ a team of "special spies" to follow in the track of the caravan and to warn him when it was to undertake its return journey.[2] Presumably this would require the spies to track the caravan all the way to Damascus, remain in or near the city for a few months until the caravan was ready to make its return journey, and then ride ahead to warn Muhammad of its coming.

The plan makes no sense on purely military grounds. Courier riders atop well-bred riding camels were the only means of conveying messages, and the distances involved were too long to make timely warning possible. At best Muhammad would have only a few days to plan his ambush and move his troops into position, probably not enough time and far less than he would have had he tried to attack the caravan on its outbound leg. Later sources tell us that the plan became pointless when Abu Sufyan discovered that he was being observed by Muhammad's spies while still in Damascus.[3] Muhammad's plan may have been forced on him by political circumstances. Perhaps the reaction to the killings at Nakhla was much worse and took more time and effort to contain than the sources report. If so, Muhammad may have been unable to rely on sufficient numbers of Muslim followers to undertake an attack on the outbound caravan, forcing him to forgo the better tactical opportunity. In the almost six months that passed while the caravan traveled to Damascus and made its return journey, Muhammad would have had time to strengthen his grip on his following and become confident in his ability to use them in a major military operation.

On March 8, 624, Muhammad set out from Medina with a force of 314 men—83 Emigrants and 231 ansar. The Muslim force could muster only seventy camels and two horses to transport men and supplies, which suggests that many of the ansar were from the lowest economic classes and almost as poor as the Emigrants. One presumes that Muhammad's spies had reported that the Meccan caravan had left

Damascus sometime in January. It must also be assumed that other spies or scouts had reported that the caravan was drawing near to where the route passed to the east of Medina. The sources are silent on these details, however. With only a handful of animals to serve as transport "on which the men rode in turns,"[4] much of the journey was covered on foot, a rare occurrence in Arabia due to the heat and difficult terrain. Muhammad's column moved mostly during the heat of the day, also something not usually done at this time of year. He ordered that the bells hung around the necks of the camels be removed so as not to give away his position when the column moved. This might indicate that the column moved during the night at times when the heat of the day became too oppressive. The march took place during the month of Ramadan. After the second day on the march Muhammad excused his men from the required fast so that they could keep up their strength.[5] Muhammad's reaction time was slow compared to the rate of movement of Abu Sufyan's caravan, and he had no opportunity for timely tactical intelligence to reach him. There is no evidence in the sources to indicate that Muhammad was informed while on the march of the location of the Meccan caravan. This suggests that he had yet to decide where to attack the caravan.

Abu Sufyan and his caravan guard were on the alert. The discovery of the Muslim spies in Damascus had led him to be cautious. Muhammad's mobilization of his force in Medina in the usual public manner had probably been noted by his enemies in the city who would have been only too willing to inform the Meccans. As he approached the Hejaz Abu Sufyan sent his scouts forward to reconnoiter the route ahead for any enemy activity. The scouts questioned every person and rider they encountered for news about Muhammad and his men. At some point they encountered some bedouin riders who told them Muhammad had left Medina and was somewhere in the area; they professed not to know his exact location.[6] We might suppose, although the text is silent, that the reports of Muhammad's movement were also accompanied by some estimate as to the size of the Muslim force, which Abu Sufyan, himself an experienced commander, would have immediately understood to be much larger than his own caravan guard of forty men. Abu Sufyan decided to send a camel rider on ahead to Mecca almost three hundred miles to the south to sound the alarm and request that the Meccans mobilize a large force and proceed quickly up the road toward Medina to forestall Muhammad's attack. A healthy camel and an experienced rider could have covered the distance to Mecca in just under four days. It would have taken at least several more days, perhaps as long as a week, for the Meccans to mobilize a force of nine hundred to one thousand men. Moving a force of this size close to Medina more than two hundred miles away would have taken another ten to twelve days. In practical terms Abu Sufyan was on his own and could not expect help from Mecca to reach him in time.

Muhammad's route to Badr as described by Ibn Ishaq was circuitous and indirect.[7] It is clear from Ishaq's account that Muhammad was unfamiliar with the area and seems to have been forced to hire bedouin along the way to guide him. Perhaps it was these bedouin who told him about Badr, although Muhammad's experience as a caravanner might have already made him aware of the place. Badr was a good-sized village with substantial wells that sat astride the main caravan route. It was a regular halting place for the caravans, so Muhammad had every reasonable expectation that Abu Sufyan's caravan would stop there. The road to Badr from Syria entered the ring of mountains that surrounded the plain where the town was located from the northwest. Muhammad had no knowledge of the location of the Meccans, and as he approached the town from the east he sent out two of his men into Badr to scout the village and report back to him. The Muslim scouts entered the village and stopped to water their camels at one of the wells. Here they overheard two local women discussing that the Meccan caravan from Damascus was expected to arrive the following day. The villagers made a tidy profit providing the passing caravans with services, so it was not unusual that news of the Meccan caravan's arrival had already reached Badr. The scouts reported the news to Muhammad.

Muhammad and a small party set out to reconnoiter the area. They encountered an old bedouin who, the text tells us, knew that the Meccans had mobilized and had departed Mecca moving north toward Medina. Muhammad still had not located the caravan and now had to contend with the approaching Meccan reaction force as well. His knowledge of the caravan route and distances involved would have permitted him to calculate roughly the position and time of arrival of the Meccan relief force. He seems to have concluded that he had sufficient time to carry out his attack on the caravan before having to deal with the relief force. A major problem remained, however, and that was the willingness of the 231 ansar troops to fight. At Aqaba the ansar had pledged to be loyal and to serve as Muhammad's bodyguard.

Ibn Ishaq tells us that "in Aqaba they stipulated that they were not responsible for his safety until he entered their territory, and that when he was there they would protect him as they did their wives and children. So the Apostle was afraid that the ansar would not feel obligated to help him unless he was attacked by an enemy in Medina."[8] Now that a Meccan relief force was on the way, the issue for Muhammad was would his bodyguard fight or go home? Muhammad assembled the ansar and put the question to them directly. Their leader pledged the loyalty of the group. "We do not dislike the idea of meeting your enemy tomorrow. We are experienced in war, trustworthy in combat."[9] Muhammad changed his direction of march to position himself at the opening of the pass in the hills through which the caravan route entered the Badr plain from the northwest. It was here that he intended to ambush Abu Sufyan and his caravan.

Abu Sufyan's scouts had failed to locate the Muslims. Muhammad and his men were probably still approaching the hills around Badr from the east and had not yet made their way to the ambush site. The Meccan caravan meanwhile had stopped just short of the northern entrance where the road forked and ran a few miles farther west close to the Red Sea coast. Abu Sufyan probably would have preferred to halt at Badr, but he was an experienced field commander and knew that Badr was the obvious place for an ambush. Abu Sufyan decided to reconnoiter the Badr wells himself. If there was any sign of Muhammad's men inside the ring of hills that surrounded Badr, Abu Sufyan could move west and south along the coastal road and bypass Badr entirely.

At the wells of Badr Abu Sufyan asked some of the villagers if they had seen any strangers. An old man told him that two camelmen had stopped here to fill their water skins a short time ago. These camelmen were, of course, Muhammad's scouts who had arrived earlier in the day on a similar reconnaissance mission. The timing of the two incidents allows us to conclude that Muhammad was still on the east–west road to Badr and had not yet begun to move toward the ambush site. The Meccans and Muslims were stumbling around not more than a few miles apart, unable to locate one another. Abu Sufyan walked over to where the Muslim camelmen had couched their camels. "Abu Sufyan came to the spot where they had halted, picked up some camel dung and broke it in pieces and found that it contained date stones. 'By God,' he said, 'this is the fodder of Yathrib.'"[10] Bedouin camels live by grazing; only in towns and oases (like Medina) were camels fed on dates and ground pit flour. The dung told Abu Sufyan that the camels belonged to Muhammad's men. The fact that they had been at the Badr wells only a few hours before told him that the Muslim force was close by, probably somewhere just beyond the ring of mountains surrounding the town. Abu Sufyan rode quickly back to where he had halted the caravan and ordered it to take the west fork and move down the coastal road. He pressed the caravan into a forced march that lasted for two days and nights until he reached safety far to the south of Badr. Out of harm's way, Abu Sufyan sent a camel rider to inform the Meccan reaction force that the caravan was safe and that it was no longer necessary for them to continue moving north. He suggested that they turn around and return to Mecca.

Unbeknownst to Abu Sufyan, however, the Meccan column had moved more quickly than expected so that both columns, the Meccan relief force and the caravan, had passed one another, one heading south and the other north, on parallel roads about five miles apart. By the time Abu Sufyan's messenger reached the Meccan column, it was already well north of the caravan and only three miles south of Badr. By now Muhammad had reached the ambush site only to learn that the caravan had passed. At about the same time, the Meccan army reached the outskirts of Badr and had sent watermen forward to locate the wells and fill their water skins. With the caravan beyond reach, Muhammad turned his attention to locating the Meccan army.

He sent a small reconnaissance party into Badr, where they ran into the Meccan watermen and took two prisoners. Although the text says nothing about it, one supposes that the other Meccan watermen escaped to return to the Meccan camp and spread the alarm that the Muslims were already in Badr. The two Meccan prisoners were beaten and told their captors that they were part of the Meccan force just outside the village. Thinking they were part of Abu Sufyan's caravan, the Muslim interrogators beat them again until Muhammad intervened. The prisoners told Muhammad, "They [the Quraish] are behind this hill which you see on the farthest side (the hill was Al Aqanqal)." Muhammad asked how many men the Meccans had with them. The watermen could only answer "many."[11] Using his knowledge of caravan logistics, Muhammad asked the prisoners "how many beasts [camels] they slaughtered every day." The prisoners answered nine or ten, from which Muhammad deduced that the Meccan force was between nine hundred and one thousand men.[12]

Muhammad now knew the location and strength of the Meccan force. He asked the prisoners how many nobles there were with the force. The watermen rattled off the names of seventeen Meccan nobles. Upon hearing this Muhammad was gratified and he told his troops, "This Mecca has thrown you the pieces of its liver!"[13] The metaphor signifies that the Meccan contingent contained the best men or key leaders of Mecca. One might surmise that Muhammad could hardly believe his luck. He was fighting a political war, and here the enemy had concentrated its most important leaders in a single place. If he could engage and defeat the Meccans at Badr and kill many of their nobles, he would cripple the Quraish and remove the primary opposition to his movement. It was an old maxim of the guerrilla forces in Vietnam that "to kill a tiger, you must first draw it out of its lair." Fortune had provided the circumstances that lured the Meccan leadership out of their stronghold exposing them to attack. Muhammad was determined to bring them to battle.

Abu Sufyan's messenger had reached the Meccan army to tell them the danger to the caravan had passed and there was no need for a fight. Many of the Meccans had relatives and even sons who had become Muslims and were not disposed to fight their own clan kin if it was not necessary. The result was an acrimonious discussion among the clan chiefs in the Meccan contingent with some wishing to return to Mecca and others desiring to stay and fight. In the end three clans refused to take part in any fight with their Muslim relatives and turned for home. In rough numbers this probably reduced the strength of the Meccan force by about three hundred men, leaving approximately six hundred to seven hundred combat soldiers in the field. Many of those who remained, however, still had serious reservations about the need to shed the blood of their fellow clan members. Even Utaba and Shaiba, the sons of Utba ibn Rabia, whose client Abdullah ibn al Hadhrami had been killed at Nakhla, objected strongly to bloodshed. Indeed, Utaba's own son was in the Muslim ranks. But the requirements of honor and the blood feud were very strong, and when Utaba and Shaiba were reminded by the others that the blood debt of their father was also their debt, they reluctantly remained with the Meccans.

The psychological disposition of the Meccan soldiers was different from that of the Muslims. Many of the Meccans entered the battle with serious reservations; shedding clan blood without a very serious reason was an infamy. And yet the code of the blood feud pulled them in the opposite direction. It is reasonable to surmise that the élan and fighting spirit of the Meccans was low even before the battle began. Muslim fighting spirit, however, must have been high. Muhammad's men had adopted the new religious community as a replacement for their loyalties to clan and kin and had done so with sincere enthusiasm. The Muslims were fired by their belief in paradise as a reward for fighting for their faith. They had few reservations about having to fight their former clan members who, in their minds in any event, were idolaters and already condemned to hell. On a more human level, many of Muhammad's men harbored strong resentments against their former Quraish tribesmen. They had been forced to flee their homes, some had been beaten and tortured, most had been reduced to poverty with no way to make a living in Medina, and many had been separated from their wives and children—all because of their conversion to Islam. Many of the Muslim warriors who took the field at Badr were angry at their Meccan tormentors and eager for revenge. When the time came to fight, the superior fighting morale of the Muslims proved crucial to the outcome of the Battle of Badr.

Its wells and sufficient pasture made the village of Badr an excellent stopping place for caravans. One of the annual trade fairs was held there, and the village probably had a small idol shrine somewhat similar to the Kaaba at Mecca, but not as large or as well attended by pilgrims. The settlement itself sat on an oval-shaped plain about five and one-half miles long and four miles across surrounded by mountains. Access to the Badr plain was gained by one of three roads that ran through mountain passes. One of these connected Badr to Syria and approached from the northwest; a second road leading from Medina approached Badr from the east. The third road connected Badr with Mecca allowing passage through the mountains from the south. Badr is ten or twelve miles from the Red Sea. It was this road running between the sea and the mountains surrounding Badr on its western side that Abu Sufyan used to bypass the village and avoid Muhammad's ambush. The ground around the village was stony and strewn with pebbles, making it hard on the soft feet of the camels.[14] To the west, near Mount Asfal, the ground was broken by sand dunes that afforded some difficulty to the movement of troops. The Meccans were encamped about three miles to the south. Muhammad and his men were camped along the northwest road through the mountains near the ambush site. Each side was aware of the other by now.

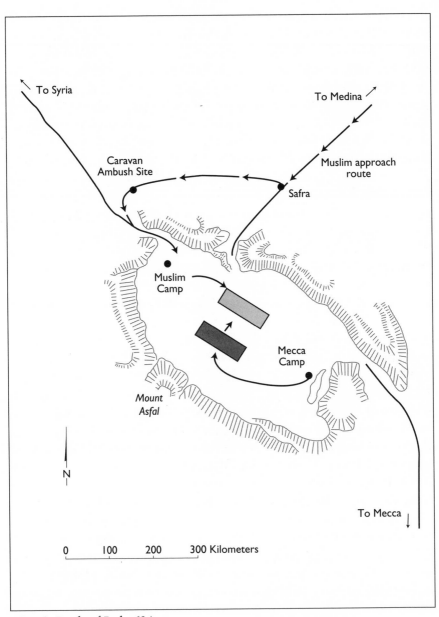

To Syria

To Medina

Caravan
Ambush Site

Muslim approach
route

Safra

Muslim
Camp

Mecca
Camp

Mount
Asfal

N

To Mecca

0   100   200   300 Kilometers

Map 6. Battle of Badr, 624 C.E.

Muhammad took the initiative and moved through the mountain pass gaining the plain from the north. He moved quickly to the center of the plain and occupied the nearest wells and ordered a halt. Here we see Muhammad on the eve of battle for the first time in command of a large body of troops. His knowledge of tactics was strikingly poor. Instead of moving farther south and seizing *all* the wells, he left the far wells unoccupied where they could be used by the Meccans when they arrived. In a desert climate water is life. The larger Meccan force required more water to sustain itself than Muhammad's contingent. Muhammad's failure to realize this was a grave tactical error and reflected Muhammad's lack of any military experience.

Fortunately for Muhammad, one of the military chiefs of the ansar clan, Hubab ibn al Mundhir, was riding with the Apostle when he drew the army to a halt and immediately saw the mistake. He turned to Muhammad and asked, "Is this the place which God has ordered you to occupy, so that we can neither advance nor withdraw from it, or is it a matter of opinion and military tactics?"[15] One of Muhammad's strengths as both a political and military commander was his willingness to listen to those who knew more than he. There can be little doubt that while Muhammad had supreme confidence in his political judgment, he was certainly aware of his lack of experience in military affairs. Muhammad responded that the troop disposition had nothing to do with revelation and that it was his idea, not God's. The chief then suggested that it would be wise to move forward and seize all the wells. There must have been a number of smaller wells forward of the Muslim position. Al Mundhir suggested these be stopped up. The wells closest to the Muslim positions were to be diverted into a cistern large enough to provide water for Muhammad's force. This done, "the Muslims would have plenty of water; then they could fight the enemy who would have nothing to drink."[16] Muhammad took al Mundhir's advice and moved his troops forward to occupy the southernmost wells. He ordered the cistern to be constructed and the remaining wells sealed. Then "his men replenished their drinking vessels" so as to have a ready supply of water when the battle commenced.

Later texts tell us that Muhammad "roamed over the plain along with some of his officers," probably to find a place to draw up his army.[17] Aside from raids and ambushes, most Arab battles of this period were set-piece affairs in which neither side made any effort to disrupt the deployment of the other. Muhammad chose a site where his men would be facing west and to the south, forcing the Meccans to face east. Arab battles usually began in the early morning when the day's heat was not yet at its height. Muhammad's choice of position forced the Meccans to fight while facing into the blinding rising sun. The Meccan army had already begun to move through the southern pass and was deploying across the plain to Muhammad's front, behind the sealed wells, where they pitched their camp. Neither side made any attempt to interfere with the other. The Meccans sent some cavalry riders to reconnoiter the Muslims' strength. They rode all around the plain looking for hidden reinforcements. Finding none, they reported back that the Muslim army consisted of "three hundred men, a little more or less. . . . They have no defense or refuge but their swords."[18]

The two armies began to arrange themselves for battle while it was still dark. One of the Meccan soldiers, angry because the wells were sealed and, perhaps, also because the army was beginning to suffer from thirst, attempted to make his way to the Muslim cistern and drink. He was cut down by the night guard. Muhammad arrayed his men in ranks; the ansar formed up by clan under their own chiefs. Muhammad arranged his troops into units of Emigrants, Awsites, and Kazrai. He inspected the troops and dressed their ranks using an arrow to prick the stomach of any soldier out of line. There is no doubt that some of the ansar, although technically converts, had come along only for the chance to obtain booty. Each unit had its own banner. Arab armies used watchwords or passwords at night to control infiltration. These watchwords were equally useful during the day. Arab armies of this period had no distinguishing uniforms or equipment, so that in the middle of an infantry melee it was often difficult to tell friend from foe. Soldiers would shout their army's password when encountering another soldier so that each could determine the identity of the other.

One of Muhammad's tactical tendencies, one that the later Arab armies of the conquest period demonstrated as well, was a preference for the defense. At Badr and in most other battles that he fought Muhammad chose to get to the battlefield first, select a strong defensive position, and wait for the enemy to come to him. At Badr he chose a position where his army was on the back edge of a field of sand dunes between himself and the Meccans so that the Meccans would be forced to make their way over the dunes before engaging his front ranks. Muhammad probably hoped that the soft sand would tire the enemy, weakening them before they engaged his rested infantry. As it turned out, it rained during the night turning the Meccan camp "into a swamp."[19] It is difficult to believe, however, that the Meccan camp was affected so severely. A rainstorm of such magnitude surely would have been mentioned in Ibn Ishaq's account, which it is not. More likely a modest rain firmed up the ground under the feet of the Muslims at the edge of the dunes while leaving most of the dunes between the Muslims and Meccans still soft in deep sand. If the Meccans were beginning to suffer from thirst, having to make their way across the soft dunes might well have consumed much of their energy before the battle even began, just as Muhammad may have calculated when he chose his position. A later text tells that Muhammad instructed his troops to collect piles of stones, the grenades of the day, to throw at the enemy. The thrown stone was an important weapon in antiquity, especially so among tribal armies. Troops arrayed in the defense could collect and throw more stones than an advancing enemy, who, having to carry their weapons and shield, could each only carry one or two stones at a time.[20]

Muhammad addressed his troops before the battle. Ibn Ishaq tells us only that "the Apostle had ordered his companions not to attack until he gave the word, and if the enemy should surround them they were to keep them off with showers of arrows."[21] Later texts have the Prophet addressing his troops in considerably more detail in the fashion of the orations of commanders found in classical texts of the West. These accounts even have Muhammad giving precise instructions. "Do not move to break your lines but stay on; do not commence fighting until I order; do not waste your arrows while the enemy is still beyond reach; discharge your arrows only when the target is within reach; when the enemy approaches, begin to throw stones with your hands; on his nearer approach use lances and spear, the sword being drawn only finally for hand to hand fighting."[22] Given Muhammad's lack of military experience, it is unlikely that he would have been able to address his troops in such practical detail. More likely the later text is a version of events redacted to demonstrate Muhammad's military prowess.

At Badr we see Muhammad's forces operating under a unified system of command, an overall field commander whose orders are followed by soldiers and clan chiefs regardless of their own tactical propensities, desire for loot, and even considerations of individual honor. At Badr the ummah fought together for the first time. Muhammad was transforming Arab warfare from war as sport, clan revenge, or individual glory into an instrument for the achievement of political goals. Muhammad intended to destroy the Quraish, not to fight for honor or loot. He could have safely returned to Medina after he failed to ambush Abu Sufyan's caravan. Instead, he remained at Badr looking for the opportunity to draw the Meccans into battle in the hopes of killing the Meccan leadership at a single opportunity. In Muhammad's intention to do just that we see the first example in Arab warfare of an army demonstrating strategic direction and unity of command under a single commander.

Muhammad and a small bodyguard climbed a low hill that overlooked the battlefield from behind the Muslim positions. A small hut or enclosure made with palm fronds was constructed for Muhammad. A number of riding camels were tethered outside to be used for Muhammad and his staff to make their escape should things go badly. Like Moses at the Battle of Rephidim against the Amalekites, the overall commander was not on the battlefield but on a hill overlooking it. The absence of the overall commander from the actual battle was an old practice in the West. It was probably Philip II of Macedon at the Battle of Cheronea who was the first field general to command his army from a position removed from the actual fighting.[23] The practice quickly caught on among sophisticated armies of the West so that we find Caesar, Scipio, and others commanding from near the battlefield but not engaged in the battle itself. But Arab warfare was tribal war in which every able-bodied man took part. This was especially so for the clan chiefs and commander of the army who were expected to set the standard for bravery and military prowess in battle. At Badr Muhammad seems to have introduced the Western practice of removed command. He had appointed his tactical commanders, selected the defensive position, developed a tactical plan, and inspected his men before retiring from the battlefield to seek a "light sleep" in the hut. General Sir Bernard Montgomery during Operation Market Garden in World War II retired to his tent to sleep after "doing all he could" to prepare his army for the battle. Like Montgomery, Muhammad left control of the actual fighting to his subordinate unit commanders.

The Meccans "marched forth at daybreak" leaving their encampment just inside the southern pass and deployed facing the Muslim ranks. In traditional Arab fashion the Meccans issued the usual challenge that the Muslims send out their best men to engage in individual combat. Three men of the ansar came forward to answer the challenge. The Meccans were Quraish and refused to accept the challengers from

Medina. They wanted to fight the men from the Quraish tribe who had become Muslims saying, "Send forth against us our peers of our own tribe."[24] The Meccans sent forth Utaba ibn Rabia, the son of the man to whom the blood debt was owed; Utaba's son, al Waleed, who took up a position on his father's left; and Utaba's brother, Shaiba, who stood to the right. Muhammad sent his uncle Hamza, a warrior noted for skill and ferocity; his cousin and recent son-in-law, Ali, who had married Muhammad's daughter, Fatima; and an old warrior, Ubaida ibn al Harith. The fight did not last long. Hamza killed Shaiba and Ali slew Waleed in hand-to-hand combat. Ubaida and Utaba hacked at one another for some minutes until both simultaneously landed near-fatal blows and fell to the ground. Hamza and Ali rushed toward the wounded Utaba and killed him. They carried their wounded comrade from the field, but to no avail. Ubaida's leg "had been cut to the marrow" and he bled to death.

The sun shined into the eyes of the Meccans who had just seen three of their best warriors slain before them. The heat, thirst, and fear must have begun to take their toll on the fighting spirit of the Meccan army, many of whose men had never been eager for a fight that day. Muslim morale had been strengthened further by the victories of their champions. The texts do not tell us who attacked first, only that a wild melee of flashing swords took place as both sides crashed into one another. Even with their fighting spirit weakened, the Meccans did not crack, and the battle moved back and forth, neither side gaining an advantage. The Meccans were unable to use their superiority in numbers to force a decision. Curiously, there is no mention of the participation of the Meccan cavalry that was surely present at Badr and had been used earlier to conduct a reconnaissance of the battlefield. The poetry and oral traditions of the battle mention that cavalry was present, in one instance making reference to fleeing "on a swift footed noble mare," and in another where the poet complains that the horses were no protection during the fight. Arab cavalry, as mentioned earlier, was not a decisive military arm and could not successfully attack disciplined infantry while it remained in formation. Like the cavalry of most armies of the ancient world, Arab cavalry hovered on the flanks picking off strays waiting for the infantry to break and run. In that event, cavalry could be put to good use hunting down and killing individual targets. The lack of participation of the Meccan cavalry at Badr suggests that the Muslim infantry retained its cohesion and continued to fight as an organized unit, just as Muhammad must have hoped the members of the ummah would do. It also suggests that Muhammad's introduction of a unified command for Muslim armies was a success.

The Battle of Badr might have been a close call, however, for it was only after the fighting had raged for some time (we are not told how long by any of the texts) that Muhammad left his hut on the hill and "went forth to the people and incited them by saying, 'By God in whose hand is the soul of Muhammad, no man will be slain this day fighting against them with steadfast courage, advancing not retreating, but God will cause him to enter Paradise.'"[25] The promise of eternal life in paradise was new to Arab thinking as it had been for the early Egyptians who may have been the first to conceive of a theology of resurrection and eternal life and for Christians who appear later to have adopted these ideas into their own theology.[26] Modern religious devotees long accustomed to this idea perhaps do not always appreciate its attraction for a people who had never conceived of such a thing before. Muhammad's promise of paradise was completely new to Arab theology and was a powerful motivational force for his soldiers.

Muhammad may have left his hut to rally his troops because things were going badly or because the outnumbered Muslims, despite holding their ground, were hard pressed by the advantage of Meccan numbers. Ibn Ishaq records that after Muhammad addressed his troops one soldier was so moved that he threw down his rations (there must have been a lull in the battle) and waded back into the fight. Another threw off his coat of mail and plunged into the battle unarmored, fighting until he was killed.[27] Muhammad stopped speaking, reached down and picked up a handful of pebbles and threw them at the enemy, and then ordered his men to attack. It was then, tradition says (but the original texts do not support), that a wind came up driving the dry sand into the faces of the Meccans. The shock of the Muslim attack broke the spirit of the Meccans, who turned and fled. A Meccan soldier who fought at Badr later described the flight of his own troops in a poem. "When I saw the army panic, running away at top speed, and that their leaders lay dead, I thought the best of them were like sacrifices to idols. Many of them lay there dead. And we were made to meet our fate at Badr."[28] With no cavalry of his own Muhammad could not pursue, and the remnants of the Meccan army were allowed to limp back to their camp unmolested.

Depending on the source, the Meccans lost either 49 or 70 dead and about the same number taken prisoner, a loss of 20 percent of the total force. By traditional Arab casualty standards this number was enormous. The Meccans had suffered a major defeat. Muhammad's contingent had suffered fourteen dead with no number of wounded recorded. If one assumes an equal number of wounded to dead, then the Muslims suffered a total combat loss of about 10 percent of strength. Nothing revealed the changed nature of Arab warfare at Badr more than the manner in which the Meccan prisoners were treated. The mercy and holding for ransom that had characterized traditional warfare in Arabia for centuries were almost completely absent at Badr. A number of prisoners were beheaded by men who held personal grudges against them. In one case a father chopped off the foot of his son who was fighting for the Meccans.[29] Other prisoners were executed for no apparent reason. "They hewed them to pieces with their swords until they were dead."[30] The ideological fervor of the Muslims is obvious when it is remembered that they were killing members of their own tribe, men who were blood relatives and sometimes even family members. Muhammad had brought a new cruelty and lethality to Arab warfare.

Whatever the military value of the Muslim victory at Badr, in Muhammad's view it was first and foremost a strategic *political* victory. Muhammad killed without mercy all the Meccan leaders that had fallen into his hands. In one case Muhammad ordered the battlefield searched for one Abu Jahal, a chief of the Beni Makhzoom clan, and an early opponent of Muhammad. Jahal had been a childhood friend of Muhammad, but later turned against him. Jahal was discovered wounded among a pile of Meccan corpses. When being taken to Muhammad he is supposed to have taunted his captor with the result that his captor cut off his head on the spot. Jahal's head was brought to Muhammad. The soldier said, "I threw the head before the Apostle and he gave thanks to God."[31] Muhammad ordered his men to dig a large pit into which the corpses of the Meccans were thrown and buried. As the bodies were being thrown into the pit, Muhammad stood on its lip and said, "O people of the pit, have you found that what God threatened is true? For I have found that what my lord promised me is true." His companions were taken aback and one of them asked, "Are you speaking to dead people?" Muhammad replied, "They hear what I say to them. . . . They hear!"[32]

On his way back to Medina Muhammad took the opportunity to settle some other old scores. Not all the prisoners had been killed. One of these was al Nadhr, who used to follow Muhammad around through the streets of Mecca mocking him and telling people that his stories were as true as Muhammad's! When Muhammad was told that his ridiculer was in his hands, he had the man brought before him. Muhammad ordered Ali to behead the man before his eyes. Later in the journey another man, Uqba ibn Muait, was brought before Muhammad. He pleaded for his life crying out, Who will care for my wife and children? Muhammad replied coldly, "Hellfire!" Some of Muhammad's behavior can be explained as pure revenge for personal slights suffered earlier. But most of the executions were nothing less than political murder to deprive the Meccans of their leadership and to weaken them strategically. The killings were coldly calculated and carried out on the grounds of political ideology and expediency. Muhammad himself seems to have suggested exactly this. When the Muslim army entered Medina some people ran up to him and congratulated him on the victory at Badr. Ali shunted them aside. "What are you congratulating us about? By God, we only met some old bald women like the sacrificial camels who are hobbled, and then we slaughtered them." Muhammad is said to have turned to Ali and smiled. "But nephew, those were the chiefs."[33] In this exchange Muhammad revealed his clear understanding of the political nature of warfare as conducted by an insurgency, something that was completely different from the warfare to which Arabs had been previously accustomed.

Two important events followed the Battle of Badr: Muhammad's reform of the marriage laws and his first attack on the Jewish tribes of Medina. The reform of the marriage laws was probably in response to the relatively large number of Muslim males killed at Badr. While we cannot be certain, it might have been that the greater number of the dead were suffered by the Emigrants, thus leaving a considerable number of women widows and children orphans with no one to care for them. Soon after Badr Muhammad had a revelation that reformed the traditional Arab customs governing marriage. The instruction appears in the Quran and says, "If ye fear that ye may not act with equity in regard to the orphans, marry such of the women as seem good to you, two or three or four—but if ye fear that ye may not be fair (to several wives), then one only or what your right hands possess."[34] Muhammad was not placing a limit on some previous Arab practice of unlimited polygamy as is sometimes thought. On the contrary, he was encouraging men who had only one wife to marry up to four. Muhammad's injunction was not a restriction of an old practice, but the introduction of a completely new one.[35]

The immediate stimulus for Muhammad's reforms of the marriage laws was the need to find husbands and fathers for the wives and children of the men that had been killed at Badr. The losses at Badr had thrown into sharper relief a problem that had plagued Arab societies for centuries. What with male deaths suffered in raids and personal combat, and lost to disease, and the generally higher survival rates of female babies, it is likely that there was always a surplus of females in Arabia. The surplus was somewhat held in check by the old bedouin practice of female infanticide in times of famine. Even so, the problem of how to care for women in general and widows and orphans in particular was chronic. This was one reason why girls as young as ten years old were sometimes "married" to older men who promised to take care of them. Men frequently married widows and orphans for their dowry or property left by the previous spouse, only to treat them badly and steal their wealth. This left widows and orphans in a worse state than before.[36] Muhammad's reforms, which also forbade female infanticide, were designed to correct both these problems by permitting men to have as many as four wives but only on the condition that all wives and children be treated fairly and equitably. It was the losses at Badr, however, that may have prompted Muhammad to proclaim the reforms when he did.

The second major event following closely upon the Battle of Badr was Muhammad's attack on the Qaynuqa, one of the Jewish tribes of Medina. The immediate result of the victory at Badr was a tremendous increase in the prestige and morale of the Muslims. No one could deny that they had defeated a powerful Meccan tribe in open battle, killing off much of its leadership and taking weapons, armor, and camels as loot. Muslims are correct when they regard the Battle of Badr as the most significant military event in the history of their religion, for had they lost at Badr the Muslim movement might well have collapsed. In Muslim eyes it was a victory owed to God's intercession and is called "*the day of the furqan*," or day of proof. The victory at Badr is seen by Muslims as the equivalent of God's intervention to save his chosen people by parting the waves of the Red Sea so that Moses and the Israelites could escape pharaoh's chariots. For many at the time the victory at Badr confirmed or "proved" Muhammad's claim to be God's Messenger, with the result that conversions increased and Muhammad's following grew. Most important to Muhammad's decision to move against the Jews of Medina was the fact that large numbers of the Aws and Kazrai tribes of Medina converted to Islam, thereby forswearing their previous alliances with the Jewish tribes.

Muhammad moved quickly to consolidate his power in Medina. His hatred of poets was well known and he immediately ordered the assassination of two Medinan poets: Asma bint Marwan, a married woman with five children; and a man, Abu Afek, were both killed on Muhammad's order. Here we see assassination for political ends. These killings were political murders carried out for ideological reasons or personal revenge. Muhammad believed he was doing God's work, and all those who opposed him or his faith had to be eliminated. To permit poets or anyone else to ridicule him or the new ideology of Islam was to undermine the primary reason why Muhammad was conducting the insurgency. At the same time, however, Muhammad hired his own poets to spread his propaganda among the tribes. One of these was Hassan ibn Thabit. When Muhammad asked him if he could defend him from the attacks of his enemies, ibn Thabit is said to have stuck out his tongue and replied, "There is no armor which I cannot pierce with this weapon."[37]

Muhammad now turned against the Jews in Medina. They had become increasingly hostile to his claims to be a prophet, publicly held him up to ridicule, and confronted him with arguments to refute his claims. There had been few conversions among the Jews, and the three Jewish tribes, when taken together, could mount a formidable armed force against him. Of the Jewish tribes—Beni an-Nadir, Beni Qurayzah, and Beni Qaynuqa—the Qaynuqa alone were said to have three hundred soldiers with armor and four hundred without armor.[38] The other two Jewish clans were either larger in absolute numbers or had stronger alliances with the Aws and Kazrai Arab tribes, which made them too powerful for Muhammad to attack. He seems to have chosen to confront the weakest of the Jewish tribes. The Beni Qaynuqa were goldsmiths and armorers and owned no fields; they had their own compounds and a small marketplace where they traded and sold their wares.

The immediate cause of the break with the Jews was an altercation that occurred in the Qaynuqa marketplace involving some sort of indecency to a Muslim woman. Both Hamza and Ali, two of the Apostle's closest companions, were involved, leading one to suspect that the confrontation was deliberately provoked. The Jews reacted to the threat by arming their men and withdrawing to their fortified compounds to await a Muslim attack. The Beni Qaynuqa had alliances with clans of the Aws and Kazrai and expected them to come to their aid against Muhammad. But most clans of both Arab tribes had already converted to Islam and made it clear that their new loyalties abrogated their previous pledges to the Jews. Isolated and with no possibility of military aid, the Beni Qaynuqa surrendered after a siege of two weeks during which there was no fighting and no casualties on either side.

The question now was, what to do with the Jews? Ibn Ishaq's account suggests that Muhammad wanted to kill them.[39] A leader of a clan of the Kazrai, one Abdullah ibn Ubay, an influential leader in Medina and a man known for his reasonableness, went to Muhammad. Ibn Ubay was a Muslim convert and begged Muhammad to show mercy to the Beni Qaynuqa who had once been his allies. In the Kazrai wars with the Aws the Jews of the Beni Qaynuqa clan had sided with his clan, and one of them may have saved ibn Ubay's life on the battlefield. Ibn Ubay said to the Apostle, "Oh Muhammad, deal kindly with my allies." Muhammad rudely turned his back on him. Ibn Ubay seized Muhammad by the cloak and spun him around. Ibn Ishaq tells us, "The Apostle was so angry his face became almost black. He said, "Confound you, let go of me!" Abdullah replied, "No, by God, I will not let you go until you deal kindly with my clients. Four hundred men unarmored and three hundred in armor protected me from my enemies. Would you cut them down in one morning? By God, I am a man who fears that circumstances may change!"[40]

Abdullah's words to Muhammad—"Would you cut them down in one morning?"—suggest that Muhammad had planned to execute the Jewish males. They were, after all, his ideological enemies; any hopes for Jewish conversions were slim. The Jews of Medina would always be his enemies. Why not deal with them now once and for all? The time would come when Muhammad would have all the males of another Jewish tribe beheaded in Medina's public square. Ibn Ubay was clearly threatening Muhammad when he said, "I am a man who fears that circumstances may change!" He was a powerful chief of the Kazrai tribe, and although a Muslim, he seemed to be saying he was prepared to support his old allies and observe the traditional tribal obligations instead of his obligations as a Muslim. He was threatening Muhammad with civil war. Muhammad grasped the calculation of interests immediately.

He could not hope to outfight a coalition of the Kazrai and the Jews. If he attempted to do so, he risked losing the support of other Arab clans and even some converted clans of the Aws who had until recently also been allies of the Jews. Muhammad drew back from the confrontation. "You can have their lives," he said, and walked out.[41]

Muhammad's opposition to the Jews of Medina seems to have arisen from a number of factors. Whether Muhammad was an anti-Semite as some have claimed remains a question beyond the scope of this work. But once the Jews of Medina were dealt with Muhammad ordered special protections for Jews and Christians, even going so far as to forbid that they be targets of Muslim proselytizing. Muhammad was, however, a committed revolutionary ideologue. There was no doubt that on this score the Jews could not be permitted to undermine Muhammad's claim to be God's Messenger. To do so would undermine the fundamental reason for the insurgency. The Jewish tribes of Medina were also a formidable military threat if they chose to use their strength against the Muslims. Muhammad's control over Medina would never be complete so long as these competitors for military power were permitted to retain their forces. Moreover, Muhammad could never hope to expand his insurgency beyond Medina or to move with military force against Mecca unless his base of operations in Medina was completely secure. To achieve this he had to reduce the threat of the Jewish forces in the city. Finally, Muhammad's sensitivity to personal ridicule seems also to have played a part in his motivations. During the time of the quarrel with the Beni Qaynuqa Muhammad had a revelation that seems to explain his anger at the Jews in precisely these terms. Sura 5, verse 57, of the Quran says, "Oh you who believe, do not take as allies those who received the Books before you [Jews and Christians] but who treat your religion as a joke and a game." As with all revolutionaries, past and present, ideological opponents were always seen as the worst enemies, more so when they made the mistake of not taking a revolutionary idealist seriously.

The Jews of the Beni Qaynuqa were ordered to leave Medina and to leave most of their property and wealth behind. Muhammad expressly commanded that they leave their metalworking tools and equipment with which they made weapons and armor. Muhammad now had his own armory. The houses, property, fields, and animals of the Beni Qaynuqa were distributed among the Muslims, which helped lift them out of the terrible poverty they had endured for so long. The Jews migrated north to Syria. Never a man to overlook details, Muhammad turned to another personal matter. An Arab poet, Kaab ibn al Ashraf, was living with his mother's Jewish tribe and was thought to be a Jew himself. Ibn al Ashraf had composed a poem lamenting the death of the Meccans at Badr. Muhammad's intelligence service also suspected that he was traveling regularly to Mecca, where he was urging the Meccans to take revenge for Badr. According to Ibn Ishaq, Muhammad said to his companions, "Who will rid me of Ibn al Ashraf?"[42] A half-brother of the poet who had become a Muslim was used to lure al Ashraf into the night, where he was murdered. Muhammad was becoming a man with a reputation for not suffering insults easily.

7

BATTLE OF UHUD
March 625

The Meccan leadership had been decapitated, and one can only imagine Abu Sufyan's shock upon learning that so many of the city's leaders had been killed at Badr. Many of the old chiefs were quickly replaced by their less experienced sons, leaving Abu Sufyan the only Quraish leader of stature to direct the civic and military affairs of the city. The older leadership had been divided on how to deal with Muhammad, with many being reluctant to use force against him. The devastating defeat at Badr, the rise of the younger chiefs, and Abu Sufyan's public outrage and oath to take revenge changed that. Many Meccans were now convinced that Muhammad could be dealt with only by force. Within a month the Meccans assembled a raiding party of 150 to 200 men under Abu Sufyan's command to undertake a raid on Medina. The small size of the raiding party suggests that its purpose was mostly psychological, to serve notice that the Meccans were still a force to be reckoned with and were ready to fight. The point may also have been to send a message to the bedouin tribes who controlled the caravan routes and on whom the Meccan trade depended for its safe travel. The Meccans now regarded Muhammad as their archenemy.

In April 624 Abu Sufyan's raiders approached Medina. In Arab fashion they prepared to attack in the early morning, switching from camels to horses. Ibn Ishaq is silent on the details of the raid, but it appears to have been a minor engagement with only a few workers caught tending the fields killed and two houses burned before the raiders withdrew. The Quba section of Medina where the raid took place lies south of the town and was densely settled so that compounds, date palm groves, and walled gardens made cavalry maneuver difficult by canalizing the raiders into narrow files. Once the alarm was sounded, the Meccans broke off the attack and returned to their camp, switched mounts to their camels, and moved quickly south along the road to Mecca. It took some time for Muhammad to assemble a reaction force and give chase. The Meccans had a significant lead but were slowed by the need to attend to their horses tethered behind the camels. At some point the Muslims must have gotten close. To lighten their load and increase their speed the Meccans jettisoned some of their baggage, including several sacks of dried barley used for making porridge. In Muslim chronicles Abu Sufyan's foray and retreat is known derisively as the "Porridge Raid." The Muslims broke off their pursuit, having given chase mostly to save face and not to engage the Meccans.

In May 624 Muhammad sought to capitalize on the increased prestige afforded by his victory at Badr by assembling a force of two hundred men and leading raids against two bedouin tribes, the Ghatafan and the Beni Sulaym. The Ghatafan bedouins lived between Medina and Kheibar, the main Jewish oasis to the north of Medina. The Beni Sulaym lived to the south of Medina, astride the main caravan route from Mecca. These raids accomplished little but the capture of five hundred camels from the Ghatafan. No fighting took place. In June 624 Muhammad assembled a larger force of 450 men and set out to raid the Ghatafan again. The Ghatafans detected his advance and moved farther into the desert to avoid contact. In August 624 Muhammad led three hundred men against the Beni Sulaym but once more was unable to find them and bring them to battle. These failures throw into sharp relief the inability of Muhammad's intelligence service to perform adequately. Given their locations along the main caravan route, both the Ghatafan and Beni Sulaym tribes must have had long-standing commercial relations to provide lodging, forage, and protection for the Meccan caravans. They were also, of course, pagans. Muhammad's attempt to attack these tribes was not motivated by religion, but by his desire to weaken the transportation infrastructure of inns, wells, feeding places, and the friendly tribes that controlled them that the Meccan caravans required to carry out their journeys. Muhammad was attempting to strangle and isolate Mecca economically and politically.

The strategy seems to have had some success. Ibn Ishaq tells us that the "Quraish were afraid to follow their usual route to Syria after what had happened at Badr, so they went by the Iraq route."[1] A poet later described the difficulty that the Meccans faced in getting their caravans by Muhammad's blockade. "You can say good-bye to the streams of Damascus, for in between are swords like the mouths of pregnant camels who feed on arak trees."[2] The sources describe the Meccan caravan in 625 as carrying a rich load of silver and other goods, a description that suggests it was the annual spring caravan. But this seems unlikely. The guard was too small for such an important caravan and was easily driven off by the Muslim force of only one hundred men. If Muhammad had planned to attack the spring caravan, he would have put a much larger force in the field to deal with the strong guard that would have attended it in light of his own recent attacks. Most likely the caravan was a small one and the figures regarding its captured cargo were inflated by the Muslims for propaganda purposes.

Muhammad's intelligence source in Mecca, his uncle Abbas, seems to have supplied the information necessary to make the raid a success by permitting Muhammad sufficient time to assemble a force and position it where it could ambush the caravan.[3] The raiding party consisted of only a hundred men under the command of Zayd, the former Christian slave whom Muhammad had adopted as his son. The caravan was attacked while it watered at a well near Qarda in Jejed, the guard driven off, and its cargo seized. Zayd returned to Medina with the booty. There were no Muslim casualties. The news of the caravan's capture reached Mecca to widespread outrage. The new Meccan leadership seems to have understood that Muhammad's attacks had now become a strategic threat to their livelihood and economic survival. There was no alternative but to break Muhammad's blockade with force. Abu Sufyan, the most prominent man left in Mecca since Badr and an experienced military commander, was selected to raise an army to destroy Muhammad once and for all.

In late January 625 an army of three thousand men and two hundred horses made up of the Quraish, an assembly of bedouin client tribes, and some "black troops" who were probably Abyssinian mercenaries marched out of Mecca toward Medina to bring the war to Muhammad.[4]

The Meccan army took twelve days to reach Medina. Their route of march took them west of the city itself and then north where they camped at a place known as the Two Springs on an open plain at the foot of a rocky outcropping called Mount Uhud. The reason the army did not come directly at Medina from the south was due to the terrain. Medina is situated on a lava plain about ten miles wide and ten miles long surrounded on three sides by steep mountains. Access from beyond the mountains to the plain itself is through a few narrow easily defended passes. The approach from the south was through Quba, an area thickly populated with clan compounds, walled gardens, and date palm groves, all of which make movement by units in formation difficult. The lava fields to the southeast rendered the terrain unsuitable for cavalry and difficult for infantry and camels as well. To the southeast lay the compounds of the Jewish tribes, and the west was thick with more groves and gardens. Any attempt to move the Meccan army through the southern pass at Quba would be difficult and expose it to the risk of ambush.

Medina could only be approached from the north over open ground free of obstacles. Much of the land between Medina and Mount Uhud was saline and unfit for cultivation.[5] Once past the foot of Mount Uhud, however, there was a good well at Zaghabah and sufficient grass to feed horses and camels. There were also some small crop fields where the Meccan animals could feed. The old riverbed running through the area was full of soft sand that was a comfort to the camels' feet. The Meccan army went into camp just north of the foot of Mount Uhud. The arrival of the Meccans was no secret, and Muhammad immediately dispatched Muslim scouts to keep watch on them. He called for a general mobilization to deal with the threat. About a thousand men reported for duty.[6]

Muhammad knew that he was greatly outnumbered and that giving battle on the open plain would relinquish the advantage to the Meccans. Worse, there was no Muslim cavalry while the Meccans had two hundred mounted horsemen under the command of Khalid al-Walid and Ikrimah ibn Abu Jahl, later to become two of the most famous Muslim generals in the wars of conquest. Muhammad called his staff together for advice. He was, as always, disposed to the defense and wanted to draw the enemy into Medina itself in house-to-house fighting. In this he was supported by Abdullah ibn Ubay, the chief of the Kazrai and an experienced warrior. Ibn Ubay said, "Oh Apostle, stay in Medina, do not go out to them. We have never gone out to fight an enemy but we

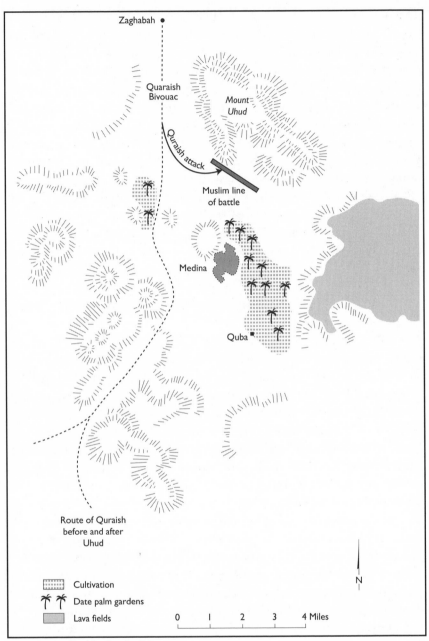

Map 7. Battle of Uhud, 625 C.E.

have met disaster, and none has come in against us without being defeated." (Ibn Ubay's references to past battles were to the tribal wars, not to any previous Muslim engagements.) "If they stay, they stay in an evil predicament, and if they come in, the men will fight them and the women and children will throw stones on them from the walls, and if they retreat they will retreat low-spirited as they came."[7] Ibn Ubay was inclined, as Ibn Hisham tells us, "to fight it out in the streets."[8]

Medina was full of obstacles to both cavalry and infantry movement deployed in large formations; the palm groves, springs, walled gardens, and the fortified compounds with their towers made the use of Meccan cavalry impossible while at the same time making it difficult for the Meccans to bring their superior infantry numbers to bear. The terrain and obstacles would force the Meccan units to break up into smaller ones, making them vulnerable to ambush and to piecemeal engagement by the Muslims. Moreover, the Meccans had no siege machinery. If the Muslims withdrew into their compounds and refused to give battle, it would only be a matter of time before the Meccan army, lacking any supply train, would have consumed what crops were still in the fields before being forced to withdraw. Both Muhammad and ibn Ubay showed considerable grasp of tactics in their analysis of how to deal with the Meccan threat.

Muhammad failed, however, to put his original tactical plan into operation. A crowd gathered around Muhammad's house and clamored to be led out to meet the Meccans in open battle. Many of the younger men, perhaps seeking martyrdom, were particularly adamant in their desire for an open fight, perhaps believing that the God that had granted them victory at Badr would do so again. The debate continued for two days before Muhammad finally put an end to it by agreeing to lead his men into battle against the Meccans on the open plain. Muhammad retired to his house and put on his armor and retrieved his weapons. When he emerged he found that the crowd had changed its mind and now wanted to stay in the city and fight![9] But Muhammad was now resolute in his decision and ordered his men to assemble in the cul-de-sac at the foot of Mount Uhud.

As the Muslim soldiers retrieved their armor and weapons from their houses and straggled toward the assembly area, two interesting events occurred. Depending on which source one reads, a contingent of Jews from the remaining tribes had assembled to help Muhammad because they were allies of Abdullah ibn Ubay; they showed up to fulfill their traditional tribal obligations to defend their allies. One of the Muslims told Muhammad that the contingent were Jews. Muhammad is said to have replied, "It is not right to invoke the aid of polytheists to fight other polytheists."[10] The other version of the story is that one of Muhammad's officers, no doubt reflecting on the fact that the Muslims were outnumbered, asked Muhammad directly, "Oh Apostle, should we not ask help from our allies, the Jews?"[11] Muhammad replied, "We have no need of them."[12] It is unlikely that the first version is correct. Muhammad certainly knew that the Jews were not poly-theists and never seems to have referred to them as such even though it became somewhat common for later Muslim sources to refer to both Christians and Jews as polytheists. The second version rings true and is interesting in that it reflects Muhammad's view of war as ideological and not based in traditional clan obligations. In terms of numbers, Muhammad surely could have made good use of the Jewish warriors. He chose not to on ideological grounds. War was a God-directed activity of the faithful, not merely a military exercise.

The second event was potentially more ominous. Abdullah ibn Ubay strongly disagreed with Muhammad's decision to offer battle in the open plain instead of engaging in house-to-house fighting in the streets of Medina. He withdrew his contingent of Kazrai tribesmen, about three hundred men or "a third of the men," and rode back to Medina.[13] Ibn Ubay seems to have realized that Muhammad's choice of an assembly area at the foot of Mount Uhud had uncovered the approaches to Medina itself exposing it to attack. When formed for battle the Meccan army had a clear avenue of advance toward Medina. Ibn Ubay may have cal-culated that if Muhammad was driven from the field, a not unrealistic expectation in light of the relative strengths of the armies, there was nothing to stop the Meccans from taking the city, looting it, and putting it to the torch. Ibn Ubay thought this too great a risk and retired with his men to his own clan compound, where he prepared to defend it against the Meccan attack that he expected would come in the wake of Muhammad's defeat.

Upon the arrival of the Meccans Muhammad ordered a picket line to be thrown across the northern approaches and nightly patrols con-ducted to warn of enemy activity. Muhammad surrounded himself with a bodyguard of fifty men. The withdrawal of ibn Ubay's troops left Muhammad with only seven hundred men. Of these one hundred had coats of mail. The Meccans had three thousand men and two hundred horses; seven hundred Meccans had coats of mail armor.[14] There were also contingents of "black troops" among the Meccans, probably Abyssinian mercenaries who were known as good javelin men. By any reasonable military calculation the Meccan army was larger, better equipped, more experienced, and led by experienced cavalry and infantry officers. Only a commander like Muhammad who believed that God was on his side and would determine the outcome of the fight would have engaged the Meccans under these circumstances and upon open ground. From a military perspective his decision bordered on incompetence.

Map 8 depicts the battlefield of Uhud and the relative positions of the Muslim and Meccan armies. Muhammad made no attempt to take advantage of any natural obstacles and deployed his forces for a direct infantry engagement. He realized that his defensive position was exposed to cavalry attacks on both flanks and that some way had to be found to neutralize the Meccan cavalry. Across the field the Meccan cavalry had deployed in a somewhat unorthodox manner. One troop under the command of Ikrimah ibn Abu Jahl was deployed forward of the main Meccan infantry line and was likely intended to skirmish with the Muslim front line using their lances from horseback. The more serious threat to Muhammad's position was the second troop, probably larger, under the command of Khalid al-Walid that deployed far to the right of the Meccan infantry line. Its mission was to turn Muhammad's flank.

The terrain to Muhammad's left and in front of al-Walid's troops was broken by palm groves and walled gardens, but insufficiently so to prevent a movement in formation by the Meccan cavalry. To prevent al-Walid's cavalry from turning his flank, Muhammad posted fifty archers on the Ainain Hill, hereafter called the Hill of Arrows in Muslim chronicles. Later texts state that Muhammad sent a few mounted men to help fill the gap between the hill and the groves.[15] The earliest texts tell us, however, that Muhammad had only two horses available and he was mounted on one. What might have occurred is that some Muslim soldiers arrived late and may have brought a few horses with them. In any event it was a paltry force and no match for al-Walid's cavalry. If Muhammad was to prevent the Meccans from turning his flank, it would have to be with the indirect fire from the archers positioned on the Hill of Arrows.

That Muhammad recognized the importance of the archers' position to his chances of success is clear from the instructions he issued

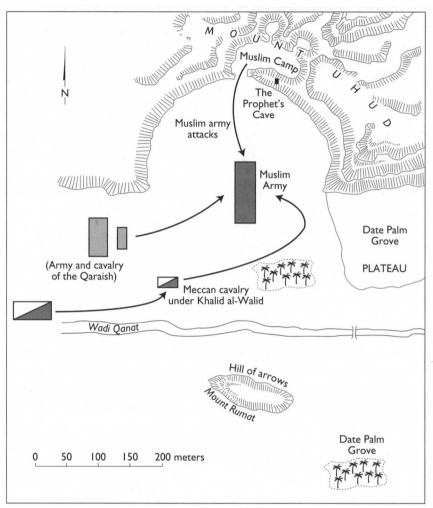

Map 8. The Battlefield of Uhud

to Abdullah bin Jubayr, their commander. Ibn Ishaq records that
Muhammad instructed his commander to "keep the cavalry away
from us with your arrows and let them not come on us from the rear
whether the battle goes in favor or against us; and keep your places so
that we cannot be got at from your direction."[16] In short, hold the
position to the last man or until relieved. Later sources record a more
dramatic instruction. The archers were ordered not to leave their
positions "even if the vultures perch on the corpses of the Muslims."[17]
Muhammad seems to have realized that if his flank were turned,
defeat would be inevitable and, as Abdullah ibn Ubay had predicted,
the road to Medina would be open.

Ibn Ishaq tells us that when Muhammad emerged from his house
in full armor, "the Apostle wore two coats of mail on the day of
Uhud."[18] The story makes little sense for a double shirt of mail would
weigh close to seventy pounds and would have made movement very
difficult. This said, when Muhammad had been knocked to the ground
during the battle one text tells us that "he had put on two coats of
mail so when he tried to get up he could not do so" and had to be lifted
up and carried to safety.[19] A later source says that Muhammad did
not put on two coats of mail but exchanged his armor with one of his
soldiers, one Ka'b ibn Malik, "apparently for the purposes of disguise
and security on the day of the battle."[20] This is a more plausible expla-
nation, and as events turned out it was Muhammad's disguise that
saved his life that day.

Muhammad reviewed his troops on horseback and moved them
into position on the battlefield. The sources do not tell us the time of
day the battle began, but there is no reason to suspect that it was any
other time but late morning. The two lines of infantry drew up opposite one another. The battle began when a Meccan warrior stepped
forward challenging the Muslims to send forth a champion to meet
him in individual combat. Ali rushed from the Muslim ranks, attacked
the Meccan, and killed him with a single slash of his sword. A great
cheer—"*Allah akbar*" (God is great!)—rose from the Muslim ranks.
The brother of the slain warrior rushed from the Meccan ranks to
attack his brother's killer. Before he could reach Ali, the fierce Hamza
stepped between them and cut down the Meccan. Three more men
from the Meccan line challenged Hamza, one after another; all three
met their deaths. Excited by the victorious combats taking place
before their eyes, the Muslim ranks charged the Meccans engaging

them in fierce hand-to-hand combat "until the battle grew hot."[21] The wounded were slain without mercy.[22] As the battle raged a Muslim soldier, Abu Dujana, cut his way through the enemy ranks reaching the Meccan camp. It was common Arab practice for the clans to bring their women to the battlefield where they would sing, bang tambourines, and shout poems to encourage their men to fight well.[23] Abu Dujana rushed headlong into the camp scattering the women, who fled for their lives.

Hamza, meanwhile, prowled the battlefield looking for Meccan warriors to fight and seems not to have taken part in the Muslim charge. A Meccan, Abu Niyar, passed close to him and Hamza challenged him to a fight saying, "Come here, you son of a female circumciser!"[24] The two warriors began fighting. Off to the side watching the combatants was Wahshi, an Abyssinian slave armed with a javelin. While Hamza's attention was focused on his opponent, Wahshi threw his javelin at Hamza; Wahshi recalled that "it pierced the lower part of his body and came out between his legs. He came on towards me, but collapsed and fell. I left him there until he died, then I came and recovered my javelin."[25] What happened to Hamza was a classic case of Arab blood revenge. Wahshi had been hired by a woman named Hind, Abu Sufyan's wife and daughter of Utaba ibn Rabia, who had been killed by Hamza at the Battle of Badr. His daughter had sworn revenge for her father's death. It was she who hired Wahshi and promised him his freedom if he killed Hamza. The highly personal nature of Arab warfare was further demonstrated when Wahshi, having killed Hamza, retrieved his weapon and then "went off to the camp, for I had no business with anyone but him."[26]

The ferocity of the Muslim attack succeeded in breaking the Meccan line at several points permitting groups of Muslims to penetrate and begin isolating segments of the Meccan ranks, hacking them to pieces. For a while their superior numbers allowed the Meccans to hold on. Eventually, however, they began to waver and finally to fall back in a semidisciplined fashion. It was at this point that the Muslims pressed the attack with great force penetrating completely through the Meccan ranks "until they cut them off from their camp and there was an obvious rout."[27] With Muslim soldiers behind them and in the midst of their ranks, the Meccan defense collapsed. Once more Muhammad's disciplined infantry had proven that a smaller highly motivated force could defeat a larger less motivated force in close combat. Had the Muslims even a small cavalry contingent with which to attack the scattered Meccan ranks, the Battle of Uhud would have been a disaster for the Meccans and a great victory for Muhammad.

What happened next is a matter of some debate. Later Muslim historians suggest that the gap between Muhammad's left and the Hill of Arrows was narrow and marked by uneven terrain and palm groves that made passage by cavalry difficult and easily covered by indirect arrow fire.[28] There is a hint in these later accounts that the Meccan cavalry under Khalid al-Walid had tried several times to attack through the gap and had been driven back by arrow fire. These historians suggest that at some point al-Walid decided to ride completely around Mount Uhud and come at the Muslims from the rear. A ride of this distance would have been at least ten to twelve miles, taken more than an hour to complete, and arrived on the battlefield with horses unfit for battle.[29] The account is implausible on military grounds and may have been devised to put a gloss on what seems to have been a breakdown in Muslim discipline exposing Muhammad to the charge of incompetence in leaving his critical left flank so poorly defended.

Ibn Ishaq's earlier account of events seems more likely. He suggests that even after the Muslim attack had broken the Meccan ranks, the enemy cavalry had not engaged at all. In typical fashion it had hovered near the flanks ready to strike if the Muslim ranks broke, hoping to pursue and kill the fleeing remnants. But when the Meccan ranks broke exposing their camp the Muslim attack lost its momentum as its soldiers abandoned the fight and began to plunder the camp.[30] Seeing their fellow soldiers sacking the camp, the Muslim "archers turned aside to the camp when the enemy had been cut off from it making for the spoil."[31] Only a handful of archers held their posts on the Hill of Arrows. When al-Walid saw the Muslim archers leaving to sack the Meccan camp, he rallied his cavalry and led it at full gallop through the now unprotected gap turning Muhammad's flank and striking his forces in the rear. Ibn Ishaq says, "Thus they [the archers] opened our rear to the cavalry and we were attacked from behind.[32]

Two hundred Meccan cavalrymen struck the Muslim rear with such force that it brought the Muslim infantry attack to a halt. Attempting to regroup along the line of departure, the Muslims broke off their looting and turned around. This provided breathing room for the Meccans to reform and return to the attack. Khalid al-Walid continued to wreak havoc behind the Muslim positions, his horsemen riding about the rear striking targets of opportunity with their long lances. The Muslim infantry began to lose its cohesion and flee. "The Muslims were put to flight and the enemy slew many of them. It was a day of trial and testing in which God honored several with martyrdom."[33] The Muslim defense collapsed.

Events went from bad to worse. Muhammad and his bodyguard were now surrounded by Meccan soldiers pressing the attack with great force. As the din of combat swirled around Muhammad, he was struck in the face with a slingstone that shattered one of his teeth and cut his lip and cheek; blood ran down his face.[34] Another account says that a slingstone struck the cheek plate of his helmet with such force that it drove it into Muhammad's face. The force of the impact knocked Muhammad off his feet. The Meccans closed in on the small group of Muslim soldiers protecting Muhammad. At some point he was struck on the head by a blow from a sword knocking his helmet down over his eyes. Muhammad fell to the ground dazed and covered with blood. His bodyguard was being cut to pieces. "They fought in defense of the Apostle man after man, all being killed until only Zayed (or Umara) was left fighting until he was disabled. At that point a number of Muslims returned and drove the enemy away from him."[35] One imagines a pile of bodies and wounded strewn around the wounded Muhammad as Abu Dujana "made his body a shield for the Apostle. Arrows were falling on his back as he leaned over him, until there were many stuck in it."[36] A few more moments and Muhammad might have been killed, perhaps putting an end to Islam as well.

Suddenly the rumor swept the battlefield that Muhammad had been killed. A cheer arose among the Meccans, who broke off their attack in celebration. The remaining Muslim contingents, thinking their chief dead, began to flee. What seems to have happened is that a Muslim standard-bearer, one Mus'ab ibn Umayr, had been killed by a Meccan who, upon seeing Umayr dressed in Muhammad's armor, thought he had killed the Apostle himself. For whatever reason, Muhammad had switched armor with another soldier earlier that day. The logic is compelling that it must have been with Umayr, but no source testifies to this fact. In any event, the news of Muhammad's death brought the battle to an end. Muhammad was safe under a pile of bodies protected by a few stalwart Muslim warriors.

Ali, Abu Bakr, Umar, and a few others were close by and began searching for Muhammad. One of the men, Ka'b ibn Malik, "recognized his [Muhammad's] eyes gleaming from beneath his helmet and . . . called out at the top of my [his] voice, "Take heart, you Muslims, this is the Apostle of God."[37] Muhammad realized that he had only survived because the Meccans had not recognized him and told ibn Malik to stop shouting and be quiet. Muhammad's men helped him to his feet and carried him up the rocky slopes of Mount Uhud, where they concealed themselves in a shallow glen. "When the Apostle reached the mouth of the glen Ali came out and filled his shield with water from al-Mihras [a well located nearby on Mount Uhud] and brought it to the Apostle, who refused to drink it because its evil smell repelled him. However, he used the water to wash the blood from his face and as he poured it over his head he said, 'The wrath of God is fierce against him who bloodied the face of His prophet.'"[38] Later, Muhammad's wounds were cauterized by a hot iron,[39] a procedure that would surely have left Muhammad with a scar on his face. There are no early portraits of Muhammad or descriptions, however, that indicate such a scar.

The view from the glen might have disheartened even so fervent a believer as Muhammad. Below the Muslim army was scattered all over the field. Meccan cavalrymen rode around the battlefield skewering Muslim infantrymen with their lances. "The army had fled away from the Apostle," Ibn Ishaq tells us.[40] The Meccans were mutilating the dead and killing the wounded. Abu Sufyan himself ran his lance into the mouth of the dead Hamza saying, "Taste that, you rebel."[41] For sheer horror, however, no one matched Abu Sufyan's wife, Hind, in her thirst for revenge. "Hind and the women with her stopped to mutilate the Apostle's dead companions. They cut off their ears and noses and Hind made them into anklets and collars and gave her anklets and collars and pendants to Wahshi, the slave. . . . She cut out Hamza's liver and chewed it, but she was not able to swallow it and threw it away. Then she mounted a high rock and shrieked at the top of her voice."[42] Hind's attempt to eat Hamza's liver seems a curious vestige of some pre-historic animism, wherein one devours the liver of one's enemy in the hope of acquiring his strength. Even among the primitive Arabs, Hind's actions would have been shocking.

The Meccan army formed up and began to move toward its camp. Abu Sufyan and a small troop of cavalry rode up to a vantage point on Mount Uhud where he was sure he could be seen and heard by the remnants of the Muslim army. Nearby Muhammad and his small band of companions kept hidden in the glen. Abu Sufyan cried out, "Victory in war is like a bucket in a well, going alternatively up and down. Today is in exchange for Badr. Show thy strength, O Hubal."[43] Inexplicably, Muhammad ordered Umar to get up and answer Abu Sufyan's boast, risking revealing his hiding place. Umar shouted back, "We are not equal. Our dead are in paradise; your dead in hell."[44] Abu Sufyan must have spotted Umar for he called to him to approach. When Umar came near, Abu Sufyan asked, "By God, Umar, have we killed Muhammad?" Umar replied, "By God, you have not, he is listening to what you are saying now." Abu Sufyan must have known that Muhammad was nearby. He could easily have ordered the cavalrymen with him to seek him out and kill him, putting an end to the entire nasty business. But in Abu Sufyan's view war was sport and honor was central to its practice. To kill Muhammad now that the battle was over and he had already been beaten was not the valiant thing to do. And so Muhammad survived.

Abu Sufyan's chivalric view of war was also evident when he called out to Muhammad. "There are some mutilated bodies among your dead. By God, it gives me no satisfaction, and no anger. I neither prohibited nor ordered mutilation."[45] As Abu Sufyan and his small troop of cavalry turned to ride down the mountain, he called out, "Your meeting place is Badr next year." The Apostle told one of his companions to answer, "Yes, it is an appointment between us."[46] The battle had been a good day's manly sport. Both sides would meet again next year to continue the game. Seventy-four Muslims and twenty-three Meccans were killed at Uhud. Of the Muslim dead only four or five were Emigrants; the rest were ansar.

The defeat of the Muslims at Mount Uhud opened the road to Medina. Had the Meccans regarded war as Muhammad did, as a means of obtaining strategic goals in the service of God's will, the logical step after defeating the Muslim forces in the field would have been to march on Medina and put it to the sword. Even if not all the Muslims in Medina were slain, the city's destruction would have at least put an end to Muhammad's ability to interrupt the Meccan caravan trade. Such a disaster befalling Medina would have weakened Muhammad's claim to prophethood, and it is not inconceivable that Islam as a religiosocial movement might have collapsed entirely. Had their positions been reversed, Muhammad would almost certainly have attacked and destroyed Mecca. But Abu Sufyan was a traditional Arab chief, not the leader of an ideological insurgency, and for him war was a means of settling conflicts between men in a chivalric manner. Instead of attacking Medina, Abu Sufyan ordered his troops to pack up and begin making their way back to Mecca.

No sooner had Abu Sufyan ridden down from Mount Uhud and ordered the Meccan army to begin moving than Muhammad emerged from his hiding place and ordered Ali to follow the Meccans and see if they were heading for Medina. Muhammad knew that if the Meccans were making for Medina only a few miles away, they would be riding their horses and leading their camels; if they were preparing for the long journey to Mecca, they would be riding their camels and leading their horses. Ali followed the Meccans for a few miles and then returned yelling with joy that the Meccans were riding their camels and heading home. Surprisingly, Muhammad sent no one to follow the Meccans to make sure that Ali's report was true. The Meccans had traveled only a few miles from the battlefield when Ali turned back, and they could just as easily have changed their minds and turned to attack Medina. Once more Muhammad's luck held.

Muhammad and his officers came down from Mount Uhud to find the battlefield littered with Muslim dead and wounded. He searched for and found the body of Hamza "with his belly ripped up and his liver missing, and his nose and ears cut off."[47] Muhammad flew into a rage and cried out, "If God gives me victory over Quraish in the future I will mutilate thirty of their men."[48] Other Muslims took up the vengeful cry saying, "[W]e will mutilate them as no Arab has ever mutilated anyone."[49] Muhammad was no Buddha, and was quite capable of working up a murderous rage against his enemies. The threat to mutilate his enemies was not an idle boast. Later, however, Muhammad had a revelation in which God urged him to punish his enemies proportionately; "if you punish, then punish only as you have been punished."[50] Muhammad forbade mutilation. Some Muslims wanted to carry their dead and bury them in Medina, but Muhammad ordered the dead buried where they had fallen. Sometimes two or three corpses were buried together.

The Battle of Uhud had been fought on Friday; on Sunday morning Muhammad ordered the remnants of his army to assemble. From Medina he marched south along the road to Mecca halting at Hamra ul-Asad, about eight miles from Medina. There he ordered every man to build a campfire so that at night the fires would give the impression of a much larger army. Muhammad was in no position to pursue anyone, certainly not the victorious Meccans. What he was attempting to do was to

deceive the Meccans that he was ready for a fight should they decide
to return to Medina. Muhammad's deception made sense only if the
Meccans could see his campfires at night. The Meccans had been on the
march only three days after reassembling their army, and could not have
been more than two or three miles ahead of Muhammad. This meant
that they were no more than ten to twelve miles from Medina, a distance easily covered if they decided to turn around and attack the city.

As events turned out Muhammad's concern was well founded.
The Meccans began to rethink what they were doing, and some young
chiefs were in favor of returning to Medina and exterminating the
Muslims. And then there occurred a remarkable stroke of fortune. A
group of bedouins of the Khuza'a tribe was making their way down the
road when they came across Muhammad's camp. The Khuza'a were
still idolaters, but had made a compact with Muhammad at some time
in the past in which they agreed that "they would not conceal from
him anything that happened here."[51] The leader of the bedouins,
Ma'bad bin Abu Ma'bad al-Khuza'a, had a conversation with Muhammad. There is little doubt that it was Muhammad's idea to use Ma'bad
as an agent of deception.

The bedouins left Muhammad's camp moving south until they
encountered the Meccans and Abu Sufyan's camp. Abu Sufyan asked
Ma'bad what the news was about Muhammad and the Muslims that
the bedouins had just passed. What happened next must be counted as
one of the great tactical deceptions of ancient military history. Ma'bad
told Abu Sufyan that "Muhammad has come out with his companions
to pursue you with an army whose like I have never seen, burning with
anger against you. Those who stayed behind when you fought them
have joined him; they are sorry for what they did and are violently
enraged against you. Never have I seen anything like it. . . . God I do
not think that you will move off before you see the forelocks of his
cavalry."[52] Ma'bad's tale was a complete fabrication. Muhammad was
on his last legs militarily. Had the Meccans turned around it is likely
that Muhammad would have been destroyed. Apparently, the Meccans
had already decided to turn back and attack Medina! Abu Sufyan
replied to Ma'bad's tale, "But we have determined to attack them to
exterminate their survivors." Ma'bad replied, "I would advise against
that."[53] And so it was that "these words turned back Abu Sufyan and
his followers," who thus marched on to Mecca. The Meccans had
missed their best chance yet to destroy Muhammad and his movement.

UNCONVENTIONAL WAR

The Battles of Badr and Uhud attracted the attention of the bedouin clans in and around Medina and Mecca. The conflict between Muhammad and the Meccans was a major event that might shape the future of any bedouin clan if one's opportunities were seized. Whether out of self-interest, the desire for loot, genuine interest in the new creed of Islam, or the pull of old alliances, the bedouin clans were now paying close attention to events in Mecca and Medina. The awareness of Muhammad's insurgency was spreading from the cities to the countryside, and clan chiefs waited to see what would happen next and how they might take best advantage of events.

Two months after Uhud, in May 625, a group of tribesmen from the 'Adal and al-Qara clans, allies of the Hudhayl tribe, came to Muhammad saying that some of their clan had already become Muslims and that others wanted to convert. They requested that Muhammad send some Muslims to instruct them in the new religion. Seeing an opportunity to strengthen his position with a new clan, Muhammad agreed to send six disciples with them. At a place called al-Raji the Muslim party was betrayed by their fellow travelers and ambushed by members of the Beni Lihyan clan of the tribe of Hudhayl. Of the six Muslims, three died fighting and three were taken prisoner. One of these was later killed trying to escape. Why the Muslims were betrayed is not clear, but it may have been that the Hudhayl tribe were allies of the Quraish. The location of their territory near Ta'if, only thirty miles or so from Mecca, suggests this might have been the case.[54] The fact that the Muslim prisoners were turned over to the Quraish also suggests an alliance. How such an alliance could have escaped Muhammad's attention is not clear. Perhaps he knew of it and saw the request for Muslim missionaries as an opportunity to weaken it. The two Muslim prisoners were turned over to the Quraish, who delivered them to families who had lost members in the fighting at Uhud. One of the Muslims was tied to a tree with ropes and crucified; he was stabbed with a spear by the young son of a man who was killed at Uhud. The other prisoner was decapitated.

Muhammad was furious at the death of his missionaries and immediately took steps to avenge himself on the Hudhayl by assassinating their chief, Sofian ibn Khalid. Muhammad sent one Abdallah ibn Unays to the Hudhayl camp, where he gained the chief's trust by criticizing

Muhammad. Ibn Khalid offered ibn Unays to sleep in his tent. During the night ibn Unays cut off ibn Khalid's head and fled. Traveling only at night to avoid capture, ibn Unays returned to Medina, where he flung ibn Khalid's head at Muhammad's feet.[55] Muhammad was pleased and gave ibn Unays a wooden rod as a reward. When the assassin asked what the meaning of the rod was, Muhammad replied that on judgment day it would be a sign of the special relationship between Muhammad and a chosen few. "There shall be few then who hold a rod."[56] Muhammad could not have been clearer: assassination in the service of religion was permitted.

In the absence of military victory, assassination was becoming Muhammad's primary tool of influencing events in precisely the same way that political murder and terror bombing became basic tools for later insurgents. It was, of course, the tool of the weak. Had Muhammad been able to deliver his adversaries a fatal military blow he would surely have done so. Weakened militarily, Muhammad shifted the struggle to political grounds using assassination as a means to inflict violence. Muhammad sent two men to Mecca to assassinate Abu Sufyan, the leader of the Meccans at Uhud and his major opponent in Mecca. The killers were recognized and the plot foiled, but not before they had killed two Meccans and taken another prisoner. Muhammad's use of political murder was truly an innovation in Arab politics, and went well beyond the blood feud. In blood feuds it was not the custom to assassinate enemies, but to meet them in combat. As Sir John Glubb observes, "In all the voluminous accounts of the Prophet's life, there does not seem to be any mention of anyone else sending assassins to murder anyone."[57] Once Muhammad demonstrated the practical value of assassination, however, "ever since assassinations have exercised an unhappy influence on Islamic societies. Political murders have always been tragically numerous in Muslim countries."[58]

In June 625 Muhammad was approached again, this time by a tribal chief named Abu Bara, head of the clan called Beni Amir. He told Muhammad that he wished to become a Muslim and that he and his whole clan would convert to the new creed. He asked Muhammad to send some Muslim missionaries to instruct his people. According to Ibn Ishaq, Muhammad agreed to the request and sent "forty of his companions from the best of the Muslims."[59] Later sources place the number of missionaries at seventy.[60] At a place called Bir Maoona some fifty miles southeast of Medina the party was attacked by the Beni

Sulaym clan as the missionaries were drawing water from the well. All but one of the Muslims were killed. A year earlier Muhammad had led raids against the Beni Sulaym in an effort to demonstrate his influence and shake their loyalty to the Meccans. Both times the Beni Sulaym had avoided battle. Muhammad may have wondered if his raids had had the intended effect. Now, at Bir Maoona, he received his answer.

The loss of forty (or seventy) Muslim warriors was a major setback. In four months Muhammad and the Muslims had suffered three successive reverses—Uhud, al-Raji, and Bir Maoona. The insurgency was not going well in the countryside, and there had been no major defections from the status quo to the Muslims. Muhammad himself was probably undeterred by these setbacks, but it is reasonable to suspect that his prestige among non-Muslims had fallen and that some defections from the Muslim cause may have occurred. Muhammad desperately needed a success, some gesture of power and ability to influence events, to hold his own ranks fast, and to convince the idolaters that he was still a man to be feared. Once again he attacked the Jews of Medina.

ATTACK ON THE BENI AN-NADIR

Muhammad approached the tribal leaders of the Jewish Beni an-Nadir tribe on the pretext of asking them to raise money to settle a blood-wit owed by one of the Muslims for killing two members of the Beni Amir clan. He was received cordially and told to wait while the Jews discussed the issue. According to Ibn Ishaq, the Jews were plotting to kill Muhammad by sending someone to the roof of the house along whose wall Muhammad was waiting and drop a stone on his head. But "news came to him from heaven about what these people intended, so he got up and went back to Medina."[61] There he told his companions about the treachery of the Jews and "ordered them to prepare for war and to march against them."[62] But had the Jews wanted to kill Muhammad they could have done so directly; there was no need to hide the deed by a surreptitious attempt to drop a stone on his head. The account of a warning from heaven, apparently unaccompanied by the usual physical symptoms, is suspicious as well. The account, probably added later to Ibn Ishaq's work by his editor, is likely a fabrication to justify Muhammad's practical stratagem of scapegoating the Jews to bolster his own political support.[63]

The Jews of Medina still had Arab allies, among them Abdullah ibn Ubay, who had pleaded the case for mercy when Muhammad had earlier expelled the Jews of the Beni Qaynuqa. Muhammad maneuvered to neutralize these alliances and isolate the Beni an-Nadir. He sent some of their allies who had become Muslims to inform the Jews that "hearts have changed and Islam has wiped out old alliances."[64] Ibn Ubay, however, appeared ready to observe his obligations to his Jewish allies. "Stand firm and protect yourselves, for we will not betray you," he told them and advised them to fight.[65] In time-honored fashion the Jews retreated to their strongholds and awaited Muhammad's siege. For three weeks, from August to September 625, Muhammad and his troops besieged the Jewish strongholds, at one point cutting down some of the date palms to demonstrate his resolve. No Arab allies, including ibn Ubay, came to help the Beni an-Nadir. The Jews sued for peace and came to an agreement with Muhammad, who permitted them to leave Medina. Many went to Kheibar; others to Syria. They were permitted to take with them as much property as their camels could carry. Their armor and weapons, however, were confiscated. Muhammad himself inventoried the military equipment: fifty coats of mail armor, fifty helmets, and 340 swords were turned over to the insurgency's armory. The land, houses, groves, and other property were distributed by Muhammad among the Emigrants. Muhammad kept some barley-growing land and a date grove for himself. Muhammad had his victory. The defections stopped, and those outside Medina once more paid attention to the man in Medina.

THE SECOND BATTLE OF BADR

At Uhud Abu Sufyan had challenged Muhammad to return to Badr within a year for another fight to settle matters. In April 626, at the time for the annual spring trade fair at Badr, Muhammad arrived with fifteen hundred men and a small number of cavalry to answer the Meccan challenge. Abu Sufyan and a Meccan force of two thousand men and fifty cavalry left Mecca for Badr only to turn back after a few days. It was a drought year and the animals were weak and there was little forage with which to feed the animals.[66] Later sources say the Meccans came to Badr but stayed out of town.[67] To force the animals over a march of two hundred miles during drought risked their deaths, and the horses would be useless in a fight by the time they arrived at Badr. Muhammad's army had only to travel eighty miles from Medina to reach Badr over ground that was better provided with forage for their mounts. When the army returned to Mecca they were greeted with derision. They were called the Porridge Army who "merely went out to drink porridge."[68] Muhammad gained an important psychological and political victory at Second Badr, as the "battle" has become known in Arab chronicles. He had arrived to meet the challenge for all to see, and the Meccans had not shown up. Moreover, the Muslim army of fifteen hundred men was twice as large as it had been the year before. Whatever defections had occurred had apparently been more than made up for by conversions. Islam was finally gaining a foothold among the bedouin clans outside of Medina itself.

Muhammad continued the political war. He was greatly concerned that the Meccans might be shoring up their support among the bedouins and trying to assemble a large coalition of tribes with which to attack Medina. He moved to preempt this with a campaign of assassinations and raids. In May 626 Muhammad sent a small group of assassins to murder Abu Rafi, one of the chiefs of the Beni an-Nadir tribe that had been driven from Medina. Abu Rafi had gone to Kheibar, where he attempted to gather support for an attack against the Muslims. The assassins killed him in his bed. The assassination of another Jewish leader in Kheibar occurred a short while later. Muhammad sent a hand-picked "commando unit" of thirty killers to Kheibar disguised as an official diplomatic approach to the Jews there. The Muslims negotiated with their leader, Usayr ibn Razim, and convinced him to come to Medina to negotiate with Muhammad. The Muslims offered to guarantee his safety with their own escort of thirty men. Among Arabs, nothing is more valued than a man's word, his pledge of safety and protection, so ibn Razim felt safe. Somewhere on the road to Medina, however, the Muslims fell upon the Jews and killed them all.

When the leader of the commandos returned to Medina he was met by Muhammad, who congratulated him on his work.[69] Muhammad was earning a reputation for ruthlessness and an ability to kill at a distance just as the size of his army was increasing and he was becoming better able to support his followers economically. The message to his opponents outside the cities was that they, too, were not safe as long as they failed to join him.

In June 626 Muhammad turned his attention once more to the important Ghatafan tribe and led a strong force to attack them. At Dhat al Riqa, 60 miles northeast of Mecca, he encountered the Ghatafan. Dhat al Riqa is 180 miles from Medina. Muhammad's ability to project military power over considerable distances was becoming impressive. To be able to conduct military operations so close to Mecca was also politically impressive to the other tribes as well. Muhammad was taking the offensive. Nevertheless, the Ghatafan contingent must have been substantial, and both sides thought it better to withdraw rather than to fight. Even so, Muhammad had made his point.[70] Two months later, in August 626, Muhammad and a force of one thousand men marched to raid the oasis of Dumat al-Jandal some 350 miles north of Medina. Once again he encountered the bedouin tribes, but once more no fighting took place. The purpose of the raid was more political than military, a demonstration of force and the will to use it to preempt the bedouins from joining the Meccan coalition. A few months later, perhaps in December, Muhammad led another large raiding party against the Bani Mustaliq near the shore of the Red Sea.[71] This time Muhammad struck with force. Taking the enemy by surprise at a well, he quickly put them to flight and captured their baggage train of two thousand camels, five thousand head of sheep and goats, and two hundred women.[72]

Within Medina the expulsion of the second Jewish tribe and the conversion of many of the Kazrai and Aws to Islam had considerably weakened Abdullah ibn Ubay's influence leaving Muhammad the city's most important chief. His base of operations was now secure. The preemptive raids against the potentially hostile bedouin tribes all along the caravan route and close to Mecca probably had some effect in reducing the military manpower that was available to the Meccan coalition. A number of Muhammad's influential and outspoken opponents had been silenced by assassination, a warning to any bedouin chief who might be tempted to side with the Meccans. If the size of Muhammad's raiding parties was any measure, it seems reasonable that Islam was gaining adherents at a substantial pace, increasing Muhammad's military manpower base. In less than a year Muhammad had reversed the humiliation of Uhud, and the insurgency was once again active and on the offensive.

But a storm was brewing in Mecca.

8

THE BATTLE OF THE DITCH
March 627

For almost a year Muhammad had been conducting assassinations and raids against those bedouin tribes who had long-standing commercial ties with the Meccans in the hope of dissuading them from joining the Meccan military coalition. At the same time he made efforts to secure the support or neutrality of other tribes through negotiation. In these efforts politics always took precedence over religion, and he formed several alliances with pagan tribes without requiring a promise of conversion. Muhammad also reconstituted his military forces that had been badly mauled at Uhud. His raids involved larger and larger forces over greater and greater distances, often reaching close to Mecca itself and sometimes even south of the city.

The result was that Muhammad was effectively able to close down both the northern and eastern caravan routes used by the Meccans. Even smaller caravans moving from Mecca southeast around Ta'if and Nakhla were raided. Two years after Uhud, Muhammad's influence and reputation had increased considerably and reached far to the south of Mecca to Najd and as far east as Yamamah. This last alliance with the chief of the Yamamah territory provided Muhammad with a powerful economic lever against Mecca. Yamamah was the granary of southern Arabia and the main source of Mecca's grain.[1] The sources do not tell us if the chief of Yamamah was a Muslim or not, but at Muhammad's request he ordered that grain shipments to Mecca be stopped.[2] Even the weather favored Muhammad when a severe drought struck the region. The drought and the embargo created severe food shortages in Mecca. In a clever political maneuver Muhammad sent money to Mecca to purchase food for the poor and starving. Among Arabs generosity was one of the most important virtues a man could possess. Muhammad's generosity toward the Meccan poor (even as he was the indirect cause of their sufferings in the first place) went a long way toward convincing many Meccans that he was a fair and just man. Muhammad surely knew that many of his converts had come from the lower social orders of Arab society, and that feeding the poor of Mecca could only increase the attraction of Islam and support for him. By November 626 word had reached Muhammad from Mecca that Abu Sufyan and the Meccans were planning a major military campaign. The source of this information was probably Abbas, Muhammad's uncle and agent-in-place among the Meccan leadership.

Muhammad was away leading a raid through the territory of the Ghatafan moving toward their main trading town at Dumat al-Jandal when word reached Medina that the Meccans had taken the decision to raise an army and attack his base of operations.[3] A camel courier was immediately dispatched to inform Muhammad. The rider caught up with him just outside Dumat al-Jandal. Muhammad and his raiders turned around and began making the fifteen-day journey to Medina, where he immediately undertook to plan a defense.[4] Muhammad's success in rebuilding his military capabilities and in cutting off Mecca's commercial routes was strangling the Meccan economy. By now it was likely that Abu Sufyan realized that his display of chivalry in not hunting down and killing Muhammad after the Battle of Uhud had been costly indeed. The accusation made by Ibn Ishaq and repeated by later writers that it was the Jews of Kheibar who originated the idea of an attack on Mecca and then convinced the Quraish to adopt it seems nothing more than Muslim propaganda. The economic situation in Mecca was becoming critical and Abu Sufyan, himself the chief opponent of Muhammad from the beginning, hardly needed urging from the Jews of Kheibar to see that Muhammad had to be removed as the source of Mecca's discontent.

The Meccans raised an army of ten thousand men comprising four thousand Meccans and their local allies, two thousand Ghatafan bedouins from north of Medina, and some seven hundred others from the Beni

Sulaym tribe, which harbored a personal grudge against Muhammad. The remainder were drawn from various small bedouin tribes, some fighting for pay, others attracted by the prospect of loot.[5] Ibn Ishaq says that there were contingents of "black mercenaries" as well.[6] As at Uhud these were probably Abyssinian professionals. The coalition had six hundred cavalrymen, two hundred of which were Meccans under the command of Khalid al-Walid; the rest were bedouin contingents under their clan chiefs. Muhammad could muster three thousand men and thirty-five cavalrymen. Although smaller than the Meccan force, Muhammad's army was still considerably larger than what he had been able to put in the field at Uhud, suggesting that his efforts to reconstitute his military capability after the defeat there had met with considerable success. By any traditional Arab standard an army of three thousand men under the command of a single chief was a formidable military asset, one that also testified to the prestige of its commander.

After the defeat at Uhud there was no question of meeting the Meccan army on the open plain. Outnumbered three to one, Muhammad wisely chose to defend Medina by taking maximum advantage of its geography and the season of year. Muhammad knew that it would take the Meccans several months to recruit and assemble their army and that it was unlikely they could arrive outside Medina much before March 627. Muhammad had arrived back in Medina probably in early December, giving him almost four months to prepare for the attack.[7] By March the harvest in Medina would have already been collected and the barley and dates safely stored within the city. There would be nothing for the Meccan horses and camels to eat in the barren fields. A ten thousand-man army required almost sixteen thousand camels to transport men and supplies, not to mention the six hundred–horse Meccan cavalry. With the fields around Medina barren of crops the Meccan army could sustain itself in the field for only a short time before its animals began to die.

The terrain around Medina offered good defenses on three sides. The large lava plains to the east and west were mostly impassable except for a few wadis too narrow to accommodate large military formations. The southern approaches were also through wadis, one of which was sufficiently wide to accommodate an army. However, this route emptied into a heavily settled area of clan compounds, walled gardens, and fortified towers where "the passages between the gardens was zig-zag, and so narrow that no formation except in long columns

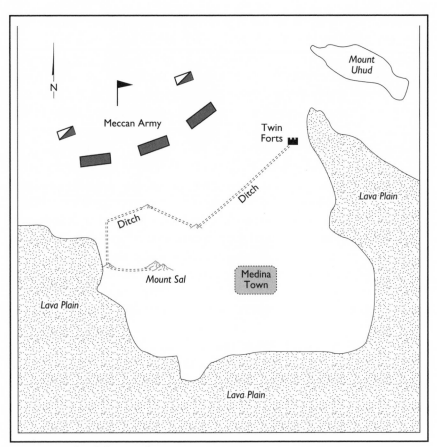

Map 9. Battle of the Ditch, 627 C.E.

was possible for the enemy . . . [N]aturally even small outposts could stop . . . these long columns."[8] The problem for Muhammad was the approach from the north. Here the lava fields opened onto a large plain offering the Meccan army a clear approach to Medina over relatively unobstructed ground. The gap in the "horns" of the lava fields was almost four miles wide, plenty of room for the Meccans to deploy. The open ground also offered an excellent range of maneuver for the Meccan cavalry. If Muhammad deployed against the Meccans on the northern plain, the numerically superior Meccan lines would easily overlap his flanks leaving plenty of room on either side for the Meccan cavalry to envelop the Muslim army with little effort. If Muhammad was to defend Medina, some way had to be found to block the northern approach.

It does not seem to have been Muhammad's idea to dig a ditch across the northern approaches to block the Meccan advance. Ibn Ishaq says that Muhammad overheard a discussion among some men wherein a ditch was mentioned. Later Muslim historians attribute the idea to one Salman al-Farsi.[9] Salman was a Muslim convert. The son of a Persian landowner who converted to Christianity as a boy, he had gone to Syria to study religion. When his teacher died Salman set out for Arabia, where he had heard that a new prophet (possibly a reference to Muhammad) had appeared. On the way his caravan was ambushed, and he was taken into slavery and sold to a Jew in Medina. As was his practice Muhammad helped Salman raise sufficient money to purchase his freedom, and he became a Muslim. Muslim historians make much of the fact that the use of a ditch as a defensive fortification was of some novelty in Arabia during Muhammad's time. If so, then it is possible that Salman's sojourns in Persia and Syria might have acquainted him, if only in a general way, with this type of fortification since it was familiar to both Persian and Byzantine armies. The fact that Muslim chronicles call the ditch by its Persian name, *khandaq*, suggests that the story that the ditch was Salman's idea may be true.

It is one thing to dig a long ditch; it is quite another to construct it in a manner where it can serve as a military obstacle to both cavalry and infantry. To cover the northern gap between the horns of the lava fields required a trench that was at least three and one-half miles long running in a roughly N-shaped line in order to incorporate the few natural obstacles into its course.[10] There are no references in the original sources as to its width and depth, only that a single laborer could dig a hole "five cubits in length and five cubits in depth" in a day.[11] It was of great concern to the defenders that the trench be sufficiently deep and wide to prevent cavalry horses from carrying it in a single jump. The key is the relationship between the depth of the trench and its width. A trained jumper horse can barely carry itself over a twenty-foot ditch; a typical cavalry mount of the period would be lucky to make an sixteen-foot leap successfully. However, if the ditch was too wide and, say, only a yard deep, the horse could jump *into* the ditch and then jump out the opposite side. Taken together a ditch about sixteen feet wide would seem to be adequate, especially if the dirt taken from the ditch were used to construct a two-foot parapet on the far side, forcing the animal to jump uphill. A depth of a little over six feet would make it difficult for a horse to jump into and out of the ditch.[12] Obviously a ditch of these dimensions would at the same time constitute a formidable obstacle to infantry attack. Defenders from behind the ditch's parapet would have the advantage of height and steepness of slope from which they could rain down stones and arrows on the attackers while remaining somewhat safe from counterfire. Under these circumstances the Meccan numerical advantage in infantry would be considerably reduced.

The ditch required almost four months to construct with everyone in Medina including Muhammad working on it. It is of interest that the sources tell us that the Jews of the Beni Qurayzah tribe, the last Jewish tribe left in Medina, also lent a hand in the digging.[13] Later Arab historians note that the Muslims borrowed "digging implements" from the Jews.[14] That the Jews would help Muhammad after the expulsion from Medina of the other two Jewish tribes may seem curious. In this regard it must be remembered that the Jewish tribes in Arabia were indistinguishable from Arab tribes in their values and customs in all respects except religion. The Jewish Qurayzah tribe had been sworn allies of the Aws, who were allies of Muhammad, and faithfully observed their obligations to Muhammad even when their fellow Jews, with whom they had no such obligations, had been expelled. All the evidence supports the view that the Beni Qurayzah had correctly observed their obligations to Muhammad and had given him no reason to suspect their loyalty. Indeed, if Muhammad had any such misgivings, he would certainly have taken steps against them *before* the Meccans arrived. Although the southern approaches to Medina were difficult, it was in the southern neighborhoods where the Jewish strongholds were located. Moreover, the Jews could put a thousand men in the field. If

Muhammad had any reason to suspect the Beni Qurayzah, he would hardly have permitted them to remain behind his defenses as he prepared to fight the Meccans.

On the eve of the battle Muhammad and his troops were in good shape. Muhammad placed his command post on a low ridge on Mount Sal, the only significant high ground on the plain that offered him a commanding view of the battlefield. The ditch had been completed in time, and it provided a great advantage in neutralizing the Meccan superiority of numbers and cavalry. Muhammad's army had a sufficient supply of food and water while the Meccans had limited supplies for their troops and animals. The fields were bare so that "the enemy horses found on that account nothing except what their masters had brought with them."[15] Muhammad also had the advantage of interior lines, which permitted him the important capability of being able to shift troops to counter concentrations of Meccan force wherever they assembled along the ditch. This gave Muhammad control of the decisive points of concentration along the entire battle line and the ability to neutralize the Meccan numerical superiority at these points. Sometime in March 627 the Meccan army arrived outside Medina. Following the track they had taken at the Battle of Uhud, the Meccans avoided the southern approaches, passed west of the city, and encamped at two locations on the plain north of Medina.

Abu Sufyan must have been furious when he found his way blocked by Muhammad's ditch. He had come prepared for a traditional Arab battle of infantry and horse on open ground, a repeat of the Battle of Uhud. He had planned to feed his army and animals on the fodder and crops around Medina. With the fields bare, he must have realized that this had been a terrible mistake. It was only a matter of time, perhaps two or three weeks, before his camels and horses would begin to weaken from starvation and die. Moreover, the Meccan army was a coalition with some of its contingents motivated by concerns other than revenge and Meccan commercial interests. If it became clear that there was no booty to be had or that one's flocks had been left untended for too long, some of these contingents might begin to drift away. Time was working against Abu Sufyan and the Meccans.

As noted earlier, Arab warfare until Muhammad's reforms was primitive in its applications, so much so that often a simple wall of a few feet was sufficient to block military movement. Whereas the Byzantine or Persian army (or almost any other army of antiquity!)[16] would have easily forded the ditch, it proved an insurmountable obstacle to the Meccans. The Muslims guarded the trench day and night with sentries and armed groups of men ready to react to any attempt at a breech. Muhammad had only thirty-five cavalrymen to patrol the length of the ditch.[17] Occasional attempts were made by the Meccans to overcome the obstacle by having their cavalry jump over it. Most of these seem to have been little more than pointless attempts at individual bravado, and none succeeded. At no time did the Meccans attempt to carry the obstacle with simultaneous attacks at different points along the length of the trench, the most obvious tactical solution to the problem. A few halfhearted attempts were made by small groups of infantry to fight their way across, only to meet disaster. No large-scale infantry attacks seem to have been attempted. After three weeks both sides were reduced to remaining in their positions and hurling insults at each other. Hamidullah observes that "there was never a pitched battle, but only the shooting of arrows was resorted to on both sides from time to time."[18] At the end of a month the siege had resulted in only three Meccan and five Muslim dead.[19]

And then a critical event occurred. Some of the Jews that Muhammad had earlier expelled from Medina had settled in the Kheibar oasis north of Medina. The Meccan stocks of food for their troops were running dangerously low when a caravan attempting to resupply the Meccans arrived from Kheibar laden with twenty camel-loads of barley, dates for the troops, and husks for the animals. Later sources report that the caravan was captured by Muhammad's men, although just how this might have been accomplished is not stated.[20] The important point is that since the Jews of Kheibar were supporting the Meccans Muhammad began to suspect that the Beni Qurayzah Jews of Medina, who were at his back, might somehow be in league with their kinsmen in Kheibar and preparing to attack him from the rear. For the moment Muhammad did nothing; but his fear of a surprise attack by the Jews lingered in his mind.

The siege of Medina dragged on for another week with no results for either side. By now the armies had been in the field for more than a month. Muhammad could have continued to let the passage of time take its inevitable toll on the Meccans' supply situation. But he was never one to react to events if he could shape them, and his political and strategic mind was at work with ways to disrupt the political cohesiveness of the Meccan coalition. Later sources tell us that Muhammad opened negotiations with the chiefs of the Ghatafan tribe, whose contingent numbered two thousand men. Using "secret agents" as go-betweens, Muhammad attempted to negotiate a separate peace with the Ghatafan. The talks succeeded in reaching an agreement in which Muhammad promised the Ghatafan one-third of the date crop of Medina if they would defect from the Meccans and return home.[21] But when Muhammad gathered the "garden-owners" of Medina together, he was unable to convince them that the agreement was in their interest and the matter was dropped.[22]

Abu Sufyan had apparently come to the same conclusion as Muhammad that a military resolution to the stalemate was unlikely. Consequently, the Meccans attempted a political solution of their own. They were aware of Muhammad's history with the Jews of Medina and certainly knew that Muhammad was aware of the attempt by the Jews of Kheibar to send supplies to the Meccan army. It was a reasonable guess, therefore, that the Jews of Medina might be convinced to attack Muhammad from their compounds located to the rear of the Muslims' positions. The Meccans made an approach to the Beni Qurayzah probably using one of the Jews from Kheibar as an intermediary. Ibn Ishaq says it was Huyai ibn Akhtab, a chief of the Beni an-Nadir tribe. The approach failed, and all the evidence indicates that the Jews refused to break with Muhammad and remained neutral.[23]

Word of the Meccan approach to the Beni Qurayzah must have reached Muhammad, and he seems to have believed that the Beni Qurayzah could not be trusted to stay out of the fight. Muhammad certainly understood that the Beni Qurayzah were the key to victory or defeat. If they joined the Meccans, he was finished. Given the gravity of the threat, Muhammad cannot be faulted for trying to make certain that the Beni Qurayzah did not ally with the Meccans. To this end he sent one Nuaim ibn Masood, a Muslim defector from the Ghatafan, to the Beni Qurayzah. Apparently ibn Masood was known to the Jews "in the heathen days" as a trustworthy man.[24] He warned the Jews not to trust the Meccans. The Jews, he said, had much more to lose than the Meccans who could return to their homeland if things went badly leaving the Jews alone to face the angry Muslims. So, ibn Masood suggested, "do not fight along with these people until you take hostages from their chiefs who will remain in your hands as security that they will fight Muhammad with you until you make an end of him."[25] Ibn Masood then went to the Ghatafan chiefs telling them that the Jews

were going to side with Muhammad, and that to convince him of
their loyalty they were planning to deliver several Quraish chiefs to
Muhammad. Ibn Masood warned that "if the Jews send to you to
demand hostages, don't send them a single man."[26] And so it was that
"God sowed distrust between them" and any concerted action became
impossible. Muhammad's back was safe.

The siege had now dragged on for over a month, and some of the
Meccan horses and camels were dying for lack of fodder.[27] The army
was running low on rations; camel milk and dates were still available,
but barley for cakes and porridge was almost gone. Some bedouin clans
worried that they had already been gone for too long from their flocks
and women. A general malaise set in among the soldiers as it was now
evident to all that there was no way to overcome the ditch. The chances
for loot and glory had disappeared. Ibn Ishaq tells us that "they [the
Meccans] had no permanent camp," by which he means that there had
been no attempt to build shelters or routinize the provision of food.[28]
This was the typical state of affairs of Arab clan-based armies, each
clan and its soldiers providing for themselves. The Meccans had expected
a quick pitched battle in open country and were ill prepared for a long
siege. It remains a mystery why no one on the Meccan side thought
about attacking Medina from the south. Although the terrain there
would have made an attack difficult, it was not an impossible course
of action and certainly much better than watching the Meccan army
atrophy with each passing day.

Then even the weather seemed to side against the Meccans. They
were continually exposed to the elements even as they were weakened
by a lack of food. One night a violent storm struck the area accompanied
by a strong wind and a cold soaking rain. The wind blew down the
Meccans' tents and scattered the campfires, sending the cooking pots
rolling across the desert. The sudden rain and cold probably took a
considerable toll on the already weakened animals, with many dying
where they were tethered. The weather was so miserable that when
Muhammad asked for a volunteer to cross the ditch and reconnoiter
the Meccan positions, "not a single man got up because of his great fear,
hunger, and the severe cold."[29] Even Muhammad's promise that the
volunteer would "be my companion in paradise" should he be killed on
the mission produced no one. Finally, Muhammad ordered a man to go.

The morale of the Meccan army was finally broken by the fierce
weather, and Abu Sufyan himself addressed his troops. "O Quraish, we

are not in a permanent camp; the horses and camels are dying, the Beni Qurayzah (the Jews) have broken their word to us and we have heard disquieting reports of them. You can see the violence of the wind which leaves us neither cooking-pots, nor fire, nor tents to count on. Be off, for I am going!"[30] He then mounted his camel and rode off. Besides the general discomfort and military failure, the annual pilgrimage and fair season at Mecca was only a month away and there was business to be done and money to be made. Once the Meccans departed, the rest of the coalition quickly came apart and the clans "broke up and returned to their own country."

THE MASSACRE OF THE BENI QURAYZAH

The ruthlessness of Muhammad's political intellect was demonstrated by what happened next. On the very day that the Meccan army began withdrawing from its positions, Muhammad moved against the last remaining Jewish tribe in Medina. Sometime around noon Muhammad is said to have met the angel Gabriel, who told him that the angels had not yet laid down their arms. Gabriel said, "God commands you to go to the Beni Qurayzah."[31] Muhammad immediately issued orders to his troops to assemble at the compounds of the Qurayzah Jews. The urgency of his command was evident in Muhammad's injunction that no one was to pray the afternoon prayer until they had assembled at the compounds with their weapons.[32] Muhammad intended to deal with the Jews of Medina once and for all.

Muhammad's decision to annihilate the Beni Qurayzah was rooted in cold-blooded politics. Ibn Ishaq, the earliest source for these events, offers no reason for Muhammad's action other than that God had commanded him "to shake their castles and strike terror in their hearts."[33] Later accounts claim that the Meccan approach to the Beni Qurayzah to attack Muhammad from the back had in fact succeeded and that a small number of Jews, said in the tradition to be eleven men, actually went into action against Muhammad.[34] There is no evidence that this attack ever occurred, and Rodinson is probably correct in saying that "the tradition had every incentive to exaggerate the incident as an excuse for the massacre which followed."[35] In fact, the Jews had resisted the Meccan approach to attack Muhammad and had remained in their compounds observing their obligations to their Aws allies, who were also Muhammad's allies. Ibn Ishaq makes no mention of the Jews acting against Muhammad, something we might be reasonably certain he would have mentioned had it occurred. Hamidullah, citing later Arabic accounts, also does not mention any Jewish betrayal of Muhammad. To the contrary he notes that one reason Muhammad was confident that the ditch would succeed was that the Meccans could not attack him through the Jewish areas to his rear because "relations with them [the Qurayzah] were for the time being correct."[36]

In the absence of any reliable account of Jewish treachery we might reasonably conclude that Muhammad decided to exterminate the Beni Qurayzah because the opportunity had finally presented itself to rid Medina of a major competitor for influence and because it would strengthen the insurgency politically. Muhammad was certain that the Beni Qurayzah would never become Muslims and, like other non-Muslim tribes and clans, would have to be dealt with sooner or later. Their military strength was considerable and represented a threat to Muslim security within Muhammad's base of operations. The previously exiled Jews had turned Kheibar into a hotbed of anti-Muslim activity, and some Jewish chiefs there had supported the Meccan assault on Medina. If the Beni Qurayzah were permitted to leave, many would settle in Kheibar and that source of opposition would grow even stronger. Muhammad seems to have decided that only the dead do not return. The massacre of the Beni Qurayzah would also help frighten and discourage the Jews of Kheibar and any other enemies. It would enhance Muhammad's already considerable reputation for ruthlessness among the bedouin tribes who Muhammad knew were the critical factor in gaining the ultimate victory. Politically speaking, then, the massacre of the Jews of Medina was an excellent solution to one of Muhammad's more serious problems.

Muhammad laid siege to the Jewish compounds for twenty-five days, during which only a few skirmishes between archers took place. Ibn Ishaq tells us that Huyai ibn Akhtab, the chief of the Beni an-Nadir Jews in Kheibar and the person who probably was used by the Meccans to approach the Jews of Medina and suggest they betray Muhammad, was still in the Beni Qurayzah compounds when Muhammad and his men laid siege to them. Once it became clear that Muhammad intended to make his point, ibn Akhtab is said to have suggested that the Jews had three alternatives to their present difficulties. The first was for the Beni Qurayzah to convert to Islam "and then your lives, your property, your women and children will be saved."[37] The second was "kill your wives and children and send men with their swords drawn to Muhammad and his companions leaving no encumbrances behind us, until God decides between us and Muhammad."[38] Both these alternatives having been rejected, ibn Akhtab said, "[T]onight is the eve of the sabbath and it may well be that Muhammad and his companions will feel secure from us then, so come down, perhaps we can take Muhammad and his companions by surprise."[39] This, too, was rejected. With the siege dragging on and with no real chance of lifting it, the Beni Qurayzah sought to come to terms with Muhammad. They sent word that they wanted to talk and requested that Muhammad send one Abu Lubaba of the Aws tribe. The Aws were still technically allies of the Beni Qurayzah, and the Jews trusted Abu Lubaba, with whom they had previous dealings.

The chiefs of the Beni Qurayzah met with Abu Lubaba and asked, "[D]o you think we should submit to Muhammad's judgment?" Now Abu Lubaba was a Muslim convert, but he was enough of a traditionalist to remain loyal to his previous commitments to his Jewish allies, who, after all, had fought on the side of the Aws in their battles against the Kazrai. Abu Lubaba said "yes" to the question but simultaneously drew his finger across his throat indicating that if they surrendered they would be massacred.[40] It is important to note that both the earliest and many later sources agree on the essentials of the story; all agree that Abu Lubaba had drawn his finger across his throat. How, then, are we to explain the story of Abu Lubaba if not by the suspicion that the fate of the Jews had already been decided and that everyone around Muhammad knew it? The evidence indicates that Muhammad planned all along to kill them. When the Beni Qurayzah chose not to go down fighting and surrendered to Muhammad the next day, they had sealed their fate. The siege had lasted twenty-five days.

Although the Aws had become Muslims, some of their chiefs felt a loyalty to their old comrades-in-arms and pleaded with Muhammad to show mercy to the Beni Qurayzah. Muhammad probably anticipated that the Aws would try to protect their allies, and he maneuvered to deal with their objections. "Will you be satisfied, Oh Aws, if one of your own number pronounces judgment on them?" he asked.[41] They agreed and Muhammad had just the right candidate for the job, Sa'd ibn Mu'adh. Mu'adh had been one of the unlucky few wounded during the siege. An arrow had struck him in the arm, and the wound was now in an advanced state of infection. Mu'adh, a devout Muslim, was feverish and near death when he was asked by the Messenger of God to judge the Jews. It is clear that he intended to die an obedient Muslim; having been wounded in battle, he would also die a martyr. When one of the Aws whispered to him to be lenient with the Jews, Ibn Ishaq tells us he replied that "the time has come for Sa'd in the cause of God, not to care for any man's censure." But the more damning evidence comes from the Muslim historical tradition that says Sa'd made a prayer before judging the Jews in which he said, "Oh Allah, if you make the war with Quraish last a little longer, spare me so that I may join in it . . . and do not let me die before I have comforted myself at the expense of the Beni Qurayzah."[42]

There is no evidence from the texts that Muhammad told Mu'adh how to render his judgment. At the same time, however, the incident with Abu Lubaba suggests that Muhammad's wishes to dispose of the Jews were already well known among the Muslims. The choice of a devout Muslim wounded in battle whose wound was now causing his death and who wished for paradise to render judgment on the Jews could hardly have been accidental. Perhaps with one eye on history's judgment, Muhammad got what he wanted: to condemn the Jews and levy the responsibility for the decision on someone else.

Sa'd ibn Mu'adh rendered his decision. First he asked, "Do you covenant by Allah that you accept the judgment I pronounce on them?" The Aws said yes. "Then I give judgment that the men should be killed, the property divided, and the women and children taken as captives."[43] "Then they surrendered, and the Apostle confined them in Medina in the quarter of al Harith. Then the Apostle went out to the market of Medina and dug trenches in it. Then he sent for them and struck off their heads in those trenches as they were brought out to him in batches."[44] Taken literally, Ibn Ishaq may be suggesting that Muhammad himself took part in the beheadings of the victims. If so, then this is the first place in Arabic accounts of his life where Muhammad actually is said to have killed someone with his own hand. "There were 600 or 700 in all, although some put the figure as high as 800 or 900. . . . This went on until the Apostle made an end of them."[45] Every adult male of the Jewish tribe of Beni Qurayzah was killed that day. The property of the Jews was distributed among the Muslims, and the women and children were sold and the money divided or used to purchase arms. And so it was that the Beni Qurayzah of Medina were annihilated. Muhammad was struck by the beauty of a particular Jewish girl named Rayhana and took her as his concubine. The Apostle became quite fond of her and offered to marry her "and put the veil on her." But "she had shown repugnance towards Islam when she was captured and clung to Judaism" and refused Muhammad's offer of marriage.[46]

The impact of Muhammad's victory at Medina cannot be overestimated. It was a great political and military triumph. All of Arabia had been watching the events at Medina, especially those tribes who were not yet committed to either side. A mighty coalition of ten thousand soldiers had failed to defeat Muhammad; if they could not do it, then perhaps no army could. Perhaps Muhammad was God's Messenger after all. Muhammad's prestige and aura of political legitimacy increased considerably, and tales of the victory at the Battle of the Ditch spread throughout the Hejaz. The Muslim state at Medina and its brilliant leader had proven themselves a force to be reckoned with.

Muhammad understood that the defeat of the Meccans would weaken their ability to retain the loyalty of their allies and increased his opportunities to woo them over to his side. For the next year Muhammad turned his attention to a political war of attrition trying to win the loyalty of those tribes along the caravan routes and close to Mecca. Those he could not convince he threatened using assassination and raids to make his point. Shortly after the victory at Medina, he dispatched a group of killers to Kheibar to kill Sallam ibn Abu-l'huqayq, one of the Jewish chiefs who had helped convince some of the tribes near the oasis to support the Meccan attack on Medina.[47] Muhammad was certainly one to hold a grudge, and he used murder and the torture of prisoners to take his revenge.[48] However, like other successful revolutionaries who have come after him, Muhammad's use of violence was usually in the service of political ends and never just sadistic.

The year following the victory at Medina was a successful one for Muhammad and the cause of Islam. Within a few weeks of the Meccan withdrawal, Muhammad struck. A force of seven hundred men was sent under the command of Abd-al-Rahman ibn Awf to raid Dumat al-Jandal, the great trading center on the road to Syria where an important annual fair was held.[49] Muhammad had attempted a raid more than a year earlier when he tried to prevent the Ghatafan from joining the Meccans. Dumat al-Jandal was the territory of the Christian tribe of Kalb, but was the major trading post for the Ghatafan bedouins. The Christian chiefs saw no interest in opposing Muhammad, who, as he often did when it was to his advantage, did not require the Christians to become Muslims. The old tribal values were still very much in force, and the

Christian chief concluded an alliance with the Muslims and gave his daughter to Abd-al-Rahman ibn Awf to seal the deal.[50] Two months later, Zayd, Muhammad's adoptive son, was sent on a raid to the north with 170 men and successfully captured a Meccan caravan returning from Syria.[51] Muhammad continued to forge alliances with the clans closest to Medina apparently without any demand that they convert to Islam. Muhammad respected the terms of these alliances to the letter and expected others to do the same. When they did not, as when his territory was violated or when his camel herds were raided, Muhammad responded quickly and forcefully. On one of these raids Ali was sent against the Beni Saad, from whom he captured five hundred camels and two thousand sheep.[52]

Six months after the events in Medina, Muhammad set out to attack the Beni Lihyan, the tribe that had earlier killed his missionaries and turned two Muslims over to the Quraish for execution. By now Muhammad had come to appreciate the need for operational security, and he mounted the raid in secret. Many bedouins had become Muslims and could act as desert guides, so that Muhammad's ability to move troops over long distances without being detected had improved considerably. Muhammad announced that his intention was to march north and raid Syria. Medina was still full of spies to report his movements. About twenty miles north of Medina he turned left and headed south hoping to catch the Beni Lihyan by surprise where they were encamped near Usfan.[53] But the Beni Lihyan had been warned of Muhammad's approach and "took up strong positions on the tops of the mountains" where they prepared to resist.[54] Having come all this way only to be frustrated, Muhammad nevertheless made good use of the expedition. He sent two hundred riders on ahead to approach the outskirts of Usfan. Ibn Ishaq tells us Muhammad said, "Were we to come down to Usfan the Meccans would think that we intend to come to Mecca."[55] Muhammad undertook a show of force to keep the Meccans in a state of apprehension. He even sent a small group of riders farther along the road to Mecca as if they were reconnoitering the route for an impending attack by Muhammad's raiders. Then he turned around and went back to Medina.

All this activity was gradually shifting the balance of loyalty among the bedouin tribes in Muhammad's favor. We have no way to estimate the rate of conversion of these tribes, although it is clear that some became Muslims and that their conversions were genuine. Of military significance were the conversions of two experienced Meccan field commanders, Khalid al-Walid and Amr ibn al-A'as. It had been al-Walid's daring cavalry charge through the Hill of Arrows gap at Uhud that turned the battle in favor of the Meccans and almost succeeded in killing Muhammad. A bold commander with an excellent grasp of strategy and tactics, al-Walid rose quickly through the Muslim ranks. It was he who won many of the critical battles during the War of the Apostates (Riddah) following Muhammad's death that preserved Islam through a brutal civil war. And it was al-Walid who later defeated the Byzantines and conquered Syria earning himself the title The Sword of Allah. Amr ibn al-A'as had also been at Uhud. He, too, fought bravely and well during the civil war. It was Amr ibn al-A'as who later led the Arab conquest of Egypt. The addition of these two officers added considerably to Muhammad's military expertise and capability.

Sometime in January 628 Muhammad's intelligence agents obtained information that the Bani Mustaliq were planning a raid on the Muslims. The Muslims caught them at a watering place at Al Muraisi near the seashore.[56] There was a brief fight in which the bedouins were surprised and several were killed. Muhammad captured a considerable number of their women and children, animals, and flocks. One of the women, Juwairiya, was the daughter of the Mustaliq chief and went to Muhammad to plead for her release saying that her father would willingly pay whatever ransom was asked. Ibn Ishaq tells us that Juwairiya "was a most beautiful woman who captivated every man who saw her."[57] Muhammad was so taken by her beauty that he proposed marriage to her on the spot! She accepted. As soon as the word spread that Muhammad had married the daughter of the chief and that the Mustaliq had now become Muhammad's relatives, the Muslims released their prisoners. Ibn Ishaq tells us that a hundred families were released.[58] With this diplomatic marriage Muhammad's former enemies and allies of the Meccans all became Muslims. Muhammad had acquired the fealty of a major tribe without any significant cost.

Sometime in March 628, Muhammad had a dream in which he saw himself making a pilgrimage to Mecca. This was not one of Muhammad's revelations, so that the pilgrimage was apparently Muhammad's idea and not a divine command. This is interesting insofar as it suggests that Muhammad may have undertaken the pilgrimage to Mecca not on the spur of the moment as the dream story implies, but as part of his strategy to weaken the Meccans. The Battle of Uhud and the siege of Medina had made it evident that Muhammad could not be destroyed by military force. At the same time Muhammad could not yet raise an army large enough to defeat the Meccans. A long stalemate was in the offing unless something was done to alter the power relationship between the two sides. From the beginning Muhammad had waged an insurgency in which the critical circumstance was the campaign to win the hearts and minds of the general populace while his guerrilla army employed hit-and-run raids to isolate and weaken Mecca economically. As always, it was primarily a political struggle with ideology and military operations made to serve political ends. It is a reasonable guess that Muhammad may have concluded that the time had come to press Mecca on the political front. Like other insurgent leaders who came after him, Muhammad may have thought it time to confront the enemy on his home ground, relying not on military force but on the ideological attraction of the new creed to produce a groundswell of popular support within the enemy stronghold to convince them that further resistance was useless. It was the same strategic assumption that Mao Zedong made when he predicted that the cities would fall into his hands like ripe fruit, and that the Vietcong made during the Tet Offensive of 1968, and that Fidel Castro made on his first march on Havana. It proved to be equally wrong.

In early April Muhammad set out for Mecca with a force of seven hundred men.[59] The column was virtually unarmed except for the traditional defensive weapon permitted on the pilgrim's journey, the sheathed sword. Pagan (and later Muslim) pilgrimages to Mecca were of two types: the *hajj*, or Greater Pilgrimage, which could only be made on a specified day of the year, and the *omra*, or Lesser Pilgrimage, which could be carried out at any time. It was the Lesser Pilgrimage that Muhammad undertook in 628. Muhammad wore the traditional garb of the pilgrim "so that all would know that he did not intend war and that his purpose was to visit the temple and to venerate it."[60] He brought with him seventy camels, necks draped with garlands as was the custom, to sacrifice at the Kaaba.

It was a bold and dangerous gamble, and it would be naive to believe that Muhammad's purpose was to venerate the Meccan shrine that, after all, was the primary symbol of the very idolatry that he despised. Muhammad was playing for higher stakes. The news of his approach reached Mecca in plenty of time and the Meccans sent out a cavalry screen of two hundred horsemen to block Muhammad's path.[61]

The cavalry was only a tripwire to test Muhammad's intentions, and its strength was such that Muhammad could easily have swept it aside, but only by starting the very battle he sought to avoid. Muhammad must have received news of the Meccan cavalry long before they located his position, for Ibn Ishaq tells us that when Muhammad turned off the main road the Meccan cavalry commander knew this only by seeing the cloud of dust in the distance raised by Muhammad's column.[62] Using a local bedouin as a guide, the Muslims made their way through a narrow pass coming within sight of the Meccan cavalry now redeployed to block the alternate route. Muhammad called a halt on level ground at a place called Hudaibiya, nine or ten miles northwest of Mecca. Here he ordered his army to pitch camp and water the animals.[63] Hudaibiya was located at the edge of the sacred ground around Mecca within which violence was prohibited.

THE TRUCE OF HUDAIBIYA

History is sometimes cruel in presenting its actors with the circumstances with which they must deal. At the time of Muhammad's pilgrimage, Abu Sufyan was suspiciously absent from Mecca. This deprived the Meccan leadership of its most decisive and adamant voice in their counsels. Abu Sufyan had opposed Muhammad from the beginning, and there would have been every expectation that he would have insisted that Muhammad be opposed forcefully. Instead the Meccan leaders were divided between those who wanted to attack Muhammad and those who wanted to come to terms with him. The omra to Mecca in 628 turned out to be one of the most crucial events in the history of Islam. The Meccans had been unable to defeat Muhammad in the field. But here he was only eight miles from Mecca protected by only a small force with no line of retreat. It seemed that Muhammad had delivered himself into the hands of his enemies, offering the Meccans a priceless opportunity to kill him and, perhaps, even to destroy Islam. Without the counsel of Abu Sufyan, however, the Meccan leaders voted to negotiate with Muhammad instead.

There is some tentative evidence that Muhammad may have known that Abu Sufyan would be absent from Mecca at this time, but this is only speculation. The trusty Abbas was still serving as an agent among the Meccan leadership, and the chief of the Khuza'a clan who had the confidence of the Meccans and participated in the discussion was also a source of accurate intelligence for Muhammad, for the "Khuza'a were the Apostle's confidants, both their Muslims and their polytheists. They kept him informed of everything that happened in Mecca."[64] The details regarding the conduct of the negotiations are not important. It appears, however, that at some point both sides became convinced that the other was about to attack. The "spontaneous uprising" that Muhammad may have hoped to provoke by his daring entry into Mecca did not happen, and he was left in a vulnerable military position. The result was that many of the outstanding issues between the two parties were quickly resolved, and an agreement was reached that became known as the Truce of Hudaibiya.

The Truce of Hudaibiya must be counted as among Muhammad's greatest political victories in his campaign to destroy his enemies and establish Islam as the religion of virtuous Arab men. Ibn Ishaq tells us that "[n]o greater victory in Islam was greater than this."[65] The agreement called for a truce between the Quraish and the Muslims to hold for ten years. Muhammad never really had a chance of defeating the Meccans militarily, and the truce prohibited the Meccans, who certainly did possess the military capability to destroy Muhammad (even as it had been badly applied so far), from attempting to do so. With a single stroke Muhammad had removed the military threat to his insurgency. To the Meccans the cessation of hostilities also meant that the caravan routes would be reopened and commerce would resume unmolested by Muslim raids. As we shall see, this was not what Muhammad had in mind. A second provision required that any member of the Quraish who went to Medina to become a Muslim without the legal permission of their family or legal guardian was to be returned. Muslims who wanted to return to Mecca were free to do so and did not have to be forcibly returned. Some of Muhammad's advisers thought this provision humiliating, but Muhammad saw it as a small price to pay for having the Meccans deal with him as an equal and recognize his status as the leader of Islam. Muhammad finally had the prestige and recognition he both desired and required if he was to convince other chiefs to join him.

A third provision required the Muslims to depart from Mecca at once, but permitted them to make an omra in the following year during which they would be permitted to remain for three days. The Muslims were to be armed only with the traditional sheathed sword of the pilgrim; the Quraish were required to withdraw from the city for three days while the omra was going on. This seemingly minor provision was, as

Muhammad knew, a major propaganda coup. The Meccans had always argued that Muhammad was a danger because he sought to destroy the Kaaba and its pilgrimage, actions that would cause great economic harm to the city. Muhammad's demand that he be permitted to worship at the Kaaba made it clear to the Meccan populace and merchants that he intended no such thing, and that the economic interests of Mecca had nothing to fear from Muhammad and his Muslims. The provision neutralized one of the major propaganda weapons of his Meccan opponents with the result that many were now prepared to give Muhammad a fair hearing concerning Islam. Ibn Ishaq tells us that "in those two years double as many or more than double as many entered Islam as ever before."[66]

The final provision of the Truce of Hudaibiya was the most important and gave Muhammad his greatest victory. The agreement permitted all the tribes of the region the freedom to make alliances with either side. This implied, as Muhammad saw it, that all prior alliances were no longer in force or, at least, that the tribes were now free to change sides or remain neutral. If they joined an alliance, the general truce applied to them for ten years. Muhammad had been somewhat successful in gaining uncommitted tribes to his cause, but had been less successful in attracting those tribes that were already allied with Mecca who pleaded that their obligations made switching sides dishonorable. Now these prior alliance obligations had been removed.

In one deft stroke Muhammad had altered the political power balance in the region. The powerful alliance of the Quraish, the Jewish tribes of Kheibar, and the large bedouin tribes of Ghatafan and Fazarah that had so effectively opposed Muhammad was formally dissolved by the truce. Muhammad could now deal with each opponent separately without having to worry that the other's allies would come to their aid. His strategy of divide and conquer had provided Muhammad with a long-awaited opportunity. He moved quickly to bring the Jews of Kheibar under attack.

9

THE BATTLES OF KHEIBAR (628) AND MU'TA (629)

Muhammad remained in Medina for less than a month after the Truce of Hudaibiya, during which time he assembled an army of fourteen hundred men and two hundred cavalry for his attack on the Jewish settlement at Kheibar.[1] Muhammad was eager to take advantage of the political confusion that had accompanied the loosening of the old tribal alliances after Hudaibiya and was determined to strike before a new coalition could be formed to oppose him. Kheibar was a major agricultural oasis located some eighty miles north of Medina. It had a reputation for being infested with malaria, and caravans sometimes avoided it altogether for this reason.[2] The settlement was home to a number of Jewish clans whose ancestors probably introduced date farming and other agriculture to the oasis.[3] The scale of date farming was enormous. An old description of the town notes that in one farm alone there were twelve thousand trees; another later source records that the Katibah farm, the settlement's largest, contained no fewer than forty thousand trees.[4] Farming on this scale made the tribes of Kheibar among the wealthiest in the region.

Kheibar was surrounded by a number of Arab tribes, the largest and most powerful of which were the Ghatafans.[5] The Jews of Kheibar were long accustomed to paying bribes to these local tribes to reduce the bedouin propensity to raid agricultural settlements. With the Ghatafans

this protection money took the form of gifts so that the arrangement
assumed the shape of an alliance whereby the powerful Ghatafan tribe
agreed to protect their Jewish allies. It was to Kheibar that the Beni
an-Nadir tribe had gone after being forced by Muhammad to leave Mecca.
The Beni an-Nadir had been anxious to avenge themselves on Muhammad and had been instrumental in using their wealth and influence to
help the Meccans assemble the coalition that had besieged Medina.
They had been most effective in convincing the Ghatafan to join the
Meccan coalition. Muhammad was aware of this and was convinced that
Kheibar could never be neutralized through political accommodation but
would have to be reduced by force. Equally important was that Kheibar
was at Muhammad's back. Any attempt to move against Mecca first
required that this hostile base of troops and supplies be neutralized.

In May 628 Muhammad and his army left Medina and moved by a
circuitous route toward Kheibar.[6] Muhammad's intelligence service
was operating efficiently and learned that the Ghatafan intended to
come to the aid of the Jews of Kheibar. Muhammad's agents had been
active among the tribes around Kheibar, and probably as a result of
Muslim bribes, none of the tribes except the Ghatafan remained loyal
to their former allies in Kheibar.[7] This was an outrageous breach of
faith by Arab standards. Nevertheless, Muhammad's financial stratagem
had seriously weakened his adversary. According to later sources the
Ghatafan and Fazarah rushed four thousand men to Kheibar, where
they took up positions manning some of the Jewish forts.[8] This seems
unlikely, however, since we hear nothing of these fighters from Ibn
Ishaq nor are they mentioned as taking part in the battle later on.
What seems to have happened is that, having detected the movement
of some Ghatafan units on the way to reinforce Kheibar, Muhammad
changed his direction of march to place his army across the Ghatafan
route of march, blocking their way to the oasis.

Ibn Ishaq tells us that Muhammad "went forward with the army
until he halted in a wadi called al-Raji, halting between the men of
Kheibar and Ghatafan so as to prevent the latter reinforcing Kheibar."[9]
It might have been that the Ghatafan units were only an advance
guard and too weak to offer battle at al-Raji. In any event, the Ghatafans rode back to their camp. Muhammad's main force then turned
toward Kheibar. But Muhammad seems to have remained wary that
the Ghatafan might still try to come to the aid of their allies if the
opportunity presented itself. To prevent this Muhammad detached

several units, most likely cavalry to cover distance quickly, and set them in the direction of the Ghatafan with orders to demonstrate their intention to attack the Ghatafan territory, drive off the flocks, and capture the women and children. This seems to be the essence of the story as told by Ibn Ishaq, that after the encounter at al-Raji, the Ghatafan "gathered together and marched out to help the Jews against him; but after a day's journey, hearing a rumor about their property and families, they thought that they had been attacked during their absence so they went back on their tracks and left the way to Kheibar open to the Apostle."[10] The rumor was probably the result of the movement and harassment in the Ghatafan rear by Muhammad's cavalry. Following what would later be the advice of Napoleon to General Ghouci at the Battle of Waterloo to "keep the sabre in the back" of the adversary, maintain contact, and prevent the adversary from returning to the battlefield, Muhammad's cavalry commander (whoever it was) kept pressing the Ghatafan until they moved off deeper into the desert from whence they could not return and support their allies in Kheibar.[11] In a brilliant display of tactics, Muhammad had isolated his objective from any outside help and was free to attack at will.

But Kheibar was no easy nut to crack. The settement lay in a deep valley surrounded by an elevated table land and plateau. The valley below the table land was narrow, less than a mile wide, and ran on for several miles. The entire area, valley and plateau, was surrounded by lava hills that limited access to the fertile lands to only a few narrow descending passes that were easily defended and through which no army could pass in force at one time. The approaches to and the most likely avenues of the advance within the valley itself were guarded by the usual fortified clan compounds, thick date groves, and walled gardens in zigzag fashion, all of which impeded rapid military movement. Ibn Ishaq says only that there were "innumerable" small forts and compounds both on the table land and in the valley. Later sources say that Kheibar had only seven forts.[12] Hamidullah, citing these same sources, suggests that the entire area may have been divided into "seven military regions," by which one supposes he means integrated clan compounds. The size of the defensive forces at Kheibar is uncertain. Ibn Ishaq is completely silent on the matter, while later sources say the defenders numbered between ten thousand and twenty thousand combatants.[13] The numbers are clearly exaggerations and may be references to the total population of Kheibar rather than to the number of available combatants. A total population of twenty thousand souls would not be beyond reason for a settlement like Kheibar. But this population would only be able to field between five thousand and six thousand soldiers, still a sizable force and considerably larger than Muhammad's fourteen-hundred-man army (the two hundred cavalry now being unavailable). Moreover, the Jews of Kheibar had the advantage of the defense.

Muhammad staged from al-Raji and moved his column down a steep narrow trail that approached the valley floor from the east. The trail was so steep that the feet of a rider touched those of the rider in front of him.[14] A walled compound and fortified tower commanded the exit of the trail where it met the valley floor. This was the compound of the Na'im clan.[15] Muhammad's plan was to take this position and then move his main force into the valley from where he could reduce each of the forts one at a time. It required ten days for Muhammad's army to subdue the Na'im fort. With the way finally clear, Muhammad moved his main force into the valley and began attacking each of the other fortified positions in turn.

It was rough going. In one engagement fifty Muslim soldiers were wounded in a single day.[16] The Jews fought well and in traditional Arab fashion. Some of their leaders came out of their defensive positions to challenge Muslims to individual combat. This proved to be a foolhardy display of courage, and many of the chiefs of the Jewish clans were killed in this manner. Still, resistance was stiff. In a number of instances Muhammad was forced to order date palm groves cut down to clear an avenue for his troops to advance.[17] Whenever a position fell to the Muslims, the remaining defenders would fall back to another fort and continue the fight. Sometimes they abandoned their women and children to the attackers. Some clans fought vigorously, even conducting sallies to attack the Muslim positions; others fought less well. In one case a fort was betrayed by a local resident who revealed a secret tunnel leading from the walls to a place near the table land. Muhammad took the position by gaining entrance through this tunnel.[18]

As always with Arab armies, Muhammad's real problem was time. He had been engaged in the valley for more than three weeks when his army began to run short of supplies. Forage was so difficult to come by that Muhammad ordered large numbers of date palms cut down to feed the animals. The army, too, was suffering from a lack of food. A soldier went to Muhammad to complain. Muhammad turned his head skyward and prayed, "O God, You know their condition and they have no strength, and that I have nothing to give them, so conquer for them the wealthiest of the enemy's forts with the richest food."[19] As events turned out, the next day the compound of the al-Sab Beni Mu'adh clan was taken, "which contained the richest food in Kheibar."[20] It was apparently a storehouse of some sort.

The shortage of food caused a curious incident. The Muslim troops had come across a herd of domestic donkeys, which they began to slaughter and cook. Muhammad happened to pass by one of the cooking fires and saw what was happening. He immediately pronounced that it was forbidden to eat the flesh of the donkey. Ibn Ishaq tells us, "The Apostle's prohibition of the flesh of domestic donkeys reached us as the pots were boiling with it, so we turned them upside down."[21] Interestingly, "when the Apostle forbade the flesh of donkeys he allowed them [the soldiers] to eat horseflesh."[22] The order must have horrified the troops, especially the cavalry! Horses were expensive and highly valued, and were not usually eaten under most circumstances. To order his troops not to eat the donkey but to kill and eat their horses instead was bizarre, to say the least. It also made no military sense because it would reduce the number of mounts available to the army.[23]

The Muslim assault on Kheibar took more than a month before the last strongpoint was taken. Even then one of the Jewish leaders came out from the fort carrying his weapon and challenged the Muslims to a fight. The challenge was answered and he was killed. It had been a long tough fight, but the Muslims had succeeded in capturing the town that was second only to Mecca in the strength of its opposition to Muhammad. Several factors contributed to the Muslim victory. First and perhaps most important, the Jews failed to bring their man-power advantage to bear. By even conservative estimates the Jews of Kheibar outnumbered the Muslims by four to one. Had they chosen to meet Muhammad in open battle deployed across the narrow valley floor, they would have given themselves a huge numerical advantage. Instead they chose to fragment their forces into isolated groups, each deployed in and around the clan compounds. This meant that Muhammad could bring numerical superiority to bear against each defensive position subduing them one at a time. The Jewish tactical deployment granted Muhammad the advantage of economy of force at the decisive point of each engagement. Second, to defend from their clan compounds required that adequate supplies of food, forage, and water be gathered for a long defense. For whatever reason, this was not accomplished with any regularity so that the defenders were often as short of supplies as the attackers. Some compounds surrendered to the Muslims because they had run out of food. Third, the defenders of Kheibar did not conduct their defense under a unified command. Although all of the clans were Jewish, each clan fought its own battle for its own compound with little or no coordination with other clans. The absence of a unified command had plagued Arab armies for centuries, and the establishment of such a command was one of the most important reforms Muhammad had introduced to Arab warfare. Its absence at Kheibar proved fatal for the defenders. Fourth, while both sides seem to have fought bravely, one is still left with the conclusion that the Muslims were better fighters and more highly motivated than the defenders. The kill ratio was seven to one in favor of Muhammad's troops with only fifteen Muslims killed while ninety-three Jewish defenders perished.

Kheibar was a very rich oasis and the booty taken must have been enormous. Al-Maqrizi tells us that five hundred bows, one hundred coats of mail, four hundred swords, and one thousand lances were taken from the single fort of Katibah, which had taken two weeks of heavy fighting to subdue.[24] The same source says that in one fort the Muslims captured a catapult (*manjaniq*) and that in another several covered cars (*dabbabah*) or wagons used in siege operations. These siege machines were commonly known in Yemen, where they were vestiges of the long years of Persian presence and influence, but were relatively rare in the rest of western Arabia. Perhaps the leaders of wealthy Kheibar had purchased them for use in defending their forts. There is some tentative evidence that the one catapult that was captured was then used by the Muslims to attack the other forts.

It is important to note that Muhammad never seems to have planned to kill the Jews of Kheibar. All the sources agree that the first plan for dealing with the residents of the town was to expel them, "that they should leave the country [territory] with nothing except the clothes on their bodies."[25] Additional evidence to this effect is that Muhammad apparently returned all the copies of the Hebrew scriptures captured in the fighting to the Jews of Kheibar once the battle had ended.[26] The residents of Kheibar were permitted to keep their farms, date groves, and gardens with the provision that 50 percent of the harvest of the town was to be given over to the Muslims each year.

The lion's share of the booty was given to the soldiers who had been with Muhammad at Hudaibiya, with the two hundred cavalrymen receiving a double share.[27]

A few days later, Muhammad prepared to move against Wadi al-Qura, another Jewish oasis in the area, which surrendered without resistance on the same terms as Kheibar. A short time later, two other larger Jewish oases, Fadak and Tayma, settled with Muhammad on the same terms. The events surrounding the treatment of the Jews in these oases strongly suggests that Muhammad's slaughter of the Jews of Beni Qaynuqa in Medina was carried out for security reasons, that is, to remove a potential threat to his primary base of operations. He could have easily caused the Jews of Kheibar to be killed or sold into slavery. Instead he came to a traditional Arab accommodation with them; peace and protection in return for money or a share in the harvest. Muhammad was certainly capable of cold-blooded terror against any of his enemies, but he seems to have harbored no particular animus against the Jews. With the accommodation with the Jews of Kheibar, Muhammad seems to have solved his "Jewish problem" once and for all.

Muhammad returned to Medina, where he spent the rest of the year carrying out a series of small raids against the various clans around Medina and Mecca to demonstrate his power and importance. Muhammad was reminding those clans who opposed him that he was a power to be reckoned with, more so since his victory at Kheibar. Throughout this period Muhammad made numerous attempts to negotiate with the various clans as he attempted to garner their support, conversion, or promises of neutrality. Muhammad's grasp of the strategic political realities was evident in that he rarely demanded that a clan convert to Islam as the price of an agreement, being content to accept the traditional form of Arab obligation. As always, his diplomatic efforts were aimed at winning over or neutralizing the countryside as a key element in his continued prosecution of the Muslim insurgency.

In February 629, a year after the agreement at Hudaibiya, Muhammad set out from Medina to make his promised pilgrimage to Mecca and to test the sincerity and strength of his Quraish opponents there. When last he had attempted to make the Lesser Pilgrimage at Mecca he had gone without arms, placing himself in great danger. Now he set out for Mecca with a bodyguard of two thousand soldiers and a large quantity of weapons. The weapons were hidden under guard near the border of the city just outside the haram, or sanctuary where weapons and violence were forbidden. The Muslim pilgrims approached the holy shrine armed only with the sheathed sword. Muhammad led the column of men riding on a camel and surrounded by his intimate companions, including Ali, Abu Bakr, and Umar ibn al Khattab.[28] Sixty camels prepared for sacrifice accompanied the party.[29] Until this day Muhammad had not set eyes on the city of his birth for seven years.

As they had promised at Hudaibiya the Meccans withdrew from the city itself, retreating to the surrounding hills where they made camp and watched the happenings below. Muhammad made the ritual turns around the Kaaba while riding on his camel and performed "the seven circuits of the House, after which he withdrew to the foot of the little hill of Safa, and passed to and fro between it and the hill of Marwah, seven courses in all, ending at Marwah, to which many of the sacrificial animals had now been led. There he sacrificed a camel, and his head was shaved. . . . This completed the rite of the Lesser Pilgrimage."[30] Behind him and on foot, his followers did the same shouting, *Labbayk Allahumma Labbayk*, "Here I am, O God, at Thy service."[31] While in Mecca Muhammad married a girl of twenty-seven, Maymuna, the sister of one of his uncles. When the Meccans came to him and reminded him that their agreement called for Muhammad and his followers to remain in the city for three days, he replied that he would offer a wedding feast for all if he could stay a few more days.[32] The Meccans refused and Muhammad ordered his men out of the city by nightfall.

Muhammad's return to Mecca was another political triumph along the same lines as his political victory at Hudaibiya. Once again the Meccan leadership was forced to treat Muhammad as an equal, a man of authority and reputation to be dealt with accordingly. Muhammad's arrival in Mecca with two thousand followers was also a show of military force that demonstrated that he possessed the means to protect himself and his movement. Perhaps more important than both of these elements was Muhammad's observance of the traditional pagan ritual of worship at the Kaaba, which put to rest the accusation of his Meccan opponents that Islam would destroy the old shrine and the economic benefits that fell to Mecca because of it. Years earlier Muhammad had instituted the *qiblah*, the direction to be faced when Muslims pray. Originally, he had required that Muslims face Jerusalem. After his initial difficulties with the Jews of Medina he changed the direction of the qiblah so that Muslims now faced Mecca when they prayed.[33] Muhammad's performance at the Lesser Pilgrimage had gone a long way to allay the fears

of the Meccans on both economic and religious grounds. The performance was so convincing that within a few months some prominent
Meccan leaders converted to Islam and went over to Muhammad.
Among the most important of these converts was Khalid al-Walid, the
talented field commander destined for military greatness; Amr ibn al
Maimoona, who had distinguished himself on the field at Uhud, but who
had also been among the most prominent leaders of the opposition
against Muhammad in Mecca; and Othman ibn Talha, the hereditary
keeper of the keys to the door of the Kaaba itself. The conversion of these
and other important persons in Mecca probably went far to convince
many others that Muhammad's movement was the wave of the future.[34]

THE BATTLE OF MU'TA

In September 629, six months after the pilgrimage to Mecca, the first
military clash between the Muslims and the world outside Arabia
occurred with the forces of the Byzantine Empire at the small town of
Mu'ta located southeast of the Dead Sea in modern-day Jordan. This
was the first penetration of the borders of the Byzantine Empire by a
Muslim army, and for the first time in history information concerning
Muhammad can be obtained from some source other than a Muslim
one. The Byzantine historian Theophanes recorded the events that
transpired at Mu'ta between the Byzantine and Muslim armies.[35] A
Muslim army of three thousand men left Medina in early September
and made its way toward the Syrian border. Command of the army
was given to Muhammad's adopted son, Zayd ibn Harithah, with
instructions that if Zayd were slain command was to fall to Jafar ibn
Abi Talib, the brother of Ali. If both were killed, Abdullah ibn Rawaha,
an ansar of Medina, was to assume command. These were notable
people close to the Apostle himself, and their presence indicates that
Muhammad attached considerable importance to the raid into Syria.

The account of what happened at Mu'ta is one of the more obscure
to have come down to us from Muslim sources. It remains unclear
why Muhammad ordered the expedition in the first place. Three possi-
bilities exist. According to Muslim tradition Muhammad sent six letters
to the great leaders of the world outside Arabia, including the Persian
and Byzantine emperors, urging them to recognize his prophethood and
the new religion of Islam by becoming Muslims. Among the recipients
of these letters was the chief of the Beni Ghassan (Ghassanid) tribe that

had served the Byzantines as allies for more than a century and guarded the Syrian frontier against Arab raids. No reliable information on the letter's content has survived, nor do we know if the letter was ever delivered, or if there was a reply. What is known is that Muhammad's messenger was set upon and murdered, an event that Muhammad seems to have attributed to the chief of the Ghassanids himself or to one of his tribe's clans.[36] The murder of an envoy who comes carrying a letter in peace has always been regarded as a terrible crime in the Arab mind. It is possible that Muhammad decided to avenge the insult with a punitive raid against the territory of the perpetrators. The size of Muhammad's force, three thousand men, would seem appropriate to this task.

A second reason for the raid on Syria is offered by the famous scholar Philip K. Hitti and is less complex. Hitti suggests that the purpose of the attack was to raid Mu'ta itself. Mu'ta contained an armory where the famous *Mashrafiya* swords were manufactured, and Muhammad wanted to obtain a large quantity of these excellent weapons to outfit his army for his planned attack on Mecca. Gifts of these expensive weapons would also have been valuable in gaining the support of the bedouin tribes that Muhammad absolutely required to raise an army large enough to attack Mecca.[37]

Yet another reason may have been that Muhammad's success at Mecca during the Lesser Pilgrimage may have convinced him that Mecca would eventually come into the Muslim fold and that a period of benign neglect toward it was the best policy for the time being. While negotiations with the bedouin tribes in the Hejaz region continued with good success, Muhammad may have turned his attention to the north for two reasons. First, the northern area from Kheibar to the Syrian border was still in the hands of the powerful Ghatafan tribe and their allies. Muhammad may have thought that a military expedition through their territory would have the effect of demonstrating his ability to move at will through their lands. Second, there is no evidence that Muhammad ever intended to limit his movement to the Hejaz region or its major cities of Medina, Mecca, and Ta'if. Islam was to be for the Arabs of all Arabia and that included those living on the borders of the two great imperial realms.[38] Moreover, the Ghassanid chiefs had lost considerable power and influence with the Byzantine Empire as a consequence of their adoption of the heretical Monophysite Christian religion, and their control over their subtribes was weakening. It is unlikely that Muhammad was unaware of these events. Muhammad's first expedition to Syria, preceded as it was by a letter to the region's governor urging conversion to Islam, may have been a missionary expedition to spread the faith. It is not impossible that Muhammad may have had all of these reasons in mind when he sent the Muslim raiders to the north.

As so often happened with Muhammad's military expeditions, this one, too, was detected long before it reached its target. As the Muslim army approached the Syrian border, a local Byzantine official named Theodore the Vicar raised a force of Arab auxiliaries to oppose them. These Arab auxiliaries were pagans and Christians living in the region to the southeast of the Dead Sea in the old biblical land of Edom.[39] The army assembled a few miles farther east near what is now the town of Kerak, called Ma'ab by the Arabs of the day, the biblical Moab.[40] Ibn Ishaq says that when the Muslims reached Ma'ab in Syria about fifty miles south of Mu'ta, reports reached them that Heraclius himself, the Byzantine emperor, was in command of one hundred thousand Greeks encamped in Mu'ta.[41] The numbers are clearly an exaggeration, and the claim that Heraclius himself was involved is completely false. The terrain, the desert, and the water supply do not permit such large numbers, and certainly not in response to a minor border raid. More likely the Byzantine force was relatively small, perhaps comprising four thousand to five thousand Arab tribesmen stiffened by a regiment or two of Byzantine regulars or even local auxiliaries for a combined force of five thousand to six thousand men at most.[42]

The Muslims approached the town of Ma'an, where news of the Byzantine force deployed to their front reached them. A debate broke out among the commanders as to what to do. Some wanted to send a messenger back to Medina and ask the Prophet for advice. The distance between Medina and Ma'an was almost six hundred miles. The idea that a messenger could reach the Prophet and return in time was abandoned. One of the Muslim commanders, the ansar and zealot Abdullah ibn Rawaha, stood up and told the others that they had forgotten that "we are not fighting the enemy with numbers, or strength, or multitude, but we are confronting them with this religion with which God has honored us. So come on! Both prospects are fine: victory or martyrdom."[43] The other commanders and troops agreed that ibn Rawaha was right. And "then the army went forward" to engage the Byzantines.

It is likely that the first contact was made by the Muslim advance units that were ranging to the front of the army. The Byzantine units, after a brief skirmish, withdrew northward toward Mu'ta. The Muslim force followed cautiously. The terrain between Ma'an and Mu'ta is rough, narrow in places, and cut by ravines and wadis so that there are few places to accommodate open battle with even a small force of three thousand men. But Mu'ta itself was located on a small open plain large enough to accommodate the Muslim force which encamped there. Muslim reconnaissance units moved northward probing to find the main Byzantine force. At some point contact was made, and the Byzantines advanced on Mu'ta. Ibn Ishaq tells us, "When the enemy approached, the Muslims [he means the advanced reconnaissance units, which might have been of some strength and mistaken for units of the main army itself] withdrew to a village called Mu'ta. There the forces met and the Muslims made their dispositions, putting over (in command of) the right wing Qutba bin Qatada . . . and over the left wing an Ansari called 'Ubaya bin Malik."[44]

The details of the engagement are sketchy. What is puzzling is that all three Muslim commanders were killed, which suggests that the fighting may have been heavy and close in. But Ibn Ishaq and later historians record that only eight other Muslims were killed, which further suggests a sharp clash of short duration where the Arab side broke and ran. The deaths of the Muslim commanders can be explained from Ibn Ishaq's account.[45] Zayd, the Prophet's adopted son, was the first to engage and the first to die, followed quickly by Jafar ibn Abi Talib, the brother of Ali, and finally by Abdullah ibn Rawaha, who said a prayer before entering battle.[46] The Muslim top leadership was gone in a matter of minutes, probably slain in traditional Arab fashion by challenging the warriors of the opposing Arab units to individual combats wherein they met their deaths. It is not unlikely that the Muslim ranks, their leaders having been killed before their eyes, broke when struck by the Byzantine attack. As regards casualty figures, much of the army consisted of recently converted bedouins, some recruited along the way with the promise of loot, and may simply have been considered of insufficient importance to merit mentioning in the accounts of the engagement. Only the better-known Muslim fighters, those from Medina, were thought worthy of mention. Thus, only eight Muslim soldiers were reported killed.

That the Muslim army broke and ran seems beyond doubt. In the general battlefield confusion with no one to take command, the Muslim units simply came apart. Ibn Ishaq tells us that Khalid al-Walid, the Meccan cavalry commander who had almost killed Muhammad at Uhud but who had now become a Muslim, saved the day by rallying the troops, breaking contact, and conducting an orderly withdrawal. As Ibn Ishaq tells it, al-Walid "called on the Muslims to rally round one man, and when they wanted to rally to him he demurred and they rallied to Khalid al-Walid. When he took the standard he tried to keep the enemy off and to avoid an engagement. Then he retreated and the enemy turned aside from him until he got away with the men."[47] Having bloodied the Muslim raiders, the Byzantines apparently thought it unnecessary to pursue them and permitted their withdrawal without further opposition.

Mu'ta was a strategic and tactical failure as well as a personal tragedy for Muhammad, who lost his adopted son in the engagement. Reports of the defeat reached Medina before the returning army. When the army arrived at Medina the Muslim inhabitants greeted them with shouts of derision, throwing dirt on the soldiers for their disgrace in fleeing from the battlefield. In a religious worldview that sees martyrdom in battle as more valuable even than victory, a soldier surviving a defeat is difficult to understand. The defeat at Mu'ta seems to have encouraged a degree of restlessness among some of the other northern tribes, who attempted to form a coalition to attack Medina. Only a month after Mu'ta (October 629) Muhammad was compelled to send an expedition against the two northern tribes of Bali and Quada'ah.[48] Both these tribes had been part of the Ghassanid frontier defense coalition and had participated in the fighting at Mu'ta. Now they were active in helping to form a rival coalition of tribes to attack Muhammad. It is possible that Muhammad's activities had finally come to the attention of the Byzantine authorities, who may have decided to use their Arab allies as a means to attack Medina and remove the possibility of any future raids along the frontier. Muhammad learned of the situation in the north and dispatched a strong force led by Amr ibn al-A'as to attack the Bali and Quada'ah. The importance of this foray was evident in that a second force was sent to reinforce al-'As's troops that had with it Abu Bakr, Umar, and Abu Ubaydah, three of the Prophet's closest companions.[49] Details of this engagement are completely lacking, but the expedition seems to have been a success in dispersing the threatening coalition.

In the two years since Muhammad and the Meccans had signed the Truce of Hudaibiya (March 628), Muslim accounts record seventeen military expeditions carried out by Muhammad. These expeditions were of three types. (1) Expeditions against tribes that openly opposed Muhammad in the north and east of Medina. Some of these raids, like those against the Fadak and Ghatafan tribes, were failures in which significant numbers of Muslims were killed in battle. Others, like the attack on Kheibar, were major successes. (2) Expeditions against the clans of the powerful Hawazin tribe, who controlled the territory around Mecca. The Hawazin were a large tribe allied with the Meccans and openly hostile to Muhammad. These raids finally led to one of the most important battles of Muhammad's life, the Battle of Hunayn. (3) Expeditions against Byzantine provinces to the north of which the defeat at Mu'ta was the most notable. During this entire period Muhammad was content to permit Mecca to remain unmolested if only for the obvious reasons that his control of his own strategic territory and resources was not yet complete and that his army was not yet sufficiently large or equipped to take on the Meccans and their powerful bedouin allies. After Mu'ta Muhammad turned his attention once more to Mecca.

10

THE CONQUEST OF MECCA
January 11, 630

Ever since the Truce of Hudaibiya Muhammad had concentrated on building his alliances among the bedouins of the Arabian countryside. These efforts were successful among the tribes and clans of the Hejaz, while those tribes farther north remained hostile. The tribes to the south of Mecca and in Yemen remained largely unaffected by Muhammad's movement until after his death. In the Hejaz Muhammad's growing power and reputation induced many clan chiefs to seek his support against local rivals, sometimes drawing the Prophet too deeply into local quarrels. Other chiefs, some of whom were once supporters of Mecca, remained neutral out of fear of ending up on the wrong side when the clash between Muhammad and the Meccans finally came. Muhammad's astute sense of politics, his negotiating skills, and his reputation as an honest judge often permitted him to settle local disputes to his advantage with both sides declaring their allegiance to him. Two years after the Truce of Hudaibiya, Muhammad's power had grown to such an extent that the Meccans were no longer a match for him.[1] Over the decade since the Meccans first recognized Muhammad as a threat, they had failed to develop a consistent strategy to oppose him. The internal politics and personal jealousies of the city had made it impossible for anyone to assume effective leadership to oppose Muhammad. Where once Meccan aristocrats were influential throughout the region, now only Muhammad possessed the reputation and power sufficient to put forth a claim to leadership of the Hejaz. Muhammad had carefully bided his time, and now the moment had come to march on Mecca.

The Truce of Hudaibiya was only six months old when Muhammad found a way around one of its central provisions. The truce required that Muhammad would no longer attack the Meccan caravans moving over the northern route to Syria. Mecca lived by trade, and the disruption in its economic lifeline threatened its very existence. For the first six months after Hudaibiya no raids were undertaken against the northern route caravans. And then a curious series of events occurred, leading one to suspect that Muhammad had once more devised a brilliant stratagem that permitted him both to observe the truce and at the same time to carry out raids on the Meccan caravans, thus renewing the economic pressure on Mecca that had been so effective in weakening its power and influence.

The Truce of Hudaibiya required Muhammad to return to Mecca anyone who came to Islam in Medina without the permission of his family or guardians. One day a man named Abu Basir 'Utabah bin Usayd arrived in Medina seeking to become a Muslim. He had been held prisoner by his relatives in Mecca for his Muslim sympathies but had escaped and made his way to Medina in search of sanctuary. Muhammad dutifully turned Abu Basir over to the two guardians who had arrived in Medina seeking his return. On the way back to Mecca Abu Basir somehow obtained possession of the sword of one of his captors and killed him, fleeing back to Medina. Abu Basir's remaining guardian followed him to Medina, where once again he asked Muhammad to hand over Abu Basir. Muhammad dutifully offered to place Abu Basir in the custody of the guardian as required by the truce, but the guardian was terrified at the prospect of having to escort Abu Basir all the way to Mecca by himself and refused Muhammad's offer. Having twice complied with his obligations under the truce, Muhammad now washed his hands of the whole affair. Moreover, because Abu Basir technically had not yet been a Muslim when he was first turned over to the Meccans, Muhammad bore no responsibility for the bloodshed that had occurred.[2]

But what to do with Abu Basir? Muhammad knew that his own actions, although technically correct and legal under the truce agreement, would anger the Meccans and might provoke them further. Muhammad was not yet ready for a showdown with Mecca. At the same time, however, Abu Basir's loyalty to Muhammad and anger at the Meccans might yet be put to good use. Although Abu Basir was now considered a Muslim because of his presence in Medina, Muhammad made a strange request: that Abu Basir leave Medina.[3] Almost certainly with Muhammad's urging, Abu Basir left Medina and went to a place near the seacoast that overlooked the Meccan caravan route to Syria. There he gathered some seventy other men about him, presumably Meccans like himself who wished to become Muslims and did not want to be returned to Mecca.[4] Abu Basir's band of men turned to attacking the Meccan caravans with a vengeance and killing any Meccan who fell into their hands. The result was that Muhammad was able partially to restore economic sanctions against Mecca and to do so without breaking the letter of the truce. The raiders were not officially members of the Muslim community, so Muhammad had no responsibility for their raids. The Meccans were, of course, free to attack the raiders, but the ambushes occurred far from Mecca and the distance made it difficult to mount effective military operations against them. After a period of some months the Meccans appealed to Muhammad in desperation to take the raiders into his community and bring the raids to a halt. Muhammad seems to have agreed to do so, but only after some considerable delay. When a letter from Muhammad finally reached Abu Basir's camp instructing him to cease his brigandage, Abu Basir had already died. The sources are not clear whether the raids ever ended or whether they continued under a new chief. In either case Muhammad had once more brilliantly outmaneuvered his enemies. Although Muhammad's conduct had been correct under the strict letter of the truce, there were those in Mecca who were furious at what had happened and had come to the conclusion that the Truce of Hudaibiya had been a mistake. What they wanted was an excuse to break the truce and take their revenge on Muhammad. The opportunity to do both arose in November 629.

What Ibn Ishaq called "the causes that led to the occupation of Mecca" began in November 629 when the Beni Bakr, bedouin allies of the Quraish, set an ambush and attacked the Khuza'a tribe while they were resting at a well near Mecca.[5] The Beni Bakr and Khuza'a had been enemies for years and had been at each other's throats several times before the Truce of Hudaibiya. The Beni Bakr were longtime allies of the Quraish of Mecca, and the Khuza'a declared their loyalty to Muhammad soon after the truce was signed. Apparently at the urging of some Quraish who had supplied them with weapons, the Beni Bakr attacked the Khuza'a without warning, killing two of them.[6] The Khuza'a were driven back into the sanctuary zone surrounding the Kaaba. The Beni Bakr pursued the Khuza'a survivors into the sacred precinct, where the latter took refuge in two houses. The attackers laid siege to the houses and finally dragged the Khuza'a from them killing twenty of their men.[7] This was very bad business by Arab standards, and certain to lead to more difficulties between the Meccans and Muhammad. A chief of the Khuza'a tribe came to Medina and asked if Muhammad intended to keep his word as an ally and come to the aid of the Khuza'a. Nothing could have served Muhammad's ends more than a pretext to attack Mecca. He had apparently already reached the conclusion that the time was politically and militarily favorable to move against the city and dispose of the Meccan problem once and for all. Muhammad immediately began making military preparations for an attack.

The Meccan leadership seems to have realized that the Khuza'a incident risked setting off greater problems and dispatched Abu Sufyan, the leader of the Meccan army at Uhud and a longtime opponent of Muhammad, to Medina to meet with him and calm things down by reaffirming the peace obligations of the Truce of Hudaibiya. But Abu Sufyan was a practical man, and he realized that things had already gone beyond anyone but Muhammad's ability to control them. He also seems to have come to the conclusion that the time was long past when Muhammad and his movement could be destroyed by Meccan political influence with the bedouins or even by military force. Shortly after reaching Medina, where Muhammad refused to see him, he surely realized that Muhammad had every intention of conquering Mecca and bringing it into the fold of Islam. The only question was whether this would be accomplished peacefully or through violence. To a man of Abu Sufyan's intelligence it was clearly time to change sides, and there are indications that Abu Sufyan and Muhammad entered into a secret agreement to bring about a peaceful capitulation of Mecca.[8]

The seeds of Abu Sufyan's political conversion may have actually been planted two years earlier, even before the negotiations accompanying the Truce of Hudaibiya. It is difficult to imagine that Muhammad would ever have contemplated the Lesser Pilgrimage into the heart of enemy territory without having first been reassured by some powerful figure in Mecca that he would not be harmed. Most likely it was Abu Sufyan who was in a position to deliver this guarantee. Moreover, Abu

Sufyan was not present at the negotiations that produced the Truce of Hudaibiya and therefore could not be held responsible for its implementation, an excuse that would serve him well when it came time to repudiate it. Of significance, too, is the fact that shortly after the Truce of Hudaibiya was concluded, Abu Sufyan's daughter, Umm Habibah, married Muhammad, perhaps sealing a bargain between the two men who were, after all, still of the same tribe of Quraish.[9] Finally, when the truce was broken by the Khuza'a incident, it was Abu Sufyan who traveled to Medina to negotiate with the Prophet.[10] Without the supposition that Abu Sufyan and Muhammad had entered into a secret agreement, the events involving Abu Sufyan leading up to the attack on Mecca make little sense. This aside, however, Abu Sufyan was probably horrified at the prospect of a house-to-house street battle for control of the city. He seems to have come to the conclusion that resistance was futile and that the only way to save the city was to facilitate its surrender to Muhammad without violence.

Whatever was going on between Abu Sufyan and Muhammad on the political front, Muhammad continued his military preparations for an attack on Mecca. Having had so many of his past operations compromised, this time Muhammad took great care to maintain operational security, making great use of deception "so that we may take them [the Meccans] by surprise in their land."[11] The first thing Muhammad did was to seal off the exits and entrances to Medina with armed guards. To prevent anyone from warning the Meccans, no travel was permitted outside the city. It was a wise precaution, for no sooner had the guards been mounted than one Hatib bin Abu Balta tried to warn the Meccans by sending them a letter hidden in the hair of a woman. The "Apostle received news from heaven" about the letter and sent guards after the woman, who was caught and the letter found.[12] Muhammad now mounted a diversion. He assembled a small body of men, perhaps a few hundred, and sent them north toward Syria to deceive any spies still lurking in Medina into believing that the unit was either an advance party or a reconnaissance for a larger movement to the north. He hoped to convince the spies that he intended to move against the northern tribes and not against Mecca.[13]

Muhammad began to gather his army in a manner designed to conceal the assembly of the force from the Meccans. Any attempt to assemble the tribes in Medina, as he had previously done on occasion, would surely have been noticed. Instead, Muhammad sent trusted agents to each of his bedouin allies ordering them to prepare for war and to be ready to join his army as it passed through their territory or close to some nearby rendezvous point along the planned route of march toward Mecca. On January 1, 630, Muhammad set out from Medina with a force of perhaps no more than three thousand men. He was joined along the way by his bedouin allies. By the time he reached the outskirts of Mecca his army had grown to ten thousand.[14] By now, of course, it was no longer possible to conceal the fact that Muhammad had raised an army and was marching in the general direction of Mecca. It was, however, still possible to deceive the Meccans as to his intentions. To this end he encamped at a place called Marr al-Zahran, two days' march short of Mecca. Here the roads joined. From this location Muhammad could march with equal facility toward Mecca or Ta'if or the Hawazins' territory, all places where there were enemies against whom Muhammad had good reason to take military action. Even at this late time, however, the Meccans could still not be certain that Muhammad was planning to attack them, a situation that helped paralyze their decision making.[15] Finally, with his intentions still unknown, Muhammad decided to reveal his strength in an effort to strike fear into the Meccans. He ordered each man to light an individual campfire at nightfall—ten thousand campfires—giving the impression that his army was even larger than it was.

By now the Meccans were in a panic having come to the conclusion that Muhammad's objective was to attack Mecca. One can only speculate what role Abu Sufyan played in stoking the fires of fear among the Meccan leadership. But if he really was a double agent who had come to an accommodation with Muhammad to deliver the city without bloodshed, it is reasonable to expect that his role here was significant. Also significant was that Abu Sufyan was sent by the Meccan leadership to negotiate with Muhammad, a fact that suggests Abu Sufyan had not raised the suspicions of his fellow Meccans as to his true loyalty. Abu Sufyan had visited Muhammad in Medina several weeks earlier, ostensibly to negotiate an end to the crisis caused by the Khuza'a incident, but had been turned away. Now he came to Dhu Tuwa, a day's march closer to Mecca, to where Muhammad had moved his army in preparation for the attack on the city, for another meeting. He was met by Abbas, Muhammad's uncle, who had been an agent-in-place among the Meccans for almost a decade and whose cover, we may reasonably presume, was now blown. Abbas escorted Abu Sufyan into Muhammad's presence, where Umar immediately suggested that Abu Sufyan be killed on the spot! This was probably a bit of arranged theater to convince Abu Sufyan that he was no longer a free agent and had no choice but to agree to Muhammad's demands. Muhammad sent him away without speaking to him with instructions to Abbas that he be brought back in the morning.[16]

Abu Sufyan returned the next morning, and the two men got down to business. Muhammad began by asking, "Isn't it time for you to admit that there is no god but God?" Abu Sufyan, now an old man, looked about the room and did not reply to Muhammad's question. Muhammad continued, "Isn't it time for you to recognize that I am the Messenger of God?" This time Abu Sufyan answered. "As far as that is concerned, I still have my doubts."[17] Muhammad must have been somewhat taken aback at this personal affront, but it was Abbas who reacted by threatening Abu Sufyan. "Submit and testify that there is no God but Allah and that Muhammad is the Apostle of God before you lose your head," he said. And as Ibn Ishaq tells us, "he did so."[18]

The whole story, while dramatic, doesn't ring true, and may have been designed by Muhammad and Abu Sufyan to maintain Abu Sufyan's cover that he was a loyal Meccan and not an agent for Muhammad. For all his earlier opposition to Muhammad, Abu Sufyan was still a Quraish as was Muhammad. When Muhammad was a young boy being tormented by other boys, he had taken shelter in the house of Abu Sufyan. Abu Sufyan had also become Muhammad's father-in-law. Abu Sufyan had not opposed the Truce of Hudaibiya, and it was probably Abu Sufyan who had guaranteed Muhammad's safety with the Meccans when Muhammad made the Lesser Pilgrimage. Now Muhammad was to make his best use of Abu Sufyan by offering the Meccans an amnesty if they surrendered their city without a fight. Had Abu Sufyan's earlier agreement with Muhammad become known even to Muhammad's closest advisers, to say nothing of the Meccans, Abu Sufyan's value in convincing the Meccans to surrender would have been worthless.

Muhammad told Abu Sufyan that he was prepared to declare a general amnesty and that there would be no killing if the Meccans surrendered the city. Anyone who remained in their house and did not take up arms would be safe. Anyone who sought safety in the courtyard of the Kaaba would be left unmolested. He was further prepared to declare Abu Sufyan's house a place of asylum (jiwar) and to guarantee that anyone who took shelter there would not be harmed.[19] To declare

Abu Sufyan's house a place of asylum was an honor, but one that would surely compromise Abu Sufyan in the eyes of the Meccans. Perhaps asylum was offered to reassure Abu Sufyan that his loyalty would be rewarded once Muhammad was in control of Mecca while at the same time sending the message to the Meccan leadership that one of their most important leaders had already gone over to Islam and that they had little choice but to join him or die. Abu Sufyan returned to Mecca carrying Muhammad's offer.

According to Ibn Ishaq Muhammad told Abbas to delay Abu Sufyan's departure from the camp by taking him to the top of a hill overlooking a narrow part of the wadi below "so that when God's armies pass by he would see them."[20] Abu Sufyan was detained until Muhammad's entire army had passed before him in full battle kit and ready for war. "Finally the Apostle passed with his greenish-black squadron [a reference to the color of the troops' armor] in which were muhajirun and ansar whose eyes alone were visible because of their armor."[21] Muhammad's gifts of weapons and armor to his bedouin allies had produced an army in which most contingents were fully armed and armored with helmets, breast plates, and back plates.[22] Abu Sufyan was duly impressed, no doubt as much with the fact that he had chosen the winning side at just the right moment as with the size of Muhammad's army.

Delaying Abu Sufyan's departure for Mecca had more than a psychological purpose, however, for it was unlikely that Abu Sufyan needed to be convinced further of Muhammad's strength. The delay served an important *tactical* purpose as well. By the time Abu Sufyan caught up and rode past the army to reach Mecca and spread the word of Muhammad's coming, the army would have already encircled the city and cut off the exits. Neither escape nor reinforcement would any longer be possible. Even if the Meccans succeeded in getting word to their bedouin allies, itself a doubtful prospect, reinforcements would have to fight their way through Muhammad's army to reach the city. In yet another brilliant tactical maneuver, Muhammad had completely outsmarted his enemy and cut off the objective. If the Meccans chose to fight, they would have to do so alone.

When Abu Sufyan reached Mecca he quickly spread the word that Muhammad was coming in force but that the city might yet save itself by surrendering and taking advantage of the amnesty. The reaction must have been ferocious. Abu Sufyan's own wife, the infamous Hind who had chewed on Hamza's liver at Uhud, seized him by his moustache

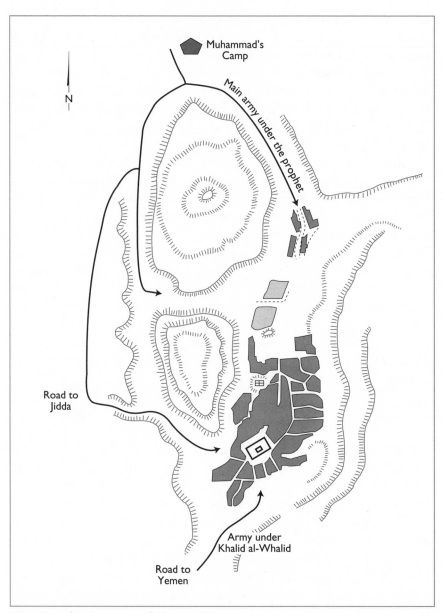

Map 10. The Conquest of Mecca, 630 C.E.

crying out, "Kill this fat greasy bladder of lard! What a rotten protector of the people!"[23] Abu Sufyan protested that all would be safe if they remained indoors or took advantage of the sanctuary granted to his house and the Kaaba. By now a crowd had gathered shouting that Abu Sufyan should be killed where he stood for his treachery.[24] But when he told them that if they remained in their houses with the doors locked they would also be safe, "the people dispersed to their houses and the mosque."[25] Meccan morale was broken, and within a few hours the streets of Mecca were deserted.

Map 10 shows that there was only one major road from the north that ran through the entire town and out the other side. Two other roads bisected the city from east and west. Muhammad divided his army into four columns, each approaching the city from a different direction. Ibn Hisham tells us that the movement of the columns was coordinated by a series of messengers on horseback who carried the commands of Muhammad to the column commanders. A special *wazir*, or marshal, was in charge of these communications and was always by Muhammad's side to relay orders.[26] The account that follows is taken from Hamidullah, who relied on Ibn Hisham and al-Tabari for his information.[27]

> The main army group of the Muslims, with the Prophet Muhammad himself in their midst, advanced from the main northern side. The high town (*Ma'lat*) is situated there. A group was led by Zubair Ibn al-Auwam on the Kada road, in order to close the escape to the sea coast, via Wadi Fatimah. A strong army group entered the city from the main thoroughfare from the south, via Lit, and occupied *Masfalah* or the low town. Maybe it was a cavalry group, and in spite of the detour, synchronized its arrival in the city at the same time as the other detachments . . . this detachment was led by Khalid al-Walid, commander of the cavalry corps. Yet another group entered the city from the Hajun road, and closed the escape to Jidda as well as to Yemen.[28]

To the south Khalid al-Walid and his cavalry met some resistance from a few diehards, but quickly swept them aside. Twenty-four Quraish and four Hudhayl were killed with no Muslims lost.[29] A small group of Muslim troops seems to have become disoriented and ran into a force of Quraish, losing two men.[30] Muhammad's columns met in the center of the city at almost the same time. For almost a decade Mecca had been gradually weakened by economic strangulation and political maneuver that had left it leaderless, without resolve, and isolated. Muhammad's show of military force was almost incidental to the city's collapse; it fell without resistance.

The occupation of Mecca by Muhammad on January 11, 630, became known in Muslim history as the *fat'h*, or Conquest. The word *fat'h* properly means "opening" but is also used with other meanings, for example, God's bestowing gifts on man or rendering a judgment between contestants.[31] Muhammad had forbidden his men to loot the city so there was no booty with which to pay the army. To compensate his troops, especially the bedouins, Muhammad took out large loans from the Meccan bankers and paid his men in cash.[32] Muhammad then went to the Kaaba, where he ordered all the idols there destroyed leaving only the images of Abraham, Jesus, and the Virgin Mary remaining. All the houses in Mecca were also required to destroy their idols.[33] Later, he dispatched special teams of Muslims to destroy the other idols and shrines that had been competitors with those in Mecca. The shrines to Manat at Mushallal (between Mecca and Medina) and to Uzza at Nakhla along with some others were destroyed.[34]

Muhammad remained in Mecca for about two weeks during which time he made a speech and invited the Quraish to come and pay homage to him. Many Meccans also became Muslims at this time acknowledging Muhammad's claim to be the Messenger of God. Interestingly, a significant number of Meccan leaders acknowledged their obligations to Muhammad in the traditional Arab manner but without becoming Muslims.[35] These Meccan leaders were important people whose talents Muhammad needed to complete his mission of converting all of Arabia to Islam.[36] Questions of religious conversions could be subordinated to political realities, at least for the time being. Elias Shoufani has observed in this regard that "Muhammad knew how to employ Meccan skill and talent in the service of his movement; and they [the Meccans], in turn, soon learned how to exploit that movement outwards. He, a religious leader first and foremost, and they, a mercantile society, had the common interest of expansion, and they joined their energies to achieve it."[37]

Although Muhammad had forbidden killing and looting by his troops, he had not promised to forgo personal revenge. Within days his secret police began tracking down and executing a number of people whose names Muhammad had placed on a list for liquidation. The offenses for which these people were executed tells us something about

Muhammad's fears and personality. The executions were a combination of settling old scores, as in the case of a man who had insulted Muhammad during his early years in Mecca eight years before; political necessity, when he ordered the execution of Ikrimah, the son of Abu Jahl, who had followed in his father's footsteps and led the opposition to Muhammad in Mecca; ideological fervor, as when two men who had renounced Islam were killed; and the purely personal, as when Muhammad ordered that two professional singing girls be killed because they had once composed songs unflattering to him and had sung them in public.[38] The executions were apparently carried out in public and deliberately so. The Quraish became alarmed that they might be a prelude to further killings now that the city was completely within Muhammad's control. The Meccan leaders sent Abu Sufyan to approach Muhammad for reassurances. Muhammad made it clear that the executions were limited, and that they would be finished in a few days. He kept his word and peace fell upon Mecca. Muhammad's conquest of Mecca was the achievement that ultimately led to the success of Islam in all Arabia. And it was the Meccans who played an important part in this ultimate success.

11

THE BATTLE OF HUNAYN
February 1, 630

Almost immediately after taking control of Mecca, Muhammad began sending parties to the surrounding bedouin tribes in the hope of reaching accommodations with them. At least three expeditions to secure the submission of the bedouin tribes of the surrounding district were sent out. No information about these expeditions has been preserved except for the third one under the command of Khalid al-Walid against the Beni Jadheema clan of the Beni Kinana living on the coastal plain south of Mecca.[1] Al-Walid was a brave and daring combat commander, but he was also headstrong and bloodthirsty when it came to matters of personal revenge. Many years before, some members of the Beni Jadheema had killed al-Walid's uncle in a dispute. When al-Walid established contact with the Beni Jadheema, he told them that since the war with Mecca was over there was no need for further bloodshed. He told them to lay down their arms. When they had done so, "Khalid ordered their hands to be tied behind their backs and put them to the sword [beheading], killing a number of them" in payment for the death of his uncle.[2] Presumably only a few of the Beni Jadheema chiefs were killed, but the record is unclear and it is possible that a significant number of the clan were executed. The fact that Muhammad was appalled at the murders and cried out to God that he had not ordered the killings lends some support to this view.[3] Al-Walid himself was not punished and was quickly assigned the mission to proceed to Nakhla and destroy the shrine of al-Uzza, which he seems to have accomplished without bloodshed.[4]

These were minor events, however, compared to the trouble that was brewing among the bedouins around Mecca and Ta'if. By all accounts the tribes and clans of the region who had previously been allies of the Meccans submitted themselves to Muhammad's governance without incident. Those that had been enemies of the Meccans, however, were another matter altogether. Among the foremost of these was the powerful tribe of the Hawazin located north and east of Mecca and whose territory sat astride the main trade route to Hira in Iraq. The Hawazin were allied with the men of the town of Ta'if, located south and east of Mecca, whose trade routes ran through Hawazin territory. This alliance had been enemies of the Meccans long before Muhammad appeared on the scene and had engaged in several wars with the Meccans probably concerning trade disputes between Ta'if and Mecca.[5] Given this history, the chiefs of the Hawazin and the men of Ta'if saw Muhammad as another powerful Quraish chief who had returned to claim the leadership of his people. The Hawazin chiefs could hardly have been ignorant of Muhammad's almost decade-long campaign to expand his power and spread the new faith of Islam, and it was a reasonable expectation that he would continue his efforts until all Arabia were brought under his control. In the Hawazin strategic view, war was inevitable. The Hawazin decided to force the issue sooner rather than later.[6]

The chief of the Hawazin, Malik ibn Auf, began to mobilize his forces for war, an activity that was immediately detected by Muhammad's agents.[7] Muhammad sent agents into the Hawazin camp to monitor the enemy's preparations and dispositions.[8] In Muhammad's eyes the Hawazin mobilization and willingness to fight was all to the good. Muhammad had a great army already in the field. Ibn Ishaq tells us that Muhammad's army comprisedthe ten thousand companions who had accompanied him to Mecca and two thousand Meccans who now joined him for a fight against their old enemy. The total force numbered twelve thousand, most of them well equipped and fully armored.[9] The Muslim force was deployed in and around Mecca, which could be used as a supply base and a good fallback location to mount a defense if things went badly. Moreover, Mecca was close enough to

Ta'if and the Hawazin homeland that if Muhammad carried the day in the field, he could readily pursue until he was in possession of the enemy's strategic heartland.

From a political point of view, the chance to defeat the Hawazin provided several opportunities. If the Hawazin were defeated, Muhammad would control all of the important caravan routes in the Hejaz. The defeat of the Hawazin would make it almost certain that Ta'if itself, the third-largest city in the Hejaz, would fall into his hands. Finally, an army of twelve thousand men under a single commander was almost unknown in Arabian warfare at this time. A victory over the Hawazin would send a strong message to other tribes that Muhammad's insurgency was unstoppable. They would be forced to come to terms. As always with Muhammad, the application of force was inevitably in the service of political objectives. The two opposing armies met at a place known to history as Wadi Hunayn on February 1, 630.

The Battle of Hunayn presents the historian with some difficulties. First, we do not know exactly where it was fought. Ibn Ishaq is silent on its location, so we have only later sources to aid us, and these are uncertain.[10] The accounts of the battle tell us that the men of Ta'if retreated to the safety of their city, only a short distance from the battlefield. Ta'if is located about sixty miles southeast of Mecca. The accounts say that Muhammad marched three days before reaching the battlefield. If so, then the battlefield was thirty-five to forty-five miles southeast of Mecca.[11] The difficulty is that there is no wadi there wide enough to accommodate the size of the armies mentioned in the later accounts. We remain uncertain, therefore, as to the exact location of the battle, being able to say only that it was probably no farther than a day's ride, about fifteen miles, from the city of Ta'if itself.

The second difficulty has to do with the numbers of troops involved. That Muhammad's army numbered twelve thousand men seems certain and is confirmed by Ibn Ishaq.[12] But there is no early source for the later claim that the opposing army numbered twenty thousand.[13] The claim is repeated in all later accounts, but one is hard pressed to believe that the figure is accurate. Ibn Ishaq tells us that the enemy army was comprised of the Hawazin, the men of Ta'if, and only a few additional clans.[14] As large as the Hawazin tribe was, it defies credulity that it could place anywhere close to twenty thousand men in the field even with the aid of Ta'if-area clans, many of whom fled the battlefield in any case. The answer may lie in the fact that the commander of the

Hawazin, the thirty-yearold Malik ibn Auf, made the decision to bring the entire tribe to the battlefield. This was an old Arab practice, the idea being that if soldiers knew that their women, children, and flocks were at risk they would fight more fiercely. The danger, of course, was that a defeat risked everything, including the tribe's physical existence. Ibn Auf seems to have deployed the tribe's women, children, and flocks at the far end of the battlefield so that when the Muslims entered the wadi they were frightened by the "black mass" of what they thought were enemy soldiers assembled at the far end of the wadi. It is possible, then, that the number of twenty thousand enemy "soldiers" was really a reference to the total size of the Hawazin tribe, including old men, women, and children. If so, a tribe of twenty thousand people could field about four thousand to five thousand soldiers at maximum effort.[15] If these circumstances obtained, then it is probable that later sources are incorrect when they say that Muhammad fought and defeated an army more numerous than his own. Rather, it was the Hawazin who were outnumbered almost four to one. As we shall see, the tactics of the Hawazin and the behavior of the Muslim army at Wadi Hunayn suggest that this was the case.

Muhammad sent his scouts to reconnoiter the Hawazin, dispatching one Abdullah ibn Abu Harad to "go among them and stay with them until he learned all about them."[16] Abu Harad did so and dutifully reported back to the Apostle. At the same time, Malik ibn Auf sent his scouts to spy on the Muslims.[17] Both commanders, therefore, had a good idea as to their positions relative to the other's, as well as a reasonable idea of the relative size of their forces. The evidence suggests that Muhammad learned that his army was considerably larger than that of the Hawazin, information that led him to be careless in the manner in which he approached the battlefield. Three events support this view. First, there is no doubt that the Muslims reached Wadi Hunayn unprepared for battle. There are no reports that the army had even donned its armor. Muhammad himself certainly had not.[18] Second, when the Hawazin attacked, Muhammad was still on his "white mule" far back in the column. If he were prepared for battle, he would have been on horseback.[19] Finally, as we shall see, the Muslims were taken by surprise while still in column of march. Taken together, these circumstances suggest that Muhammad was overconfident and incautious, probably as a consequence of his superiority in manpower.

Malik ibn Auf must have been greatly concerned when he learned that the Muslim army was significantly larger than his own. He had brought his entire tribe with all their women and possessions to the battlefield only to discover that he was greatly outnumbered. His entire tribe faced death or slavery if he was defeated. Moreover, stories of the fighting élan and courage of the Muslim soldiers certainly had reached his ears, no doubt convincing him that a direct infantry engagement on open ground would spell disaster. Malik ibn Auf would have to make brilliant use of terrain, deception, and surprise if he was to have any chance of defeating the Muslims at Wadi Hunayn.

The Hawazin chief took great advantage of all three factors as he prepared for battle. He selected Wadi Hunayn as the place to fight. Wadi Hunayn is a long, dry riverbed of modest width, perhaps not more than a half mile from side to side, bracketed by steep rocky walls that make descent into the wadi difficult and slow. There were openings along the wadi walls at various places leading to narrow canyons large enough to conceal cavalry units of significant size. The floor of the wadi itself, however, was free of vegetation and obstacles and was sufficiently broad and flat to permit room for cavalry to maneuver. Ibn Ishaq, quoting one of ibn Auf's officers, describes the terrain as "a fine place for cavalry. Not a hill with jagged rocks, nor a plain full of dust."[20] Ibn Auf used the night before the battle to move his forces into position in the wadi.

He deployed his forces to lure Muhammad into a trap. The bait was the Hawazin women and their flocks of sheep, goats, and camels. Ibn Auf positioned this mass of women, children, and flocks at the far end of the wadi, placing a thin infantry screen in front of them so that from a distance—say, from where ibn Auf expected Muhammad to enter the wadi—this "black mass" (as the accounts refer to it) would look like the main body of the Hawazin army arranged in formation for an infantry battle. An infantry battle would surely play to Muhammad's advantage in numbers, and ibn Auf probably reckoned that Muhammad would think precisely that when he saw the Hawazin "troops" massed at the far end of the wadi. If so, ibn Auf could reasonably expect that Muhammad would continue his column of march into the wadi taking his time to deploy his forces for a traditional infantry engagement. It was in anticipation of these developments that ibn Auf had hidden his cavalry squadrons in the canyons on both sides of the wadi. Once Muhammad's army had gained the wadi floor and was

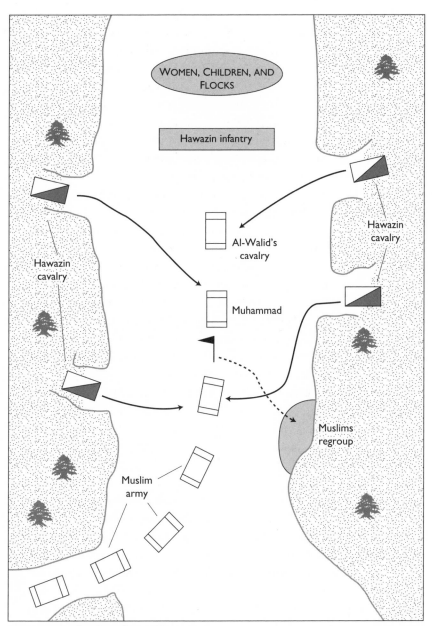

WOMEN, CHILDREN, AND FLOCKS

Hawazin infantry

Hawazin cavalry

Al-Walid's cavalry

Hawazin cavalry

Muhammad

Hawazin cavalry

Muslims regroup

Muslim army

Map 11. Battle of Wadi Hunayn, 630 C.E.

still marching toward the far end, ibn Auf planned to use his cavalry to attack the Muslim army on both flanks, driving it back upon itself until it could not move. It was a sound tactical plan.

Muhammad had camped near one of the entrances to the wadi. There is no evidence that Muhammad used the evening to prepare for battle, so that he entered the wadi riding his white mule and without his armor on. It is also a fair assumption that the rest of the army had not yet donned its armor and were riding their camels leading their tethered horses behind them. Just before dawn the Muslim column began to move down the steep path to the wadi floor. Ibn Ishaq recounts that one of the men who fought at Wadi Hunayn told him, "[W]e came down through a wadi wide and sloping. We were descending gradually in the morning twilight."[21] The vanguard of the column was led by a cavalry squadron from the tribe of Sulaym commanded by Khalid al-Walid. Sighting the "black mass" to his front, al-Walid may have become fixated on what he thought was the main body of the Hawazin army. There does not seem to have been any reconnaissance screen or scouts in advance of the Muslim van nor on the flanks. The Muslim army was moving along the wadi floor straight at the Hawazin, but was doing so without "any eyes and ears." Ibn Auf's deception had worked and Muhammad had taken the bait.

About a third of the Muslim column was already on the wadi floor with the rest still outside the wadi trying to make its way in when the Hawazin struck. Suddenly, from out of the canyons on both sides of the wadi, ibn Auf's cavalry attacked in force aiming for both flanks of the Muslim column. Ibn Ishaq tells us that "the enemy had got there before us and had hidden themselves in its bypaths and side tracks and narrow places. They had collected and were fully prepared, and by God we were terrified of them. . . . [T]he squadrons [of cavalry] attacked us as one man."[22] Al-Walid's van was struck immediately with such force that it came apart. The Sulaym tribesmen took to their heels and fled.[23] The Muslim column was struck all along the flanks by Hawazin cavalry, sending it into immediate disarray and headlong rout to the rear. Abu Sufyan, who was with Muhammad as the fleeing soldiers streamed past, cried, "Their flight will not stop until they get to the sea!"[24]

The confused mass of Muslim soldiers fled to the rear, crashing into other Muslim units that had just reached the wadi floor and sending them into disarray. The large mass of men and animals became pressed together so tightly that no one was able to gain the trail that led out of the wadi to safety. The trail was blocked by units trying to descend onto the wadi floor. Muhammad and his entourage escaped being swept away by the wave of panic by clinging to a small hill near the south wall of the wadi. To his credit Muhammad did not panic. He stood bravely in the stirrups of his white mule in full view of the enemy calling to his troops to stop and gather around him to continue the fight.[25] One by one men gathered about the Apostle until there were about a hundred around him. "Finally, a hundred were gathered by him and they went forward and fought. . . . They were steadfast in the fight and the Apostle standing in his stirrups looked down at the melee as they were fighting and said, 'Now the oven is hot.'"[26]

Ibn Auf's plan had worked perfectly to this point. But now circumstances turned against him. The sheer size of the Muslim force had produced a great mass of dismounted soldiers gathered around the clogged exit from the wadi. Had they been able to use the exit, the rout may have continued indeed until it reached the sea. But with nowhere else to go, the Muslim troops turned to face the enemy in what might have become a last stand. Muhammad's presence and bravery on the battlefield gave them assurance that the Prophet was still alive and with them. By now the Hawazin cavalry attacks had spent themselves against the jumble of massed men and animals and had lost their momentum. Ibn Auf had hoped that the rout would be complete and did not foresee that the clogged exit would stop it. The small size of his army made it impossible for him to hold any strength in reserve. Except for the small infantry screen in front of the women and animals at the far end of the wadi, there were no units available to attack the stalled enemy. As the Muslims gathered themselves together to continue the fight, the battle became exactly what Ibn Auf had hoped to avoid, a hand-to-hand infantry battle in which numbers were decisive.

As the battle raged the Muslim advantage began to tell, with the result that the Hawazin were gradually forced back and pressed on all sides. Ibn Auf himself stood and fought beside his war banner until seventy of his men were killed around him before leaving the field.[27] Some of the men of Ta'if fought bravely until the end; others only for a short time before fleeing to the safety of their city's walls. At a key point in the fight a strange incident occurred. Ibn Ishaq tells us, "Before the people fled and men were fighting one another I saw the like of a black garment coming from heaven until it fell between us and the enemy. I looked and lo black ants everywhere filled the wadi. I had no doubt that they were angels."[28] While we cannot be certain, this was probably a reference to Khalid al-Walid, who had rallied his cavalry squadron of Beni Sulaym tribesmen and was leading a fierce cavalry charge that slammed into the rear of the dismounted Hawazin cavalry now fighting as infantry and broke their resistance.[29] Elsewhere, the Nasr clan of the Hawazin held open a narrow pass at the far end of the wadi so that some of their soldiers could escape. The Hawazin infantry deployed in front of their camp seems also to have fought bravely to protect their women, families, and goods.[30] It was all to no avail. The fighting men of Hawazin were dispersed, captured, or killed, and the women, children, animals, and goods fell into the hands of Muhammad's army. As the Hawazin remnants made their way out of the wadi, Muhammad sent cavalry units in pursuit to drive them away from the battlefield so they could not mount an attempt to rescue their families.[31]

The victory at Wadi Hunayn was a turning point in Muhammad's campaign to bring Islam to Arabia. The battle was larger than any battle that anyone in the Hejaz could remember. It was an encounter that had been long in coming between Muhammad's Muslims and the bedouin tribes. The bedouins had given it their all against Muhammad and lost. The lesson was not lost on the remaining bedouin clans who had not yet pledged their loyalty to Muhammad. Most of the chiefs of the Hawazin clans and of Ta'if were still at large, but this was of no consequence. Muhammad was in possession of the Hawazin's women, children and flocks, without which their lives were meaningless. It would not take long before the Hawazin would ask Muhammad for peace and he would offer to return their families to them in the traditional Arab manner of bargaining. For the present, however, the army was still in the field and its blood was up. Muhammad struck while the iron was hot and moved to place the town of Ta'if under siege.

Ta'if was the second occasion in which Muhammad attempted to subdue a fortified town, the first being Kheibar. Kheibar possessed no surrounding walls, and the Jews of Kheibar did not fight under a unified command; therefore, Muhammad was able to overcome the settlement's interior compounds one at a time. In addition, the residents of Kheibar had not prepared for a siege with the result that food and water shortages weakened their ability to resist. Ta'if presented Muhammad with far more difficult problems. First, it was a walled city complete with

fortifications. Tradition had it that the city was constructed when the
Persians controlled Yemen, and that as a favor to the town the Persian
satrap sent engineers to Ta'if to construct its walls and fortifications.[32]
The name Ta'if means "with a wall around."[33] The town had plenty of
internal wells to supply water and there were many gardens and small
farms for food. Probably most important was that, having lost a considerable number of men at Hunayn,[34] Ta'if was prepared to resist to the
death fighting under a unified command. All of these circumstances
limited Muhammad's options in bringing the siege to a quick conclusion.

The accounts of the siege are short and confused, and it is difficult to
obtain anything but a broad outline of the events at Ta'if. Later sources
say that Muhammad had catapults and covered cars for use against the
walls and to protect his miners. Since Muhammad marched directly on
Ta'if after the engagement at Wadi Hunayn, it is difficult to see where
he may have obtained this equipment, although it is possible that it
might have been obtained somewhere in the locality of Ta'if itself. Ibn
Ishaq tells us that two of the chiefs of the Ta'if were absent from the city
because "they were in Jurash learning the use of the testudo, the catapult,
and other instruments."[35] Perhaps these machines were manufactured
in a town close to Yemen, where Persian influence and technology was
most evident and more available than heretofore thought.

At first Muhammad made a strong attempt to take Ta'if by force of
arms, but his men were beaten back by a storm of arrows. When he
attempted to mine the walls from below, the defenders dropped "scraps
of hot iron" on them that burned through the leather roof of the wheeled
platforms protecting the miners.[36] An assault on the main gate was
also repulsed with significant Muslim casualties.[37] The arrow fire from
the walls was dangerously effective. Muhammad seems to have made
the mistake of placing his camp too close to the city's walls and within
range of the defenders' arrow fire. A later source says "the arrows shot
by them from the ramparts would sometimes take a toll of the besiegers,
especially when they were off guard in the camp during the night."[38]
Muhammad ordered the construction of a *khashab*, or wooden plank
fence, around the camp to protect his troops.[39] At some point Muhammad ordered that "wooden thorned balls and fresh branches from thorn
trees be strewn all around the wall" in order to "prevent all ingress of
provisions, men, and material."[40] It is possible, however, that these
obstacles were also designed to prevent the defenders from mounting

offensive sallies against the attackers. At one point Muhammad grew so frustrated with his lack of progress that he ordered the famous and precious vineyards of Ta'if destroyed.[41]

The siege lasted about three weeks before Muhammad broke it off and retired.[42] The resolve of Ta'if remained strong, and Muslim casualties were beginning to mount. If the siege dragged on much longer without results, the army's morale might begin to weaken and the clans begin to drift homeward. The prestige of the Muslim victory at Wadi Hunayn might also evaporate if the stalemate went on too long, reducing the Muslim image for military prowess. While no source mentions it, the problem of supplying the army with food and forage must also have been a consideration. The army had fought a major battle only a few days before besieging Ta'if. Fodder for the animals must have been running short. Finally it was never Muhammad's goal to destroy Ta'if; he wanted to convert it. To this end the less blood shed the better. With the Hawazin defeated, the clans of Ta'if were isolated. Sooner or later they would have no choice but to reach an accommodation with Muhammad.

Muhammad and the army retired to a place called al-Jirana to divide the spoils taken at Wadi Hunayn. Six thousand Hawazin women and children had been captured along with thousands of camels, sheep, and other animals,[43] a number sufficient to give every man in the Muslim army four camels or the equivalent.[44] Muhammad made a public display of dividing up the animals to send the message to the Hawazin that unless they came to an accommodation soon, their women and children would also be distributed as booty.[45] While all this was taking place, an old woman named Shima who claimed to be the woman who had suckled the young Muhammad when he was sent into the desert as a baby to be wet-nursed was brought before the Prophet. Muhammad asked if she had any proof, and she showed him a bite he had given her when she carried him on her hip. The woman was a member of the Beni Saad, a clan of the Hawazin, and asked Muhammad to treat his "relatives" kindly.[46] Muhammad agreed and offered to return the women and children to the Hawazin, who in turn swore their loyalty to Muhammad.

The conversion of the Hawazin to the Muslim cause deprived the Ta'if of their last significant ally. Moreover, the victory at Wadi Hunayn had convinced other clans around Ta'if that their future lay with Islam, and a good number of them went over to Muhammad. This shift in bedouin loyalty completely cut off Ta'if from the Meccan market and exposed their caravan routes to Iraq to attack. With no options left, Ta'if sent a delegation to Muhammad asking for talks. Muhammad asked the whereabouts of Malik ibn Auf, the chief of the Hawazin. He was told that he had taken refuge in Ta'if. Muhammad promised that if ibn Auf came to him in peace there would be no punishment. Ibn Auf arrived in the Muslim camp a few days later to be greeted with respect. Muhammad returned his animals and his family to him.[47] The price of the accommodation, however, was that the pagan shrines to the idols Uzza and Lat located in Ta'if were to be destroyed and the population were to become Muslims. A year later, a delegation from Ta'if traveled to Medina and agreed to Muhammad's terms.

Muhammad remained at al-Jirana from February 24 to March 9, at which time he left and returned to Mecca to make another omra.[48] While in Mecca he lavished large gifts on the city's leaders, giving many a hundred camels each in an effort to assuage their fears and make them loyal allies. This infuriated some of the Muslims, especially the ansar who, Ibn Ishaq tells us, received nothing in the way of spoils.[49] Equally infuriating was the fact that many of the Meccan leaders remained pagans! Muhammad did not demand their acceptance of Islam, a clear indication of the importance he attached to their support. Before he left Mecca to return to Medina Muhammad appointed a young man under thirty to be in charge of his affairs in Mecca. The man, Attab ibn Asid, was a member of Abu Sufyan's Umayyah clan, evidence that although Muhammad wanted the support of the Meccan old guard, the future belonged to his loyal Muslim ally, Abu Sufyan, and his clan.[50]

The Battle of Hunayn against the largest and most powerful bedouin coalition in the region was Muhammad's greatest military success and was the first cooperative achievement of Muhammad and his new Meccan allies. In the view of some Arab historians, the victory and alliance was the real beginning of the Arab conquests that would eventually see Arab armies conquer the Byzantine and Persian Empires.[51] With Mecca, Medina, and Ta'if, the three main towns of the Hejaz, and Kheibar and the other oases in the north finally under his control and with large segments of their populations having accepted Islam, the bedouin tribes located near these settlements lost their ability to maneuver politically. There was only a single chief whose authority and power ran throughout the entire Hejaz, and that was Muhammad. No single tribe or feasible coalition of tribes in the Hejaz could hope to resist Muhammad and his Muslims through force of arms. There was no realistic choice but to submit. The bedouins of the Hejaz submitted and joined the Muslim state. So closely did they become identified with Islam that a separate history has not been recorded for them.[52] If the victory at Wadi Hunayn was Muhammad's greatest military achievement, winning the Meccans to his side was certainly his greatest political achievement. In one of the curious turns of history it was the Meccans who came to play the central role in the conquest of the rest of Arabia and, later, in the Arab conquest of the entire Middle East.

12

The Tabuk Expedition and the Death of Muhammad
630–632

In September to October of 630, ten months after the fall of Mecca, Muhammad began to prepare for a major military expedition to the north. If we can believe the sources, Muhammad mobilized between twenty thousand and thirty thousand men for the operation.[1] The army consisted of troops from Medina, Mecca, and the bedouin tribes of the surrounding areas.[2] Despite his prior success Muhammad's influence did not extend much farther than the area from which these troops were drawn. Unlike his previous military operations, Muhammad took the unusual step of publicly announcing the purpose of the expedition. It was to raid the rich border provinces of Byzantine Syria.[3] Muhammad's public pronouncement does little, however, to clear up the question of why he chose to mount such an expedition at this time of year when it is clear that a campaign against the Byzantines made no military sense.

All the sources except Ibn Ishaq are vague regarding Muhammad's motives behind the expedition. Many regard Muhammad's actions as a response to a divine command. Ibn Abbas tells us that "the prophet remained in Medina six months after his return from Ta'if. Then God ordered him to attack Tabuk."[4] Other sources say that rumors reached Medina of an impending invasion of Arabia by Heraclius, who was said to be assembling a large army for that purpose.[5] Heraclius had just won a resounding victory over the Persians, and Muhammad surely realized that his army was no match for the Byzantines fighting from behind their considerable border defenses. Heraclius's army was assembled at Emesa (Homs) and in a perfect position to defend the Syrian border against Muhammad's attack, although it is uncertain whether or not Muhammad was aware of these circumstances. The trek from Medina to Tabuk was more than 250 miles and would still leave Muhammad's army another 200 miles' march from the nearest Byzantine garrison, most of it over open desert. The same terrain and distance made it highly unlikely, and at certain times of the year even impossible, that a Byzantine regular force or their Ghassanid Arab allies could have attacked Medina. Moreover, by the time of the Tabuk expedition the Byzantine and Ghassanid alliance had all but collapsed due to religious persecution and imprisonment by the Byzantine authorities of some Ghassanid chiefs for their heretical Monophysite faith. We have no way of knowing if any of these circumstances were known to Muhammad and his advisers. But any competent assessment of these factors would have forced the conclusion that an attack against the Byzantine provinces was simply unlikely to succeed.

Equally puzzling from a military perspective was why Muhammad chose to mount a northern expedition in October. The weather in Arabia at this time of year is terribly hot and dry, making the long march of almost five hundred miles to the Syrian border extremely difficult. The heat and terrain combined to make it a "dry year," which made any travel hazardous. A delay of two months would have brought cooler weather. In October there would be insufficient grazing and water for the men and animals. October was also the time of year when the date crop was harvested. Medina and other oases relied on the crop for their livelihood. Muhammad's expedition threatened to draw off considerable manpower that was needed to help harvest the dates. Finally, the bedouins were greatly concerned that an arduous journey under such harsh climatic conditions might kill their horses and camels, a serious loss of personal wealth. If only from consideration of weather and terrain, Muhammad's northern expedition was a highly questionable endeavor. It was not for nothing that the operation became known in Arab history as *jaysh al-usrah*, the Army of Distress.[6]

Within Medina there was considerable opposition to the expedition, and many men found excuses to avoid going. The most common excuse was that their camels were already in poor condition due to the drought and would not survive the rigors of the march.[7] Others begged off because of the severe heat. Muhammad called on the richer Muslims to provide money to purchase replacement mounts for any camels or horses lost.[8] Right up to the date of departure, individuals deserted or refused to muster for the march. The difficulties associated with organizing the expedition appear to have been the subject of a revelation, now found in sura 9 of the Quran, wherein God chastised the Muslims for their lack of trust in him and their unwillingness to bear hardships in his name. Verse 38 says, "O you who believe, what is the matter with you, when you are told to go forth in the name of God, that you make such heavy weather about starting? . . . The good things of this life are but trivial in comparison with the life to come." The revelation issued a grave threat: "If you will not go forth, God will punish with a painful punishment and He will exchange you for another people and will not do Him any harm . . ."

Even with the threat of divine retribution things continued to go poorly. The night before Muhammad left Medina he pitched camp at Thaniyatu'l Wada, a pass overlooking Medina from whence he had previously set out on other military campaigns.[9] Below him Abdullah ibn Ubay and his contingent of ansar had pitched their camp. Several sources say that Ubay's camp was larger than Muhammad's, suggesting that the claim that Muhammad's army numbered thirty thousand men may be somewhat of an exaggeration.[10] When Muhammad and the army moved out the next morning, ibn Ubay did not follow but returned to Medina, where he "stayed behind with the hypocrites and doubters."[11] Most of the ansar of Medina, however, seem to have accompanied Muhammad in hopes of obtaining their share of booty.

Under these circumstances Muhammad must have had a very pressing reason to continue with the expedition, and it is unlikely that the reason was a military one. It may be telling that Muhammad ordered Ali, his most renowned soldier, to remain behind in Medina. The victory at Wadi Hunayn had been a military success, but it had turned into a political failure. In order to secure the loyalty of the Meccans, Muhammad had lavished large portions of the Hawazin booty on them. To encourage the Hawazin to pledge their loyalty to him, he had returned much of the booty that was left. The ansar, already angry that there had been no booty from the attack on Mecca, were furious at Muhammad for what seemed his preferential treatment of "his own people [Quraish]."[12] Abdullah ibn Ubay, the leader of the ansar in Medina, had never accepted Muhammad's leadership even though he had become a Muslim. It could hardly be expected that he would refrain from using the ansar's discontent to recoup some of his lost influence among the clans of Medina. His refusal to accompany Muhammad on the expedition was an ominous threat to undercut Muhammad while he was away, perhaps by assaulting the families and property of the Muslims or even leading a revolt. Muhammad's decision to leave Ali behind may have been a precaution against ibn Ubay's ambitions and to suppress any revolt that broke out. It was these ansar, then, who were referred to as the hypocrites (*nifaq*) and opponents (*munafiqun*) of Muhammad in Medina, and whom Muhammad punished when he returned.

The victories at Mecca and Wadi Hunayn had produced large numbers of supporters who flocked to Medina to become Muslims. These are referred to in the sources as *ashab al-suffah*, that is, the poor who lived on the contributions of the Muslims and the Apostle and whom the Muslims used to take along on raids so they could obtain booty.[13] It was from these impoverished converts that the *sa'alik*, groups of brigands who rallied around a leader from among themselves and lived on plunder, arose among the Muslims.[14] Muhammad did not possess the resources to support the large number of poor who flocked to Islam after the fall of Mecca. More disturbing was the potential of the sa'alik to resort to violence against him if their needs went unmet for too long. Muhammad was in danger of losing his grip on the most important asset of any insurgency, his popular base of support, through the opposition of the ansar and other opponents in Medina. The extent of the opposition even within Muhammad's own expeditionary force can be gauged by his decision to plant spies in his own ranks to report on the "murmurings" of the troops.[15]

The problems confronting Muhammad were serious and threatened the future of the insurgency. It was to resolve them, then, that he decided to attack the Byzantine border provinces and the Arab tribes of the Syrian Desert. If the expedition succeeded it would produce sufficient booty to supply the ashab al-suffah with their needs, compensate the ansar for their past efforts at Mecca and Wadi Hunayn for which they had received nothing, and satisfy the Quraish who had become restive with the loss of trade and finance that was no longer being generated in Mecca.[16] It was a bold gamble, of course, but one that could be expected of an insurgent leader who understood the primacy of political power over military concerns when it came to conducting a revolution. Muhammad was on the brink of losing all he had fought for. To rescue the situation he turned outward for a military solution to a political problem.

There were other factors that might have impinged on Muhammad's decision to undertake a major military expedition under unfavorable conditions. The triumph of Islam in the Hejaz had imposed new rules governing Arab behavior that had serious unforeseen consequences. Arabia was a poor land and could not feed itself; the bedouins especially were half starved most of the time. They survived by raiding settlements and each other's flocks, which redistributed the wealth and food supply permitting many to survive who otherwise would have perished. But now Islam forbade raiding the towns and flocks of other Muslims, greatly increasing the poverty of many bedouins. Islam also forbade the traditional practice of war to the death among Muslims to avenge personal wrongs. This ancient means of recreation and demonstration of manliness had been one of the major psychological foundations of male Arab life. Now it was gone. Even the spice trade was no longer lucrative. The Islamic laws against usury had dried up much of the commercial activity relative to the risks involved in undertaking caravans. One result was that Mecca itself, once the primary commercial center of the Hejaz, fell into serious decline. Islam's promise of paradise through jihad that had worked well enough in attracting tribes to war against idolaters now seemed empty. Without enemies to attack, how was one to become a martyr and gain paradise? All these prohibitions meant that there was no booty to be had and therefore no way to improve one's lot in life.

Consideration of these circumstances has led some to suggest that Muhammad's expedition against the Byzantine border provinces was part of a larger strategic vision, a "northern strategy" designed to find new enemies against whom Muslims could fight and pillage.[17] In this view the northern strategy was preferable to an attack against the Persian provinces in Iraq because the routes to the north were well known and more easily traversed than the longer and more difficult eastern route to Iraq. But even if Muhammad had devised such a strategy, was this the right time to attempt to implement it? Muhammad was barely in command of the Hejaz, and most Arabs remained idolaters. Moreover, the powerful tribes of the north were his declared enemies, and any northern route to the Byzantine provinces would pass perilously close to their territory. Moreover, Muhammad surely knew that his army was no match for the Byzantines. Perhaps the northern strategy was a long-term plan to be put into operation once Islam had triumphed in all Arabia, when all its manpower resources would be at Muhammad's disposal.

Given these assumptions, perhaps Muhammad's northern expedition was really a reconnaissance in force to test the enemy's defenses and see what allies might be acquired for future operations. Perhaps Muhammad also had in mind taking revenge for the Muslim defeat at Mu'ta that had taken the life of his adopted son, Zayd.[18] The difficulty with this analysis is that if the expedition was either a punitive raid or a reconnaissance mission, in neither case could it be expected to produce the booty Muhammad needed to meet the needs of his disgruntled followers. In the end the only reason that makes sense is that Muhammad did indeed intend to attack the Byzantine provinces, but circumstances prevented him from doing so.

The trek to the north was very difficult, probably much more so than Muhammad had anticipated, and took much longer than it would have taken two months later when the weather was cooler. The 250 miles between Medina and Tabuk might easily have been covered in ten to twelve days under more favorable conditions, but seem to have taken upwards of eighteen to twenty days. The heat was unbearable, and in traditional Arab fashion under such conditions the army moved mostly at night when it was cooler. This resulted in a slower pace whereby the army moved in stages over shorter distances. Fodder for the animals was scarce, and it is a reasonable conclusion that some of the animals perished in the heat. Ibn Ishaq reports that water, too, was in short supply and that the troops suffered from thirst.[19] The column stopped at al-Hijr, 180 miles into the march. The place was marked by caves and ruins from prehistoric times, and Muhammad seems to have believed the place was haunted. He forbade his men to leave the camp unless accompanied by a companion.[20] Although the army was suffering from thirst, Muhammad forbade them to drink from the well. One soldier ignored the warning and was struck with a constriction of the throat that killed him.[21] The army suffered throughout the night, and "[i]n the morning when the men had no water they complained to the Apostle, so he prayed, and God sent a cloud, and so much rain fell that they were satisfied and carried away all the water they needed."[22] By the time Muhammad's army reached Tabuk, the troops must have been exhausted, short of supplies, and in no condition to fight the Byzantines, whose nearest garrison, in any case, was still two hundred miles away.

It was probably at Tabuk that Muhammad learned for certain that Heraclius's army was bivouacked at Homs in Syria, only half the distance to the border that Muhammad would still have to cover from Tabuk to attack the Byzantine provinces. It was at Tabuk that Muhammad must have also realized that his poorly equipped army so far from home was in no condition to continue the march and engage the Byzantines. To do so risked disaster, and Muhammad's weakened hold on his base of popular support could probably not survive another military disaster like Mu'ta. Muhammad decided to call off the expedition.

Muhammad remained in Tabuk for ten days, during which time he rested his army and entered into negotiations with local chiefs forming several new alliances. "The Apostle stayed in Tabuk some ten nights, not more. Then he returned to Medina."[23] The presence of so large a Muslim army, no matter how bedraggled, was still a clear demonstration of Muhammad's power that impressed the local chiefs, and some traveled to Tabuk to treat with Muhammad. One of these chiefs, Yohanna ibn Ruba, was the "governor" of Alia (modern Aqaba) and concluded a pact with Muhammad in which he agreed to pay a tax in return for Muslim protection of the port. This protection extended to the ships as well.[24] Three Jewish towns—Jerba and Udhruh, 80 miles north of Alia in the Transjordan, and Maqna, a fishing village on the Red Sea—also entered into similar agreements.[25] Muhammad sent Khalid al-Walid and a few hundred men to the oasis of Dumat al-Jandal, where they killed the king's brother and brought back the Christian king under guard. The king agreed to pay tribute to Muhammad and was released. These agreements constituted only small victories, for the largest and most powerful Arab tribes on the Syrian border—the Ghassan, Lakhm, and Bahra—remained unremittingly hostile to Muhammad and Islam. With his army rested, Muhammad turned southward and marched for Medina.

The failure of the Syrian expedition could only make matters worse in Medina, and one can only wonder what "murmurings" went on among the ansar who had accompanied Muhammad only to return empty-handed for the third time. The ansar resentment of the Meccans increased as Muhammad now appointed more Meccans to high positions.[26] A later source tells us that one of the ansar publicly rebuked Muhammad's new Meccan advisers as having "the most voracious stomachs of us all, the newest in nobility, and are the most cowardly in battle."[27] Another said, "And these are the men who are now put over us to lead us! Muhammad is right, we are worse than donkeys!"[28] Reports of the opposition's activities in Medina must have reached Muhammad while he was still on the return march. He halted at Dhu Awan, a town about an hour's journey from Medina itself, where some Muslims had constructed a mosque that they said was for the sick and needy. Muhammad somehow knew that the mosque had become a center for the opposition and ordered it burned.[29] Some people were inside when the mosque was set afire "and the people ran away from it." The attachment to the account of a list of the twelve men who constructed the mosque suggests, however, that they may have been burned inside. Some later sources suggest that opposition plotters had met in Medina in the house of a Jew. Muhammad apparently learned of this and had the house burned immediately upon his return.[30]

Once back in Medina Muhammad moved swiftly against the opposition. Those ansar who had refused to accompany the expedition were publicly identified and banished from the city for 50 days. They were later called one by one before Muhammad (and one suspects his advisers or perhaps the suffah), where they had to publicly recant and explain why they had refused the Prophet's command. The whole episode, while vague as to details, rings suspiciously like the public show trials of later revolutionary regimes. One later source even suggests that an opposition clique plotted to assassinate Muhammad by throwing him over a cliff.[31] The plot failed and nothing is known of the fate of the plotters. But it is not too far-fetched to suggest that they may well have died amid all the odor of sanctity. We do not know what happened to the opposition parties in Medina, but it is not beyond imagination that they were liquidated by Muhammad's henchmen as a prelude to the imposition of a greater discipline upon all his followers that shortly followed. It was probably not coincidental that at this time Muhammad received a revelation in which all Muslims were instructed in the future to pray "at the tombs of the unyielding Doubters."[32]

If Muhammad needed reminding, the resistance of the troops to the Tabuk expedition and the open revolt in Medina demonstrated clearly enough that many Muslims were halfhearted converts brought into the fold when their chiefs or clan leaders had come to Medina to reach an accommodation with Muhammad. Many of these chiefs had sworn allegiance to Islam as a way of gaining support from Muhammad in their local squabbles; others saw the acceptance of Islam as an opportunity for booty. Many of Muhammad's allies were still idolaters, and all of Arabia beyond the Hejaz remained pagan. Muhammad could not hope to succeed in his mission of spreading the new faith throughout Arabia unless he first established firmer control and discipline over his own followers, Muslims and idolaters alike. The suppression of his opponents in Medina was the first step.

"WAR TO THE KNIFE"

Like all insurgencies since, there came a time when the backsliders and opportunists had to be weeded out or forced to make a genuine commitment. It was against this backdrop that shortly after returning from Tabuk Muhammad made a drastic change in his policy toward his non-Muslim allies. The Quran tells us that during that same year (631) Muhammad had a revelation instructing him to impose an obligatory yearly tax on all those who sought his support.[33] In the Quranic text the tax is called the *sadaqah*. It was later called the *zakat*. Muhammad may have calculated that while he was strong enough to impose his will in the Hejaz, he was not yet strong enough to impose his will throughout Arabia. The imposition of the tax on all those who sought his support, Muslim and non-Muslim alike, was a bold gamble. He would give the tribes of Arabia one last chance to join the movement, and payment of the tax, the traditional Arab means of showing submission to a chief from time immemorial, would be the test of their loyalty. Those who refused would be killed.

Muhammad designated Abu Bakr to lead the annual Muslim pilgrimage to Mecca, where Abu Bakr announced the imposition of the new tax. Muhammad remained behind in Medina. Shortly after the Muslims and Abu Bakr left Medina, Muhammad received another revelation. This instruction is known in the Muslim tradition as *Surat al-Bara'ah*, or "Freedom from Responsibility." It is also sometimes called *Surat al-Tawbah*, or "The Repentance," and is found in the Quran.[34] The revelation proclaimed Muhammad's new policy toward those who refused to obey him. Its importance justifies its being quoted here in full.

An acquittal, from God and his Messenger, unto the idolaters with whom you made covenant: "Journey freely in the land for four months; and know that you cannot frustrate the will of God, and that God degrades the unbelievers."

A proclamation, from God and his Messenger, unto mankind on the day of the Great Pilgrimage: "God is quit, and His Messenger, of the idolaters. So if you repent, that will be better for you; but if you turn your backs, know that you cannot frustrate the will of God. And give thou good tidings to the unbelievers of a painful chastisement; excepting those of the idolaters with whom you have made covenant, then they failed you naught neither lent them support to any man against you. With them fulfill your covenant until their term; surely God loves the godfearing.

"Then, when the sacred months are drawn away, slay the idolaters wherever you find them, and take them and confine them, and lie in wait for them at every place of ambush. But if they repent, and perform the prayer, and pay the alms, then let them go their way."

It is significant that Muhammad sent Ali to Mecca to announce the new policy. The fact that Ali was the most renowned Muslim soldier in all Arabia was probably not lost on the audience.[35]

The Arab world changed dramatically with the promulgation of the Surat al-Tawbah. It was now time to choose between the old order and the new, and Muhammad declared war against all non-Muslims. The idolaters were given four months' grace after which Muhammad declared himself free of any responsibility toward them. Muslims would then "slay the idolaters" wherever they were to be found. Those non-Muslim tribes who had existing covenants with Muhammad were safe for the time being. But even these were to be secure only for an unspecified period. No longer would Muhammad form alliances with non-Muslims. The choice for all Arabia was to join the insurgency or face "war to the knife."

Muhammad soon announced another revelation, this one prohibiting non-Muslims from making the traditional pilgrimage to Mecca. "The polytheists are nothing but unclean, so let them not approach the sacred mosque after this year of theirs."[36] Mecca was now a holy city for Muslims only, and almost two centuries of traditional Arab religious practice was swept aside. It is of interest that the promulgation of the Surat al-Tawbah is the only example of Muhammad forcing "conversion by the sword" under penalty of death, and it occurred *within* Arabia and among Arabs and not, as Westerners sometimes maintain, among Christians and Jews in those lands outside Arabia that later fell to the Arab conquest. It is important to note as well that Muhammad's threats applied only to Arab idolaters; Christians and Jews were not included and were not to be harmed.

Muhammad's threat of religious war seems to have been prompted by the political circumstances with which he was forced to deal at the time rather than any religious zeal. It was a time of crisis for Islam. Either the pagan tribes would be forced into the fold setting the stage for the religious conversion of all Arabia or Islam would remain a creed confined to the Hejaz. In the circumstances attending the later Arab conquests, conversion by the sword was forbidden. To be sure, resistance to the Arab armies was punishable by death. But once established, Islam recognized only voluntary acceptance of Islam. Taxes were required of all subjects, Muslim and non-Muslim, with Muslims paying the zakat and non-Muslims subject to a land tax (*kharaj*) and a poll tax (*jizya*). Muslims were required to perform military service in addition to the tax. Christians and Jews were exempt from military service.

When the pilgrims at Mecca returned to their tribes, they brought news of Muhammad's new edicts. The news was cause for alarm, for few chiefs doubted that Muhammad would use his large army as he threatened. The politics of Arabia made it almost certain that some tribes would also join Muhammad for the opportunity to settle old tribal rivalries. And there was, as always, the prospect of loot to be had. Muhammad had threatened to turn all of Arabia into a battlefield. Under these circumstances many of the chiefs chose to join Muhammad's movement and to profess Islam, which, in any case, was now a condition for any agreement with Muhammad. In 631 representatives from tribes as far away as Yemen began to arrive in Medina to make their peace with Muhammad and to adopt Islam. This is referred to in the tradition as the Year of Deputations. There is no doubt that many of these "conversions" were less than sincere. To many chiefs the need to swear allegiance to Muhammad and Islam was probably not seen as much different from the traditional practice of swearing loyalty to any powerful chief as had been done in Arabia for centuries. Whether sincere submission or alliance of convenience made no difference. Muhammad was now the new prince and chief of a considerable part of Arabia.

Muhammad's change in policy and the pressure he imposed on the tribes and clans left them with little choice but to submit to his authority or take up arms against him. When Muhammad's agents began arriving in the tribal territories to collect the zakat, resentment surfaced immediately. The weaker tribes and those close to Mecca and Medina had little choice but to promise to pay. The stronger tribes, however, defied Muhammad's ultimatum and stood in unconcealed hostility to him. Even while representatives of some tribes were streaming into Medina during the Year of Deputations to swear allegiance, the stronger tribes—al Aswad in Yemen, Musaylimah in Yamamah, and Talhah in Asad—all openly declared their animosity to Muhammad, his allies, his tax, and his religion.[37] When Muhammad died less than a year later, these tribes were still in open defiance. Muhammad never sent an army to deal with their recalcitrance. The powerful tribes of the north, the Ghatafans, and those along the Syrian border never came under Muhammad's influence during his lifetime. It is probably with good reason that tradition says that until he died Muhammad complained bitterly that many Muslims were less than observant and some even outright hypocrites.

Whatever its limitations, Muhammad's authority and manpower base from which to raise an army was much greater than before, and he began to plan for another expedition against the Byzantines.[38] While the expedition was still in its planning stages, Muhammad undertook his famous *Hijjat al-Wada*, or Farewell Pilgrimage, to Mecca. On March 9, 632, he gave a sermon in which he repeated the injunctions from God that were to govern the behavior of all Muslims. At the end of the sermon he asked the gathered crowd, "Have I not told you what to do and completed my mission?" The crowd responded with a roar, "Yes, by God, you have." Muhammad raised his eyes to heaven and cried out, "O God, bear witness!"[39] He left Mecca never to return.

MUHAMMAD'S DEATH

Upon his arrival in Medina he continued his preparations for the expedition against the Byzantines, appointing the eighteen-year-old Usamah, son of Zayd ibn Harithah, to command. The boy's youth was the subject of much complaint among the more experienced soldiers, but Muhammad remained firm in his decision. The appointment of such a young and inexperienced soldier is puzzling. Perhaps Muhammad wished formally to avenge the death of his adopted son, Zayd, who had been killed at Mu'ta by appointing the young Usamah, Zayd's only son, to command the army that would exact that revenge.[40] The choice of commanders is difficult to explain in purely military terms.

One night in June 632 Muhammad called to one of his companions and told him that God had ordered him to go to the cemetery and pray for the dead. He prayed at the cemetery for some time and then returned home, where he fell asleep. The next morning Muhammad was struck with a violent headache. Some sources say that he had been suffering from fever and headaches for some time, perhaps brought on by fatigue from the pilgrimage.[41] Despite his pain Muhammad continued spending the night with each of his wives in turn. He sent for Usamah, and two days later he was strong enough to perform the public ceremony of bestowing the war banner on Usamah and his troops. Ibn Ishaq tells us that "the Apostle went out walking between two men of his family. . . . His head was bound in a cloth and his feet were dragging."[42] There was sufficient concern for his health that Usamah delayed the scheduled departure of the expedition to Syria.

Muhammad was moved to his wife Aisha's apartment so she could care for him. He seems to have suffered from a burning fever and a terrible headache. He instructed one of his companions to "'[p]our seven skins of water from different wells over me so that I may go out to the men and instruct them.' We made him sit down in a tub and we poured the water over him until he said, 'Enough! Enough!'"[43] One witness told Ibn Ishaq that "when the Apostle's illness became severe he and the men came down to Medina and he went in to the Apostle who was unable to speak."[44] Despite these difficulties Muhammad went to the mosque "with his head wrapped up," where he permitted Abu Bakr to lead the prayer. On the tenth day of his illness Muhammad suffered a high fever and his body was racked with pain. Those around him thought he might be suffering from pleurisy the symptoms of which are similar to pulmonary edema and adult respiratory distress syndrome that is sometimes accompanies long-term malarial infection.[45] The next morning he arose and went to the mosque and sat down in the courtyard to rest. Then he returned to his bed in Aisha's apartment and cleaned his teeth.

At some point he asked for writing materials with which to write a document to keep the faithful from error, but there is no evidence that Muhammad ever executed such a document.[46] He lay down with his head in Aisha's lap and talked to her for a while. Suddenly his head grew heavy and his eyes became fixed. "Lord, grant me pardon," he said and slipped away into death "with the heat of noon that day . . . on the very day that he came to Medina as an emigrant, having completed exactly twelve years in his migration."[47] There was some dispute among the Muslims as to where to bury the Prophet. Some wanted to bury him in the mosque, while others wanted him buried with his companions in the cemetery. Abu Bakr settled the matter when he claimed "I heard the Apostle say, 'No prophet dies but he is buried where he died'; so the bed on which he died was taken up and they made a grave beneath it. . . . The Apostle was buried in the middle of the night of the Wednesday."[48] And that was the end of Muhammad ibn Abdallah.

Muhammad's death was not, of course, the end of his influence on history. He had founded a new religion that would sweep the Middle East within a few short years of his death. Over the centuries Islam would spread to peoples and countries yet unknown in Arabia and to the West until it came to be among the world's great religions. Within Arabia itself Muhammad had shown the way toward a new form of government, administration, and social life that would eventually replace the old tribal system by subsuming it into the new ummah, or community of the faithful. Islamic law and moral instruction eventually replaced many of the harsher aspects of Arab custom with far less attendant loss of life than was previously the case. But all these things were only partially achieved at the time of Muhammad's death, and would probably not have been achieved at all had it not been for Muhammad's other important achievement, his transformation of the Arab armies and their manner of warfare. It was this legacy, his military legacy, that provided his successors with the means to conquer the rest of pagan Arabia and impose Islam on it, reform the Arab social order along the lines of Islamic morality and law, and embark on the great Arab conquests that destroyed the Persian and Byzantine Empires and replaced them with the Empire of Islam.

13

MUHAMMAD'S
MILITARY LEGACY

The fragile unity of the Islamic insurgency that Muhammad had managed to hold together during his lifetime began to crumble even before his death. Now it threatened to come apart altogether. At the time of Muhammad's death no more than perhaps one-third of Arabia had been exposed to Islam in any way, and far less than a third of the population, perhaps no more than 20 percent or so, had actually professed it. Beyond Mecca, Medina, and Ta'if and the bedouin tribes in the immediate vicinity of these towns, the pull of Islam was weak if extant at all.[1] Even within the insurgency many professed loyalty to Muhammad himself more than to the creed. In the traditional fashion of Arab covenants, upon Muhammad's death many tribal and clan chiefs no longer felt bound by their old agreements with the Prophet. The crux of the problem was the zakat, the annual tax that Muhammad had imposed. The zakat had been announced at the Meccan pilgrimage, but Muhammad died before the tax could be collected from all but the tribes nearest Medina and Mecca. Some of the allied tribes sent delegations to Medina to negotiate new agreements with Abu Bakr, who had been elected to succeed Muhammad, promising to remain Muslim and say the daily prayer in exchange for repeal of the tax. Abu Bakr refused saying, "By Allah, if they withhold a rope of a camel they use to give its due zakat to Allah's Messenger, I will fight them for it." The result was the Riddah, or the War of the Apostates.

It was Abu Bakr who was responsible for the ultimate success of Islam by using the Arab armies to suppress all opposition to it and to enforce conversion on all Arabia by military means. During the two-year period of the wars of the Riddah we see Muhammad's reformed armies operating on a larger scale over greater distances than ever before with several campaigns taking place at once, all of them operating under unified command to implement a single strategic goal formulated by Abu Bakr. The same operational characteristics that became typical of the armies of the later Arab conquests were first revealed during the Riddah, and it was Abu Bakr who was the political and military genius behind it.[2]

Abu Bakr assumed leadership of the insurgency when the movement was on the verge of collapse. He reckoned correctly that to accede to the tribes on the issue of the zakat meant the end of centralized control over the movement, opening it to schism, eventual disintegration, and perhaps, even absorption by other monotheistic religions. To prevent this Abu Bakr declared war on all those who would not obey. He proclaimed withdrawal from Muhammad's coalition to be a denial of God's will (the concept of *kufr*) and declared secession from the coalition and the ummah as apostasy (*riddah*) that was punishable by death. Once the tribes had joined Muhammad, he asserted, they were no longer free not to be Muslims. Nor could they be loyal to God under any leader whose legitimacy did not derive from Muhammad. This fusion of two once separable phenomena, membership in Muhammad's community and faith in Islam, became one of Islam's most distinctive features. Perhaps to forestall the influence of others claiming to be prophets who had already arisen in Arabia during Muhammad's lifetime, Abu Bakr declared Muhammad to be the last prophet that God would send. Although these tenets were originally devised and introduced as part of Abu Bakr's *political* strategy to isolate and destroy the enemies of the insurgency, over time they became important *religious* tenets of Islam.

The term *al-Riddah* has been used by traditional Arab historians who wished to cast the opposition of the tribes in religious terms, as apostasy, a falling away from the true faith and thus an attack on Islam. These traditionalists saw the war as a religious and defensive one to save the true faith.[3] But this view is only partially correct. An apostasy could only apply to those tribes and clans who had already agreed to the tax. Muhammad had died before his agents could collect the zakat, and most chiefs had never agreed to pay it while Muhammad was alive. Now that it was demanded by Abu Bakr, they saw no reason to pay it to a man in whose election they had played no part. These chiefs could only be deemed apostates under Abu Bakr's *new* tenets of Islam and not under the tenets with which Muhammad had governed.

While certainly a war about religion, the Riddah was also really a war declared by Abu Bakr, his Meccan allies, and the local loyal bedouin tribes to spread the authority of Medina and the faith of Islam throughout Arabia. The conquest of Arabia served the interests of the Meccan aristocracy to expand their financial and commercial markets; it served the interests of those, among them certainly Abu Bakr, who wished to spread the true faith and destroy the idolaters; and it served the interests of the loyal bedouin tribes for battle and booty. Seen in this larger context, the Riddah was not so much a war against apostates as it was a war of outright conquest driven by a combination of political, economic, and religious motives.

THE ARMIES OF THE RIDDAH

The decision to attack the "apostates" was not a popular one with many of the faithful, including some of Muhammad's field commanders and advisers. Abu Bakr removed these commanders from their positions and appointed Meccan officers who had supported his election over the opposition of the ansar and some Emigrants.[4] Once the conquest of Arabia had been accomplished, however, these commanders were reinstated and went on to play important roles in the campaigns against the Persians and Byzantines.[5] Abu Bakr appointed Khalid al-Walid as commanding general of the Muslim forces during the Riddah. These appointments and Abu Bakr's negotiations with the recalcitrant tribes occurred while Usamah was conducting the expedition against the Byzantines that Muhammad had ordered before he died. Usamah's army was a small contingent, between seven hundred and three thousand troops,[6] and it seems to have succeeded only in plundering and burning the town of Ubna in southern Jordan as revenge for his father's death.[7] Usamah returned to Medina forty days after he had left. During his absence Abu Bakr had assembled a Muslim army from the tribes around Medina and immediately marched to Dhu al-Qassah (northeast of Medina), where he attacked several of the tribes of Najd and defeated them. Abu Bakr then ordered a general mobilization of all Muslim forces and ordered his Meccan commanders to join him at Dhu al-Qassah. From there al-Tabari tells us that he dispatched eleven armies, supposedly at the same time, to all parts of Arabia with the mission of subjugating the "apostatizing" tribes.[8]

Abu Bakr's military operations were carried out simultaneously and in four different directions over almost eighteen months with the result that all Arabia fell to the Muslim armies and accepted Islam. Al-Tabari provides a list of the Muslim commanders and the tribes against which they fought.[9] (Map 12 depicts the major campaigns of the Riddah.) Campaign 1 was carried out to the east and northeast of Medina under the overall command of Khalid al-Walid accompanied by Shuranbil bin Hasanah ad al-Ala bin al-Hadrami against the Tayii, Ghatafan, Asad, Tamin, Bani Hanifah, and Rabi'ah tribes. The most famous engagement of this campaign was the Battle of Aqraba, which al-Walid fought against the Bani Hanifah under the command of Musaylimah. The Bani Hanifah supposedly put forty thousand men in the field and had already crushed two Muslim armies sent to bring them to heel.[10] Khalid al-Walid attacked with five thousand men driving the Bani Hanifah back until they took refuge in a walled orchard known to Arab history as *Hadiqat al-Mawt*, the Garden of Death. In desperate hand-to-hand combat most of the Hanifah army was slain including its commander. Muslim losses were twelve hundred dead.[11] Among the dead were a number of "Quran reciters," men who had memorized the sayings and instructions of Muhammad that would later be collected in the Quran. Had all of them been killed, the Quran might have been lost to history.

Campaign 2 was undertaken to the southeast under the leadership of Ikrimah ibn Abu Jahl, Hudhayfah bin Mihsah, and Arfajah bin Harthamah against the tribes of Oman and Mahrah. The southwest campaign (3) was led by al-Muhajir bin Abi Umayyah and Ziyad bin Labid, who conquered Yemen and Hadramawt. The north and northwest campaign (4) was aimed at the Arab tribes along the Syrian border who had once been allies of the Byzantines. Two generals, Amr ibn al-A'as and Khalid bin Sa'id, succeeded in getting some of these tribes to defect to the Muslims before undertaking a series of major operations into Palestine and Syria. By the time the Byzantines' former allies had gone over to the Muslims, some fourteen months after the start of the Riddah, most of Arabia had been pacified and Khalid al-Walid was on the border of Iraq. Abu Bakr ordered al-Walid to march to the aid of Amr ibn al-A'as in his campaign on the Syrian border. As the other

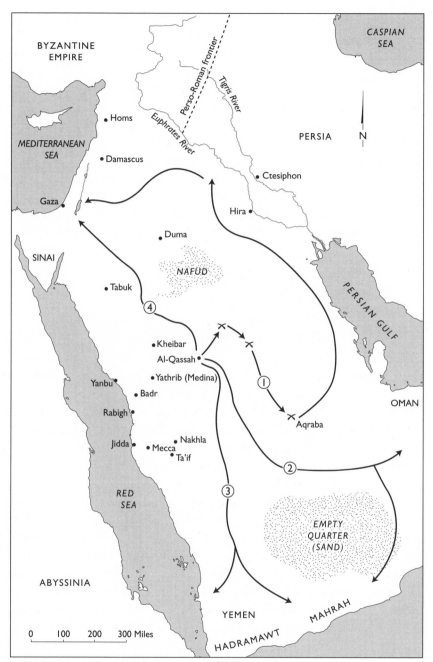

Map 12. Military Campaigns of the *Riddah*, 632–633 C.E.

victorious Muslim commanders began to return to Medina from different parts of Arabia with their armies, Abu Bakr ordered them to the
Syrian front to reinforce the Muslim armies there with troops
recruited from among the newly converted tribes in Arabia. The result
was the collapse of the Byzantine defenses on the Syrian frontier and
the beginning of the Arabs' westward conquests.

The armies that carried out Abu Bakr's campaigns left Medina as
relatively small contingents, each numbering perhaps four thousand to
five thousand men or even less, comprising ansar, Emigrants, and tribal
units of local bedouins under the leadership of experienced field commanders. Only Khalid al-Walid's army seems to have been substantially
larger, a circumstance that made sound military sense given that he
had the mission of subduing some of the larger and more powerful
tribes in Arabia. The size of the Muslim contingents seems to have
been only large enough to engage and defeat those small clans and
tribes encountered along their routes of march. These contingents were
expected to recruit more manpower along the way with religious
promises and loot. If this failed, then military action could be undertaken to inflict a defeat on the recalcitrant clan, which would then
make a peace agreement with the victors that required them to accept
Islam and join the campaign. Once within the area of the operations
of the target, Muslim commanders would seek to take advantage of
local rivalries to attract additional manpower to their armies.[12] It was
a technique Muhammad had used on several occasions, and it worked
well for the armies of Abu Bakr.

The armies of the Arabian conquest demonstrated all the operational capabilities that Muhammad had introduced into Arab warfare.
The Muslim officer corps was competent and experienced, and had
acquired in Muhammad's wars the skills needed to command large
armies over long distances. Abu Bakr, while remaining in Medina,
was able to coordinate the eleven major campaigns and to shift forces
as needed from one front to another.[13] The units within the armies,
while mostly organized on tribal or clan lines, nevertheless operated
under a unified command structure through which all subordinate
commanders were expected to carry out the missions assigned to them
as part of a larger tactical plan. Abu Bakr's campaigns demonstrated
the primacy of strategic objectives in tactical planning, something that
had been absent in Arab warfare until introduced by Muhammad. Even
the idea of a single tribe or political group conquering all of Arabia was

inconceivable until Muhammad showed the Arabs how to think in strategic terms. Logistics and supply for large armies had improved considerably under Muhammad and were put to good use in Abu Bakr's campaigns. We have no reports of serious shortages of water, fodder, or armaments in any of the campaigns of the Riddah. Muslim morale and fighting spirit were superior to that of any tribe the armies engaged with the possible exception of the Bani Hanifah who fought to the death to retain their freedom. Muslim soldiers had learned to fight as units operating within a larger tactical design, while the warriors of most tribes fought in the old manner as individuals. Finally, the quality of Muslim combat leadership, certainly at the field commander level and probably in the major subordinate units as well, was superior to their adversaries. Muslim field commanders were never selected on the grounds of piety, but always on the basis of demonstrated competence in war.

Muhammad's legacy of new operational capabilities passed intact to the armies of Abu Bakr and produced the conquest and conversion of all Arabia. The Muslim military experience against the border garrisons of the Byzantine and Persian Empires had demonstrated that both were hollow and ripe for defeat. By the spring of 633 the Riddah was over and Arabia was an armed camp full of warrior tribes ready to seek new adventures and loot. An Islamic Arabia lacked sufficient resources of food and wealth to sustain itself under the limitations that the new Islamic laws placed on the old ways of life. If new sources of wealth were not found, the Muslim state that Abu Bakr's military campaigns had brought into being would soon fragment into warring tribal groups. Muhammad's earlier raids attempted against the Byzantine border provinces provided the guiding strategic concept behind Abu Bakr's decision to use the united Arab tribes as a means to an even larger conquest. In 633 Abu Bakr ordered three Muslim armies to attack the Byzantines. The great Arab conquests had begun.

THE ARMIES OF THE ARAB CONQUESTS

The armies of the Arab conquests were those military forces of Arabian origin that established the Empire of Islam before being subsumed into the larger Muslim convert population. The original Arab armies can be said to have existed from 622 when Muhammad first formed them to approximately 842 when the Abbasid caliph, al-Mutasim, introduced the Mamluke Institution of slave Turk soldiers who replaced the original

Arab contingents in the armies of Islam. Until then the armies of Mohammad and his immediate successors consisted almost exclusively of Arabs from Arabia. It was these armies that invaded and conquered large segments of the Byzantine and Persian Empires between 633 and 656. Over the next hundred years the Arabs fought three civil wars. The first replaced the original successors of Muhammad with the Umayyad dynasty, which ruled from Syria from 661 to 750. The Umayyads survived the second civil war (684–692) but were driven from power during the third civil war (744-750) and replaced by the Abbasids, who ruled from Iraq and retained the caliphate, although in much altered form, until 1258. The Arab invasions produced a new sociopolitical order that eventually included the whole of the Arabian Peninsula, all the Persian lands, and the Byzantine provinces of Syria and Egypt.[14]

The structure of the Arab army reflected the structure of Arab tribal society. Arab society during Muhammad's day and for more than a century afterward never really developed a stable political order worthy of being called a state. There was no state per se and no administrative structure of government. Arab society remained what it had always been, a tribal society characterized by personal leadership and appointed retainers that drew no distinctions between the social, religious, and military aspects of life. Indeed, there was never a formal army as such. Instead, there was an alliance of powerful tribal chiefs who led their personal armed retinues in battle. There was no financial system, and what treasury there was came from gifts and booty obtained in raids. Government was essentially an enlarged tribal system of negotiated consensus among powerful tribal chieftains, and it was these warrior chiefs who controlled the Arab populace and the army. Governance was effected indirectly through tribal intermediaries. This system of indirect rule plagued the Muslim Empire until its end. Power ebbed and flowed from the center of authority, but no caliph ever was able to retain control of the tribal and regional armies for very long. Revolts and insurrections rooted in jealousy, political interests, religious apostasy, and blood feuds went on for centuries.[15]

Some authorities have argued that the invasion of the Byzantine and Persian Empires by the Arab tribes was comparable to the invasion of the Western Roman Empire by the Germanic tribes with the same general result, the establishment over the long run of a number of separate states ruled by powerful national kings. It seems more correct to say, rather, that the Arab invasions were unlike the tribal invasions in the West, for they were coordinated from a single center, Medina, for a specific *religious* purpose, to extend the rule of God's believers over the unbelievers as commanded by God himself. This central leadership, direction, and religious purpose led to results quite different from those of the Germanic invasions. Instead of conquering, settling, and then ruling the new lands, the Arab conquerors stayed together as soldiers living in garrison cities (*amsar*), military districts (*ajnad*), and even military monasteries (*ribat*) whose members remained celibate.[16] The Arab conquerors remained apart from the societies they conquered and showed little interest in governing the new lands, leaving the old systems, leaders, kings, and governmental officials—now converted to Islam—in place to continue to administer the conquered lands.[17]

The military garrisons remained just that, fortresses that accommodated Arab armies that could be sent forth on further conquest or used to suppress revolts. This arrangement was possible because the Arab armies, although receiving religious direction from the center, were not really structured armies at all. They were tribal coalitions led by local chieftains and made up of emigrants from Arabia who left their homes to serve as soldiers in a holy war. In Islam, all believers were soldiers. There was no Muslim army distinct from Muslim society. The Muslims were a holy army and their society, living apart from the conquered infidels with their families at government expense until called to further holy war, worked well.

The Arab armies that attacked the Byzantines and Persians may have been infantry armies, but they did not move on foot. Instead, they made extensive use of the camel in transporting their armies to the strategic objective. This provided them with superior strategic mobility enabling them to bypass enemy strong points and offer battle at times and places of their own choosing. The guiding tactical concept was to move quickly to a favorable position, establish the infantry on the ground, and then force the enemy to attack at its disadvantage. Once the horse became widely available, Arab armies continued their practice of using mounted infantry in a strategic manner. Eventually the Arab armies produced the best war horse of the day, the Syrian-Arab crossbreed combining the small strong North African Barb with the heavier Iranian mount.[18]

Once established in their new lands the Arabs attempted to remain an ethnically homogeneous, warlike, and religious society apart from the conquered infidels. But their numbers were not very large. Crone

suggests that the total size of the Arab armies that left Arabia could
hardly have exceeded one hundred thousand people, including men
and children, whereas the population of the conquered lands probably
exceeded 20 million souls![19] All Arab emigrants lived in garrison cities
or military districts and were registered in the *diwan*, or "register."
The registered soldier was entitled to monthly rations for himself and
his family, and received an annual cash stipend as did his wife and
children. Quarters were also provided for the soldier and his family. In
return these religious warriors were available for military service at a
moment's notice. As the Arab occupation stabilized, military calls to
active service became relatively infrequent. When called to service, the
soldier had to supply his own mount—horse or camel—and military
equipment that included a lance, sword, shield, bow, quiver, and armor,
usually some form of mail.[20]

Once registered on the diwan, the soldier remained on the roll for
life. There was no classical Arabic word for veteran soldier, and no special
provisions were made for them. Soldiers too old for service probably
provided substitutes or worked for the army administration. Disabled
soldiers were registered as cripples and continued to draw some portion
of their annual pay and allowance. Arab soldiers were usually forbidden
to engage in agriculture, although in rare instances it was permitted.
Such limitations on "fraternization" and economic activity worked
against the creation of an Arab "society" in the conquered lands, a
task left to the conquered infidels who converted to Islam. In some
respects the diwan may have been adopted from the military role of
the Byzantines, but with a very important difference: the diwan was
not seen by the Arabs as an institution for the maintenance of the army,
but as a social institution for the maintenance of Muslims. Stipends
were not military pay, but a right claimed by every Muslim emigrant
and his descendants as a reward for participation in the conquest of
Islam over the infidels. Islam was religion, society, and army all in one,
and the diwan was the mechanism for sustaining all three.

This attempt to sustain a separate Arab identity apart from the
infidels was bound to fail in the long run on the grounds of numbers
and conversions. Even as military manpower demands increased, the
Arabs made no effort to recruit the able-bodied men of the conquered
lands into their armies. Captives were sometimes resettled on conquered
lands, and some even served as special units, often private guards or
urban police. Gradually native peoples were permitted to lend military

service, usually ethnic or racial units serving as separate battalions. But once the conquered peoples accepted Islam, more and more non-Arabs came to serve in the Muslim armies even as the purely Arab elements remained isolated in their garrisons. Over time the Arab elements of the Muslim armies came to see the military diwan as a social stipend, and the Arab elements became a smaller and less used segment of the armies as the Arabs gradually were submerged into the Muslim armies of disparate peoples who had converted to the new faith.[21]

With gradual assimilation and widespread conversion, the old citizen armies eventually gave way to professional armies manned largely by non-Arab Muslims, although their commanders remained Arabs for many years. The regional armies of the old tribal chiefs survived for centuries, but for the most part they were confined to their garrisons supported by the diwan and were of little use. As the Arabs were submerged in a sea of Muslims, the old tribal consensual style of government became more difficult to operate and proved insufficient to constrain tribal and personal ambitions. The result was two civil wars. The second war (684–692) forced the Umayyads to abandon the old ideal of consensual rule completely, and they governed by force supported by their professional army made up mostly of Syrian troops. It was not until the last Umayyad caliph (750), however, that the armies became professionalized.

Under the Umayyads heavy cavalry became increasingly important. Originally, Arab cavalry was divided into armored and unarmored horse, or heavy and light cavalry. The heavy cavalry still comprised only a small number of units and was used mostly as shock troops along Byzantine lines. Light cavalry, when not used as skirmishers and reconnaissance, was used only to complete the destruction of already disorganized or broken enemy units. Surviving records of the period describe the full equipment of the seventh-century Arab cavalryman as lance, sword, shield, hauberk, packing needles, five small needles, linen thread, awl, scissors, horse's nose bag, and feed basket.[22] During the Umayyad period the bulk of Arab cavalry became armored in a transition toward the Byzantine model in mounts, armor, and weapons. Unlike the Byzantines, the Arab armies retained their old infantry traditions. Byzantine cavalrymen, for example, were trained for use as shock troops fighting from horseback only. Arab heavy cavalrymen were trained in the old tradition of fighting first from horseback and then being able to dismount and fight on foot. Heavy cavalry never became a truly decisive arm in Arab armies until much later, and heavy infantry remained the central combat arm. The cavalry would deploy safely behind the infantry formations and sally forth as opportunity permitted to attack the enemy only to retreat quickly behind its own infantry for protection. The idea of cavalry against cavalry in open combat was unknown to Arab commanders.

When the Arab armies encountered the Central Asian horse archer on the rim of the empire they were unable to find a tactical solution to this novel way of fighting. The Arabs did what the Byzantines and Persians had done before them: they hired whole contingents of horse archers and used them against their countrymen. The new cavalry threat forced a change in Arab cavalry equipment, most notably in the adoption of light felt armor for man and horse to protect against arrows and the introduction of the iron stirrup (over the objections of Arab scholars who claimed the device would make soldiers effete by hindering their ability to mount and dismount rapidly in battle).[23] But even with the introduction of the horse archer, infantry remained the king of the battlefield in Arab tactical thinking.

The Umayyad period was brought to an end by yet another civil war, and the Abbasids were brought to the throne by rebel armies raised in Iran. These troops replaced the Syrian troops of the Umayyads in imperial garrisons, and the capital was moved to Baghdad. These Iranian troops, or Khurasiani, were mostly horse archers, and this type of cavalry now became dominant in Arab armies. Although cavalry was now the arm of decision, infantry still played an important role on the battlefield, and close infantry and cavalry cooperation remained central to the new Arab tactical design. These new troops wore clothes similar to the eastern Christian monks and wore beards and long hair. Great reliance was placed on the bow and lance. The attack was marked by a shower of arrows as the cavalry closed with the enemy at the gallop firing as it went. Once in contact, the lance came into play along with other weapons of close combat like the curved sword, mace, battle-ax, and short sword of single-edge design.[24]

The Abbasids made no effort to broaden the base of their army or government, relying instead on those groups and tribes of mostly eastern origin that had brought them to power. The Arab armies were now mostly cavalry armies, and since horses were expensive and training took a long time, it was more efficient for the Abbasids to rely on the natural horsemen of the Khurasiani rather than to outfit and train Arabs themselves. The reliance on foreign troops and the failure to extend governmental participation to the powerful regional chiefs resulted in the imperial army being run more like a mafia than a military institution. The caliphs and the army became increasingly isolated from the society with the consequence that the Abbasids were forced to deal with frequent revolts.[25]

During one of the civil wars that threatened to topple the Abbasids, one of the participants, al-Mutasim (r. 833-842), had outfitted his army with four thousand Turkic troops whom he had purchased as slaves and then freed for military service under his command. Once al-Mutasim had become caliph, he expanded the practice of purchasing and training Turkish slaves for service in his armies, thereby bringing into existence what Muslims came to call "the Mamluke Institution." The essence of this institution was the systematic reliance of the caliphate on soldiers of servile and non-Islamic origin. The use of other foreign, non-Muslim, ethnic units in the army also increased greatly. The result was that the areas of the empire under direct imperial control were policed by these slave Turks. Over time, most of the major military commands and some important governorships were assigned to Turkic officials as well. Eventually the Mamlukes carried out a military coup against the Abbasids and took control of the caliphate.

For the next two centuries the Abbasid caliphs continued to rule from Baghdad, but mostly in name only while genuine power was exercised by Turkic military commanders who continued to pay lip-service to the rule of the caliphs. In reaction to this state of affairs, the governors of various provinces, using their regional armies as leverage, broke into open revolt time and again with one province after another seceding from the empire by force of arms. By the middle of the ninth century the old Arab empire had ceased to exist, and with it the Arab "army of God" that had swept over the ancient Mediterranean world wielding the sword of Allah also disappeared.[26]

Without doubt Muhammad's greatest military legacy was the doctrine of jihad, or holy war. It is indisputable that divinely justified warfare became a force of major importance during the early Islamic period and remained a powerful motivator for the Islamic conquests that followed Muhammad's death. This is even more amazing when it is recalled that pre-Islamic Arabia knew no notion of ideology of any sort, much less the idea of religiously sanctioned war. Pre-Islamic warfare was directly linked to the economic and social circumstances of pasturage, material wealth, and prestige, and there is no evidence of any kind to suggest any religious or ideological motivation for Arab warfare prior to the influence of Muhammad and Islam.[27] Under these circumstances, martyrdom had little meaning, and no transcendent meaning was applied to warfare as a reward for carrying out the instructions of God.[28] The idea of warfare as a command of God rewarded by martyrdom and paradise seems to have been an innovation with no precedents in Arab culture, custom, or practice brought about completely by Muhammad's thinking and influence on events.

The concept of jihad came to have many meanings over the years as a consequence of the influence of Muslim legalists, scholars, and theologians. The term derives from the root *jahada*, which is defined as "exerting one's utmost power, efforts, endeavors, or ability in contending with an object of disapprobation."[29] There are, therefore, many kinds of jihad, most of which have nothing to do with warfare. Thus, the "greater jihad" (*al-jihad al-akbar*) refers to a struggle within or against one's self while the "lesser jihad" refers to warring in the path of God.[30] Jihad, therefore, may not have always been equated with holy war, although that is the primary meaning that Muhammad seems to have given it. With regard to jihad as holy war most Muslim scholars subscribe to what is called the classic evolutionary theory of holy war: that what Muhammad meant by jihad depended on the historical circumstances and needs at different times during his prophetic mission. Thus,

> At the beginning of his prophetic career in Mecca when he was weak and his followers few, the divine revelations encouraged avoidance of physical conflict. Only after the intense physical persecution that resulted in the Emigration (*Hijra*) of the Muslim community to Medina in 622 were Muhammad and the believers given the divine authority to engage in war and only in defense. As the Muslim community continued to grow in numbers and strength in Medina, further revelations widened the conditions and narrowed the restrictions under which war could be waged, until it was concluded that war against non-Muslims could be waged virtually at any time, without pretext, and in any place.[31]

It is this classical interpretation of Islam as a "religion of dominion" that provided the ideological justification for the Arab conquests and that is very much alive in the minds of Islamic *jihadis* of the present day.

Muhammad's military legacy lives in the minds of these jihadis in their memory of Muhammad as a great general and passionate revolutionary who created and fought a successful insurgency to achieve his political and religious goals. It is this legacy of Muhammad as successful revolutionary that motivates Muslim insurgents and revolutionary leaders in Iraq, Afghanistan, and elsewhere. In their portrayal of their insurgencies as divinely sanctioned acts, these modern revolutionaries are imitating Muhammad. It can scarcely be denied that at least to some extent some suicide bombers are motivated by their desire to become martyrs in the same manner that many of Muhammad's soldiers were willing to die for their faith. The Osama bin Ladens of the Muslim world, like Muhammad, speak of creating a more moral world in which to live, a community of believers living according to the instructions given by God himself. Like Muhammad, they are prepared to use violence to bring that new moral order into being. Those who do not understand the historical roots of modern Muslim insurgencies fail to do so at great risk.

NOTES

INTRODUCTION

1. I am indebted to Michael Edwards for his thoughts that appear in his *Ibn Ishaq's Life of Muhammad, Apostle of Allah* (1964) on the difficulties encountered in researching the lives of religious figures. The book is a truncated version of Ibn Ishaq's lengthy book and is only marginally useful as a source due to its heavy editing.

2. Watt, *Muhammad: Prophet and Statesman*, 237.

3. Examples of these types of attributions can be found in Hamidullah, *Battlefields of the Prophet*. Hamidullah is a fine scholar except when he permits religious elements to cloud his military explanations, something that may be accounted for by his writing for an already religiously committed audience. This said, Hamidullah's early work is invaluable for reconstructing the terrain of Muhammad's battlefields. On a pilgrimage in 1939 Hamidullah walked the ground and provided some descriptions and primitive maps of the battlefields that can be cross-checked against the observations of others and descriptions of the terrain as they appear in Ibn Ishaq's text.

4. Huntington, *Clash of Civilizations*, 263; see also Payne, *Why Nations Arm*, 125. Huntington's paraphrase of Payne is inaccurate. Moses was an excellent military commander. Siddhartha Gautama, before he became the Buddha, was a prince of the warrior class of India and was certainly trained in warfare since this class had no other function but to fight wars. There is, however, no record of the Buddha having experienced combat. For more on Moses' combat experience as a commander, see Gabriel, *Military History of Ancient Israel*, the chapter entitled "Exodus."

5. Watt, *Muhammad at Medina*, 276.

6. What is meant politically and militarily by the term "ideology" is captured by the German *Weltanschauung*, a systematic set of ideas that provides a "total world outlook." More than just a general set of beliefs, it is a systematic, logically interconnected set that explains all of one's life, relationships, and obligations in much the same way as do the doctrine of a religious cult. Ethnic and religious differences as such do not constitute an ideology in the same way that Islam did for Muhammad's followers. For more on the Muslim influence on later Christian doctrines of war and the Crusades, see Gabriel, *Empires at War*, 3:792.

7. For more than thirty years I have argued that the military history of the ancient world did not end in 450 C.E. as is often asserted but when the last army of the ancient world, that of the Byzantine Empire, met its end at Constantinople in 1453. The argument for this point of view can be found in my *Empires at War*, 1:15, cited above. The relevance of the argument to the present work lies only in my referring to Muhammad has having lived during the ancient period of military history. I hope the reader will grant me this indulgence even while reserving judgment as to the validity of the argument.

8. Hitti, *History of the Arabs*, 17.

9. See Giap, *People's War, People's Army*, for the methods required to organize and conduct an insurgency.

10. Watt, *Muhammad at Medina*, 257.

11. The story appears in Hamidullah, *Battlefields of the Prophet*, 40, citing Ibn Hajar Isabah, no. 8336.

12. Watt, *Muhammad at Medina*, 257.

13. See Gabriel, *Subotai the Valiant*, and *Military History of Ancient Israel* as examples of the author's previous work dealing with foreign-language sources in works of military history.

14. Ibn Ishaq, *Life of Muhammad*, xxxiv (hereafter cited as Ibn Ishaq).

1. THE LAND OF ARABIA

1. Hoyland, *Arabia and the Arabs*, 3–4.
2. Ibid., 85.
3. Hitti, *History of the Arabs*, 17.
4. Hoyland, *Arabia and the Arabs*, 169.
5. Ibid.
6. Gabriel, *Military History of Ancient Israel*, 121.
7. Yadin, *Warfare in Biblical Lands*, 1:19.
8. Hitti, *History of the Arabs*, 19.
9. Ibid.
10. Ibid., 20.
11. Ibid., 25.

2. THE STRATEGIC SETTING

1. Hoyland, *Arabia and the Arabs*, 142, says the idol was of Nabataean origin. See also page 156 for Ibn Hisham's description of the idol and the rituals

used in the Kaaba. Hitti, *History of the Arabs*, 100, suggests that the idol may have been of Moabite origin, which, in any case, was close enough to Nabataea to account for the disparity in the claims. According to tradition there were more than a thousand idols in the *ka'bah* during Muhammad's day.

2. Glubb, *Life and Times*, 50.

3. For the history of the military collapse of Constantinople in 1453, see Gabriel, "Byzantines and Ottomans," *Empires at War*, vol. 3.

4. For a brief account of the life and battles of Heraclius, see Dupuy and Dupuy, *Encyclopedia of Military History*, 329.

3. ARAB WARFARE

1. Gabriel, "Ancient India," *Empires at War*, 1:235–52.

2. Gabriel, "Japanese Way of War," *Empires at War*, 3:837–72.

3. Gabriel, "Rediscovery of Infantry," *Empires at War*, 3:915–44.

4. Gabriel, *Military History of Ancient Israel*, 118. See Deuteronomy 20:16–17 for the complete quote.

5. Hitti, *History of the Arabs*, 95.

6. Glubb, *Life and Times*, 27.

7. Gabriel, "Charlemagne and the Franks," *Empires at War*, 2:659–700.

8. Gabriel, "The Crusades," *Empires at War*, 3:791–836.

9. Glubb, *Life and Times*, 220.

10. Rodinson, *Muhammad*, 223–24.

11. The idea that Muslim soldiers are bloodthirsty fanatics remains very much alive in the Western mind today largely as a result of the continuing insurgency in Iraq.

12. Hamidullah, *Battlefields of the Prophet*, 139.

13. Hoyland, *Arabia and the Arabs*, 188–89.

14. The Arabs of Arabia were primarily an illiterate and backward people. Their conquest of much of the eastern ancient world brought little to it except the Arabic language and the Islamic religion. The peoples of the conquered lands were the heirs to the art, architecture, literature, and science of the ancient world. Over time the conquered populations converted to Islam and translated their ancient texts into Arabic, which then made their way to the West. It was the knowledge and technology of the conquered peoples that transformed the Arabs, not vice versa. The Western habit of referring to all peoples who speak Arabic and observe the Muslim faith as Arabs is a gross mischaracterization and misunderstanding of both the Islamic conquests and the Arabs. See Gabriel, "Wars of Arab Conquest," *Empires at War*, 2:639–58.

15. Hitti, *History of the Arabs*, 173.

16. Nicolle and McBride, *Armies of Islam*, 11.

17. Hitti, *History of the Arabs*, 173; Hoyland, *Arabia and the Arabs*, 188 says that the bamboo shafts were assembled in al-Bahrayn, but not grown there.

18. Hoyland, *Arabia and the Arabs*, 189.

19. Nicolle and McBride, 9.

20. Hoyland, *Arabia and the Arabs*, 189.

21. Nicolle and McBride, *Armies of Islam*, 8.

22. Hitti, *History of the Arabs*, 147, suggests the real reason Muhammad attacked Mu'ta was that the *Mashrafiya* swords were manufactured there.

23. Ibid., 173.

24. Hoyland, *Arabia and the Arabs*, 189.

25. Ibid. The reference to David as a maker of iron is found in the Quran, sura 34:10–11, 21.80, which says, "We bestowed upon David Our favours . . . and made hard iron pliant for him, telling him to make coats of mail and measure their links with care."

26. The poetic text is from the *Mu'allaqat*, the seven famous pre-Islamic poems, found in Lyall, *Ten Ancient Arabic Poems*; see also the translation of same by Arberry, *Seven Odes*.

27. Nicolle and McBride, *Armies of Islam*, 13.

28. Crone, "Early Islamic World," 311.

29. From the *Mu'allaqat*.

30. Hitti, *History of the Arabs*, 173.

31. From Tufayl ibn 'Auf, *Poems of Diwan*.

32. Goldschmidt, *Concise History*, 23. See also Bulliet, *Camel and the Wheel*.

33. Gabriel, *Military History of Ancient Israel*, 81–86.

34. Gabriel, *Soldiers' Lives*, 149.

35. As reckoned by Muhammad prior to the Battle of Badr as recorded by Ibn Ishaq, 295. Interrogating a Quraish waterman to discern the strength of the enemy, Muhammad asked, "[H]ow many beasts (camels) were slaughtered every day" to feed the army. The prisoner replied, "[N]ine or ten." Muhammad calculated that "the people [enemy] are between nine hundred and a thousand."

36. Hitti, *History of the Arabs*, 21–22.

37. Goldschmidt, *Concise History*, 23.

38. Ibid.

39. Rodinson, *Muhammad*, 13.

40. Glubb, *Life and Times*, 225.

41. Hitti, *History of the Arabs*, 22.

42. Parry and Yapp, *War, Technology, and Society*, 32.

43. Roth, *The Roman Army*, 207.

44. Rodinson, *Muhammad*, 13.

45. Doughty, *Travels in Arabia Deserta*, 553.

46. Hitti, *History of the Arabs*, 22.

47. Gabriel and Boose, *Great Battles of Antiquity*, 98.

48. Ibn Ishaq, *Life of Muhammad*, 373.

49. Parry and Yapp, *War, Technology, and Society*, 36.

50. Roth, *The Roman Army*, 61–62.

51. Ibid.

52. Only the Israelites seem to have used the mule as their primary military animal. David is portrayed as fleeing Jerusalem on a mule. Ibn Ishaq reports that Muhammad sometimes rode a white mule.

53. Gabriel, *Soldiers' Lives*, chap. 12, "Cavalry."

54. Gabriel, "Wars of Arab Conquest," 646.

55. Parry and Yapp, *War, Technology, and Society*, 35.

56. Ibid.

57. Ibid.

58. Ibid., 39.

59. Hitti, *History of the Arabs*, 173.

60. Ibid.

61. Hamidullah, *Battlefields of the Prophet*, 139.

62. Ibid., 140.

63. Ibid.

4. MUHAMMAD

1. Quran, sura 14:40.

2. Hitti, *History of the Arabs*, 103.

3. Glubb, *Life and Times*, 64. According to legend Qusai was also the first warrior to tie a banner around his lance to distinguish himself on the battlefield as the leader of the clan, thus making himself a target.

4. Retreating to the desert to meditate remains a common practice among Arabs to this day.

5. Glubb, *Life and Times*, 72.

6. Watt, *Muhammad: Prophet and Statesman*, 12. The dispute is of long standing and cannot be definitively resolved.

7. Glubb, *Life and Times*, 84.

8. Ibid.

9. Ibid.

10. Ibid., 85.

11. Lings, *Muhammad*, 44–45, quoting Ibn Ishaq.

12. Watt, *Muhammad: Prophet and Statesman*, 18–19.

13. Glubb, *Life and Times*, 97, quoting Ibn Ishaq.

14. Ibn Ishaq, 279–80.

15. Ibid., 279–80; Ibn Ishaq identifies Aisha as the original source of the story.

16. Ibid., 280, quoting one Yaquba ibn Utaba as the source.

17. I wish to express my gratitude to Dr. Toby Rose, physician, pathologist, and coroner in Toronto, Canada, and Dr. Lucy Harvey of Montpelier, Vermont, for providing me with the information on the symptoms of malaria. Dr. Peter F. Weller notes, "Clinical symptoms develop about 1 to 4 weeks after infection and typically include fever and chills. Virtually all patients with acute malaria have episodes of fever. At the outset, fever may occur daily; over time, the paroxysms may develop the typical every-other or every-third day pattern. The paroxysms of fever (as high as 41.5 degrees C [106.7°F] and chills (with or without rigors) may be irregular, however. Other symptoms may be head-ache, increased sweating, back pain, myalgias, diarrhea, nausea, vomiting, and cough. . . . Cerebral involvement may lead to delirium, focal disorders, (e.g., seizures), and coma. *P. malariae* organisims can persist in the blood as an indo-lent, even asymptomatic, infection for years or even decades." See Weller, "Protozoan Infections: Malaria," 1–6.

18. Ibn Ishaq, 143.

19. Ibid., 194.

20. Ibid.

21. Ibid., 203.

22. Ibid., 204.

23. Ibid., 213.

24. Ibid.

25. Watt, *Muhammad at Medina*, 321.

26. Lings, *Muhammad*, 35. The original source for Lings's description can be found in Ibn Ishaq, 725–26.

27. Glubb, *Life and Times*, 238.

28. Rodinson, *Muhammad*, 279.

29. Watt, *Muhammad at Medina*, 321.

30. Glubb, *Life and Times*, 334.

31. Ibid., 228.

32. The term is taken from James H. Breasted, *The Development of Religion and Thought in Ancient Egypt*. Breasted used the phrase to describe the religious ferocity of Pharaoh Akhenaton, the ancient world's first true monotheist and the ruler from whom Moses may have adopted the idea of a single God. However, the first use of the phrase was to describe the famous religious philosopher Baruch Spinoza.

33. Ibn Ishaq, 157.

34. Ibid., 131.

35. Ibid., 106.

36. Ibid., 227.

5. INSURGENCY

1. Hoyland, *Arabia and the Arabs*, 170.

2. Muhammad Hamidullah, *Le Prophete de l'Islam*, cited in Glubb, *Life and Times*, 170. Hamidullah's estimate seems correct. When Muhammad destroyed one of the Jewish tribes of Medina, he executed nine hundred males of military age. Reckoning the number of wives, children, and aged relatives, the Jewish tribe could easily have numbered thirty-six hundred. Given that there were two more Jewish tribes, two major Arab tribes, and eight Arab clans in Medina at the time, it is probable that the population of Medina exceeded ten thousand.

3. Hitti, *History of the Arabs*, 104.

4. Ibid. The term means town in the sense of "jurisdiction." No doubt the identification of town with jurisdiction stems from the fact that Arab society was overwhelmingly nonurban, but highly tribal and territorial. Whether one was in a town or in the countryside, it was very important to know whose "jurisdiction" in the sense of tribal territory one was in at any given time.

5. Hoyland, *Arabia and the Arabs*, 170.

6. Glubb, *Life and Times*, 143.

7. Ibn Ishaq, 226.

8. Ibid., 232.

9. Ibid.

10. Ibid.

11. Ibid.

12. Ibid.

13. Ibid.

14. Glubb, *Life and Times*, 170.

15. Ibn Ishaq, 233.

16. Ibid., 283.

17. Ibid.

18. Glubb, *Life and Times*, 175.

19. For the figures on the range and speed of a riding camel, see Doughty, *Travels in Arabia Deserta*, 553.

20. Ibn Ishaq, 287.

21. It is not unlikely that some of Moses' massacres of his own people that are recounted as due to violations of religious ritual or divine command were attempts to suppress rebellions by some who thought his leadership incompetent. It may also have been that Moses did not reach the Promised Land because he was killed in one of these rebellions and replaced with Joshua. For more on this theory see Gabriel, *Gods of Our Fathers*, and Jonathan Kirsch, *Moses: A Life*.

22. Ibn Ishaq, 288.

23. Ibid.

24. Watt, *Muhammad at Medina*, 7, argues, "The essential part of Muhammad's sealed orders to Abdullah ibn Jahash was to go to Nakhla and ambush a caravan of Quraish. The further clause (in some versions) about bringing back a report to Muhammad is clearly a later addition intended to give the word *tarassadu* the meaning 'keep a watch' instead of 'lay an ambush.' In this way all responsibility for blood shedding would be removed from Muhammad. There can be no doubt, however, that Muhammad sent out the raiders on an errand which he realized might involve deaths among both his own men and the enemy."

25. Ibid., 6.

26. Ibn Ishaq, 287.

6. THE BATTLE OF BADR

1. Hamidullah, *Battlefields of the Prophet*, 120, citing the later source Ibn Sa'd, II/i: 4.

2. Ibid., citing Ibn Sa'd, II/i: 6.

3. Glubb, *Life and Times*, 179. Ibn Ishaq is silent on this matter.

4. Ibn Ishaq, 293.

5. Hamidullah, *Battlefields of the Prophet*, 45, citing al-Tabari, 1:1299.

6. Ibn Ishaq, 289.

7. Ibid., 293.

8. Ibid., 294.

9. Ibid.

10. Ibid., 295.

11. Ibid.

12. Ibid.

13. Ibid.

14. Hamidullah, *Battlefields of the Prophet*, 27, citing Ibn Hisham, 439.

15. Ibn Ishaq, 297. The man who warned Muhammad was named al-Mundhir, whose name means "the warner."

16. Ibid.

17. Hamidullah, *Battlefields of the Prophet*, 33.

18. Ibn Ishaq, 295–96.

19. Hamidullah, *Battlefields of the Prophet*, 27, citing Ibn Hisham, 439.

20. Ibid., 37, citing al-Waqidi.

21. Ibn Ishaq, 299.

22. Hamidullah, *Battlefields of the Prophet*, 36, citing Ibn Hisham, 443.

23. Gabriel, *Empires at War*, 1:296.

24. Ibn Ishaq, 299.

25. Ibid., 300.

26. For more on the Egyptian sources of the Christian doctrines of resurrection and eternal life, see Gabriel, *Gods of Our Fathers*, and *Jesus the Egyptian*.

27. Ibn Ishaq, 300.

28. Ibid., 355.

29. Ibid., 303.

30. Ibid.

31. Ibid., 304.

32. Ibid., 305.

33. Ibid., 308.

34. Quran, 4.3; see also Watt, *Muhammad at Medina*, 274.

35. Watt, *Muhammad at Medina*, 274.

36. Ibid., 275–76.

37. Glubb, *Life and Times*, 196.

38. Watt, *Muhammad at Medina*, 195.

39. Ibn Ishaq, 363.

40. Ibid.

41. Ibid.

42. Ibid., 367.

7. BATTLE OF UHUD

1. Ibn Ishaq, 364.

2. Ibid. The poem is taken from al-Waqidi's account.

3. Hamidullah, *Battlefields of the Prophet*, 43.

4. Ibn Ishaq, 370.

5. Hamidullah, *Battlefields of the Prophet*, 47–48.

6. Ibn Ishaq, 372.

7. Ibid.

8. Hamidullah, *Battlefields of the Prophet*, 50.

9. Ibn Ishaq, 372.

10. Glubb, *Life and Times*, 205, quoting al-Waqidi.

11. Ibn Ishaq, 372.

12. Ibid.

13. Ibid.

14. Ibid., 371.

15. Hamidullah, *Battlefields of the Prophet*, 52, citing Ibn Hisham, 560.

16. Ibn Ishaq, 373.

17. Hamidullah, *Battlefields of the Prophet*, 52.

18. Ibn Ishaq, 373.

19. Ibid.

20. Hamidullah, *Battlefields of the Prophet*, 52, quoting Isti'ab.

21. Ibn Ishaq, 374.

22. Ibid., 375.

23. Ibn Ishaq, 374. The Meccan women sang, "If you advance we hug you / Spread soft rugs beneath you / If you retreat we leave you / Leave and no more love you."

24. Ibn Ishaq, 375. Circumcision among Arabs predates Muhammad by several centuries, perhaps even by a millennium. The custom seems to have begun in Egypt, probably as a ritual in which Egyptian military conscripts were circumcised as part of an oath of loyalty to serve the pharaoh, their warrior god. The story of Abraham in Genesis aside, the first historical mention of circumcision among the Israelites occurred when Joshua circumcised all Israelite males of military age prior to crossing the Jordan and invading Canaan. That ceremony, too, was military in character in that like the Egyptian rite it was a covenant between the Israelite soldier and Yahweh Sabaoth, the Israelite god of war. Long before the Christian era, Egyptian or Moabite caravanners may have brought the custom to Arabia, where it may have taken root as a ritual associated with male military prowess. This pagan custom found its way into Muslim practice even though Muhammad was not circumcised, circumcision is not mentioned in the Quran, and it has no religious significance in Islam. For more on the subject see Lowin, "Muslims and Circumcision," 18–21.

25. Ibn Ishaq, 375.

26. Ibid.

27. Ibid., 379.

28. Hamidullah, *Battlefields of the Prophet*, 55–56.

29. Ibid.

30. The same thing happened to Ramses II at the Battle of Kadesh. His troops abandoned the attack to loot the Hittite camp with the result that he was almost killed and his army nearly destroyed.

31. Ibn Ishaq, 379.

32. Ibid.

33. Ibid., 380.

34. Ibid.

35. Ibid.

36. Ibid., 381.

37. Ibid.

38. Ibid., 382.

39. Rodinson, *Muhammad*, 183.

40. Ibn Ishaq, 383.

41. Ibid., 386.

42. Ibid., 385. In the *Iliad* Hecuba offers to eat Achilles' liver.

43. Glubb, *Life and Times*, 211. Hubal was the main idol of Mecca. Sufyan's boast was that the idol's power in battle was greater than that of Muhammad's god.

44. Ibn Ishaq, 386.

45. Ibid.

46. Ibid.

47. Ibid., 387.

48. Ibid.

49. Ibid.

50. Ibid.

51. Ibid., 390.

52. Ibid.

53. Ibid.

54. Ibid., 426.

55. Rodinson, *Muhammad*, 189.

56. Ibid.

57. Glubb, *Life and Times*, 220.

58. Ibid., 221.

59. Ibn Ishaq, 434.

60. Glubb, *Life and Times*, 222, citing al-Tabari.

61. Ibn Ishaq, 437.

62. Ibid.

63. Ibn Ishaq, 437. This is the view taken by Guillaume.

64. Rodinson, *Muhammad*, 192.

65. Ibn Ishaq, 437.

66. Ibid., 447.

67. Rodinson, *Muhammad*, 195.

68. Ibn Ishaq, 447. The reference is to *sawiq* made of crushed parched barley or wheat mixed with water or liquid butter that is drunk as a sort of thin porridge. Sawiq was a common military ration.

69. Rodinson, *Muhammad*, 249.

70. Ibn Ishaq, 445. It was here that Muhammad introduced the Prayer of Fear for soldiers; one-half of the force prayed while the other half stood facing the enemy weapons in hand and ready to do battle.

71. Rodinson, *Muhammad*, 196.

72. Ibid., 197. Muhammad's men wanted to rape the women before selling them, but Muhammad objected. Then the soldiers asked if it would be permitted for them to perform *azl*, or coitus interruptus, with the women, which in the Arab view was not technically rape. Muhammad gave his permission saying, "You are not under any obligation to forbear from that."

8. THE BATTLE OF THE DITCH

1. Hamidullah, *Battlefields of the Prophet*, 80, citing Ibn Hisham.

2. Ibid.

3. Hamidullah, *Battlefields of the Prophet*, 64, citing al-Sha'miy.

4. Ibid., 84.

5. Rodinson, *Muhammad*, 183; see also Glubb, *Life and Times*, 241.

6. Ibn Ishaq, 452.

7. Hamidullah, *Battlefields of the Prophet*, 68.

8. Ibid., 66.

9. Ibid., citing al-Tabari, 1:1465.

10. Hamidullah, *Battlefields of the Prophet*, 68; Ibn Ishaq is silent on the length of the ditch.

11. Ibid., quoting al-Waqidi.

12. I am grateful to Alison Gagliardi, an accomplished equestrian, for the information regarding the jumping capabilities of a horse.

13. Rodinson, *Muhammad*, 209.

14. Hamidullah, *Battlefields of the Prophet*, 71, citing al-Waqidi.

15. Ibid., 72, quoting al-Sha'miy.

16. For the military capabilities of the major armies of antiquity from 4000 B.C.E. to 1453 C.E., see Gabriel, *Empires at War*.

17. Hamidullah, *Battlefields of the Prophet*, 73, citing al-Waqidi.

18. Ibid.

19. Rodinson, *Muhammad*, 210.

20. Hamidullah, *Battlefields of the Prophet*, 74, citing al-Sha'miy. The story is almost certainly a fabrication. The Kheibar caravan would have been coming from the north to the rear of the Meccan positions. Muhammad's troops were ensconced behind the ditch enclosed by the horns of the lava plain. It is inconceivable that a force large enough to capture the Kheibar caravan could have somehow slipped out of Medina, passed through the Meccan positions undetected, ambushed the caravan, and then returned to the Muslim positions with the booty.

21. Hamidullah, *Battlefields of the Prophet*, 76, citing Ibn Hisham and al-Tabari.

22. Ibid. Nothing of this story appears in Ibn Ishaq's text.

23. Rodinson, *Muhammad*, 210.

24. Ibn Ishaq, 458.

25. Ibid., 459.

26. Ibid.

27. Ibid.

28. Ibid.

29. Ibid., 460.

30. Ibid.

31. Glubb, *Life and Times*, 249.

32. Ibid.

33. Ibn Ishaq, 461.

34. Rodinson, *Muhammad*, 211.

35. Ibid.

36. Hamidullah, *Battlefields of the Prophet*, 66.

37. Ibn Ishaq, 462.

38. Ibid.

39. Ibid.

40. Ibn Ishaq, 462; Glubb, *Life and Times*, 250; Rodinson, *Muhammad*, 212; the latter two sources cite later Arabic accounts.

41. Ibn Ishaq, 463.

42. Ibid. See also Rodinson, *Muhammad*, 214, quoting Ibn Hisham, 679, for Sa'd's prayer.

43. Ibn Ishaq, 464.

44. Ibid.

45. Ibid.

46. Ibid., 466.

47. Ibid., 482.

48. Rodinson, *Muhammad*, 249. See also Ibn Ishaq's account (515) of Muhammad's order to torture a chief at Kheibar who would not reveal the location of the town treasury. Hamidullah, *Battlefields of the Prophet*, 114 (citing al-Maqrizi, 1:320), provides an account of the same incident confirming the use of torture.

49. Glubb, *Life and Times*, 248.

50. Ibid.

51. Ibid.

52. Ibid., 249.

53. Ibn Ishaq, 485.

54. Ibid., 485–86.

55. Ibid.

56. Glubb, *Life and Times*, 262; Ibn Ishaq, 490.

57. Ibn Ishaq, 492.

58. Ibid., 493.

59. Ibid., 500; Ibn Ishaq also cites reports from some men who claimed to have been there that the number of soldiers was fourteen hundred.

60. Ibid., 500.

61. Ibid. Interestingly the Meccan cavalry screen was commanded by Khalid al-Walid, who apparently had not yet converted to Islam. The strength of the cavalry screen as comprising two hundred horses is Rodinson's estimate, in *Muhammad*, 250.

62. Ibn Ishaq, 500.

63. Rodinson, *Muhammad*, 250.

64. Ibn Ishaq, 501.

65. Ibid., 506–507, for details regarding the provisions of the truce.

66. Ibid., 507.

9. THE BATTLES OF KHEIBAR (628) AND MU'TA (629)

1. Rodinson, *Muhammad*, 253; Ibn Ishaq, 522.

2. Hamidullah, *Battlefields of the Prophet*, 109.

3. Rodinson, *Muhammad*, 253.

4. Hamidullah, *Battlefields of the Prophet*, 109, citing al-Maqrizi, *Imta'*, 1:320.

5. Hamidullah, *Battlefields of the Prophet*, 111.

6. Ibn Ishaq, 511.

7. Rodinson, *Muhammad*, 253.

8. Hamidullah, *Battlefields of the Prophet*, 111.

9. Ibn Ishaq, 511.

10. Ibid.

11. Hamidullah, *Battlefields of the Prophet*, 112 (citing al-Sha'miy, *Sirah*, chapter on Kheibar), says that the Ghatafan had already reached Kheibar before Muhammad shifted his route of march toward their territory.

12. Hamidullah, *Battlefields of the Prophet*, 108, citing Yaqut's *Geography*, 108.

13. Hamidullah, *Battlefields of the Prophet*, 113 (citing al-Ya'qubi, 11:56), says the population of Kheibar was twenty thousand; al-Maqrizi, 1:310, says the population was ten thousand.

14. Ibn Ishaq, 511.

15. Ibid. Hamidullah, *Battlefields of the Prophet*, 114 (citing al-Maqrizi, *Imta'* 1), says it was the region of Natat.

16. Hamidullah, *Battlefields of the Prophet*, 115, again citing al-Maqrizi.

17. Ibid., al-Maqrizi, 311.

18. Hamidullah, *Battlefields of the Prophet*, 112, citing al-Sha'miy, *Sirah*.

19. Ibn Ishaq, 514.

20. Ibid.

21. Ibid., 511.

22. Ibid., 512.

23. "The Apostle prohibited four things that day: carnal intercourse with pregnant women who were captured; eating the flesh of domestic donkeys; eating any carnivorous animal; and selling booty before it had been duly allotted." Ibn Ishaq, 512.

24. Hamidullah, *Battlefields of the Prophet*, 115, citing al-Maqrizi, *Imta'*, 1:319–20.

25. Hamidullah, *Battlefields of the Prophet*, 116, citing al-Maqrizi; Ibn Ishaq (515) agrees.

26. Hamidullah, *Battlefields of the Prophet*, 113, citing al-Maqrizi, *Imta'*, 1:325.

27. Ibn Ishaq, 522.

28. Glubb, *Life and Times*, 286.

29. Lings, *Muhammad*, 146. Lings says seventy camels were sacrificed.

30. Ibid., 281.

31. Ibid., 280.

32. Ibn Ishaq, 531.

33. Watt, *Muhammad: Prophet and Statesman*, 99.

34. Glubb, *Life and Times*, 288.

35. Rodinson, *Muhammad*, 256.

36. Glubb, *Life and Times*, 289; Ibn Ishaq is silent on the whole matter of a letter, and it is possible that the story is a later invention complete with forgeries.

37. Hitti, *History of the Arabs*, 147.

38. Shoufani, *Muslim Conquest of Arabia*, 66.

39. Rodinson, *Muhammad*, 256.

40. Glubb, *Life and Times*, 290; Ibn Ishaq, 532.

41. Ibn Ishaq, 532.

42. Glubb, *Life and Times*, 290. Glubb was himself a professional soldier who spent more than three decades serving with Arab units in the Middle East. His estimate deserves serious consideration as being correct.

43. Ibn Ishaq, 533.

44. Ibid., 534.

45. Ibid., 534–35.

46. Ibid.

47. Ibid., 535.

48. Watt, *Muhammad at Medina*, 55.

49. Shoufani, *Muslim Conquest of Arabia*, 39.

10. THE CONQUEST OF MECCA

1. Shoufani, *Muslim Conquest of Arabia*, 22.

2. Watt, *Muhammad at Medina*, 61, citing both Ibn Hisham and al-Waqidi as sources. Interestingly, Ibn Ishaq makes no mention at all of this important incident.

3. Ibid.

4. The suspicion arises, of course, that Muhammad may have supplied some men to Abu Basir. It is unlikely that a sufficient number of would-be Muslims from Mecca would have been wandering around the countryside to join Abu Basir's raiders without being mentioned in some other source.

5. Ibn Ishaq, 540.

6. Watt, *Muhammad at Medina*, 62, citing al-Waqidi.

7. Rodinson, *Muhammad*, 258.

8. Shoufani, *Muslim Conquest of Arabia*, 24.

9. Ibid., 25, citing al-Baladhuri, a much later source (ca. 892 C.E.).

10. The argument that Abu Sufyan was probably a double agent is made most forcibly by Shoufani and Watt.

11. Ibn Ishaq, 544.

12. Ibid., 545.

13. Watt, *Muhammad at Medina*, 66, citing al-Waqidi.

14. Ibid., citing Ibn Hisham, 810, and al-Waqidi, 332. The latter also provides a partial list of tribes and the number of troops each committed to Muhammad's army.

15. Ibn Ishaq tells us that the "Quraish were completely ignorant of the fact and did not even know what he [Muhammad] was doing." Ibn Ishaq, 546.

16. Ibid., 546–47.

17. Ibid., 547.

18. Ibid.

19. Ibid., 548.

20. Ibid.

21. Ibid.

22. Glubb, *Life and Times*, 307.

23. Ibn Ishaq, 548.

24. Ibid.

25. Ibid.

26. Hamidullah, *Battlefields of the Prophet*, 85, citing Ibn Hisham, 818.

27. Ibn Ishaq agrees with the account in substance but offers fewer details.

28. Hamidullah, *Battlefields of the Prophet*, 85.

29. Watt, *Muhammad at Medina*, 66.

30. Ibn Ishaq, 550.

31. Watt, *Muhammad at Medina*, 66.

32. Ibid., 67.

33. Watt, *Muhammad: Prophet and Statesman*, 260.

34. Watt, *Muhammad at Medina*, 68.

35. Ibid., 68.

36. Rodinson, *Muhammad*, 262. The importance of political considerations over even personal vengeance can be gauged from the fact that the infamous Hind—wife of Abu Sufyan, who had paid a slave to kill Hamza at Uhud and then mutilated his body and chewed his liver—was not killed.

37. Shoufani, *Muslim Conquest of Arabia*, 26.

38. Rodinson, *Muhammad*, 261.

11. THE BATTLE OF HUNAYN

1. Watt, *Muhammad at Medina*, 70.

2. Ibn Ishaq, 561.

3. Ibid.

4. Ibn Ishaq, 565–66.

5. Watt, *Muhammad: Prophet and Statesman*, 71.

6. Shoufani, *Muslim Conquest of Arabia*, 26, suggests that the initiative for the battle came from Muhammad, who was strongly pressured by the Meccans to do battle. The manner in which the military events unfolded suggests that it was the Hawazin who initiated the war.

7. Ibn Ishaq, 567.

8. Ibid.

9. Ibid.

10. Hamidullah, *Battlefields of the Prophet*, 91–99, identifies these later sources as al-Maqrizi, Ibn Hisham, Ibn Hajar, al-Baladhuri, and Ibn Sa'd.

11. Hamidullah is the only Muslim historian of whom I am aware who actually walked the ground in an attempt to locate the battlefield at Wadi Hunayn.

12. Ibn Ishaq, 567–68.

13. Watt, *Muhammad at Medina*, 72, citing al-Waqidi, 368.

14. Ibn Ishaq, 566.

15. This estimate was calculated by using the method outlined in Yadin, *Warfare in Biblical Lands*, 1:19, according to which the number of males of military age in a tribal society of the Middle East during antiquity was approximately 20 percent of the total population of the tribe. For an example of the use of Yadin's method, see Gabriel, *Military History of Ancient Israel*, 114. Yadin's method of calculation supports Glubb's contention that the size of the Hawazin army at Wadi Hunayn was between four thousand and five thousand men. See Glubb, *Life and Times*, 321.

16. Ibn Ishaq, 567.
17. Ibid.
18. Ibid., 569.
19. Ibid., 570.
20. Ibid., 566.
21. Ibid., 569.
22. Ibid.
23. Watt, *Muhammad at Medina*, 72, citing Ibn Hisham, 850.
24. Ibn Ishaq, 569.
25. Ibid., 570.
26. Ibid.
27. Glubb, *Life and Times*, 323; Ibn Ishaq, 572.
28. Ibn Ishaq, 572.
29. The reference to "black ants" may reflect the Arab tradition of wearing black robes when dressed for war. Al-Walid's tribesmen may have been wearing black robes. In addition, the Beni Sulaym always resented the accounts of the battle in which they were portrayed as having fled. To counter the charge, a Sulaym poet authored a long poem emphasizing the bravery of his tribe. One of the verses strongly suggests that they were the men who saved Muhammad by taking part in the cavalry charge that broke the Hawazins' morale. The poem is cited in Ibn Ishaq, 582, and reads in part, "Until we came on the people of Mecca with a squadron / Glittering with steel, led by a proud chief / Composed of Sulaym's sturdiest men."
30. Watt, *Muhammad at Medina*, 72, citing al-Waqidi.
31. Ibn Ishaq, 572.
32. Hamidullah, *Battlefields of the Prophet*, 96, citing al-Aghani, 12:48–49.
33. Ibid.
34. Ibn Ishaq (572) says that the men of Ta'if lost seventy. Perhaps these were the same men who died alongside Malik ibn Auf defending the war banner.
35. Ibn Ishaq, 587.
36. Ibid., 589.
37. Ibid.
38. Hamidullah, *Battlefields of the Prophet*, 99, citing al-Baladhuri, *Ansab*, 1:367.
39. Hamidullah, *Battlefields of the Prophet*, 99, citing Ibn Sa'd, II/i: 114.
40. Ibid.
41. Ibn Ishaq, 589.
42. Watt, *Muhammad at Medina*, 73; see also Hamidullah, *Battlefields of the Prophet*, 99 (citing Ibn Sa'd, 11/i: 114), which says the siege lasted for forty days.
43. Ibn Ishaq, 592.
44. Watt, *Muhammad at Medina*, 73.
45. Ibid., 75, citing al-Waqidi, 385.
46. Glubb, *Life and Times*, 324.
47. Ibn Ishaq, 593.
48. Watt, *Muhammad at Medina*, 75.
49. Ibn Ishaq, 596.

50. Watt, *Muhammad at Medina*, 75.

51. Shoufani, *Muslim Conquest of Arabia*, 27.

52. Watt, *Muhammad at Medina*, 87; see also Lewis, *The Arabs in History*, 51.

12. THE TABUK EXPEDITION AND THE DEATH OF MUHAMMAD

1. Shoufani, *Muslim Conquest of Arabia*, 42, citing al-Waqidi, 822, and Ibn Sa'd, II/i: 98. The figure of thirty thousand men is also cited by Rodinson, *Muhammad*, 275. It was certainly the largest army Muhammad had ever commanded in the field.

2. Caetani, *Annali dell'Islam* 2. Caetani's ten-volume work is regarded as one of the classic Western works on the history of Islam based in original sources.

3. Ibn Ishaq, 602, tells us, "This was the sole exception."

4. Shoufani, *Muslim Conquest of Arabia*, 40, citing Abbas; Watt, *Muhammad at Medina*, 180.

5. Shoufani, *Muslim Conquest of Arabia*, 40, citing Ibn Sa'd, II/i: 119.

6. Shoufani, *Muslim Conquest of Arabia*, 39, citing al-Waqidi, 990, and Ibn Sa'd, II/i: 120.

7. Ibn Ishaq, 603.

8. Ibid.

9. Ibid., 604.

10. Ibid.

11. Ibid.

12. Ibid., 596.

13. Shoufani, *Muslim Conquest of Arabia*, 40.

14. Ibid., citing al-Aghani, 3:70–83.

15. Glubb, *Life and Times*, 321.

16. The argument is presented in its entirety by Shoufani, *Muslim Conquest of Arabia*, 42.

17. Caetani, *Annali dell'Islam*, 1:307–308.

18. Rodinson, *Muhammad*, 274.

19. Ibn Ishaq, 605.

20. Ibid.

21. Ibid. In a footnote, Guillaume explains the event as a case of disease or infection known to the Arabs as *khunaqiya* that attacks men, horses, and sometimes birds in the throat.

22. Ibn Ishaq, 605. Heavy spontaneous cloudbursts are not rare occurrences in Arabia even in October.

23. Ibid., 608. Other later sources cited by Rodinson, *Muhammad*, 275, say Muhammad stayed in Tabuk for twenty days.

24. Ibn Ruba was not a "governor" in the sense of a Byzantine official. He was a local prince or tribal chief. It should not be thought, therefore, that Muhammad was negotiating with officials of the Byzantine Empire.

25. Rodinson, *Muhammad*, 275. There is some unresolved difficulty here in that Glubb says the three villages were not Jewish but Christian.

26. The success of the Meccans in reaching high positions under Muhammad and the later caliphate is exemplified by the position of Abu Sufyan, Muhammad's onetime archenemy, was now one of Muhammad's trusted advisers. Abu Sufyan placed his family into prominent positions. It was this family that later became the famous Umayyad dynasty. Abu Sufyan's son, Yazid, was appointed governor of Tayma, and his other son, Mu'awiya, became the Prophet's secretary. Later, Abu Bakr replaced many Muslim commanders with Meccan officers.

27. Rodinson, *Muhammad*, 277, citing al-Waqid, 3:1066.

28. Ibid.

29. Ibn Ishaq, 609.

30. Rodinson, *Muhammad*, 277. It seems clear from these incidents that Muhammad's intelligence service in Medina was working well during his absence.

31. Ibid., citing al-Waqidi, 3:1066.

32. Quran, sura 9:85.

33. Ibid., 9:104.

34. Ibid., 9:1–6.

35. Ibn Ishaq, 619.

36. Quran, sura 9:28.

37. Ibn Ishaq, 648–49; Shoufani, *Muslim Conquest of Arabia*, 46.

38. Ibn Ishaq, 652, says Muhammad began planning the expedition after his return from the pilgrimage; Shoufani, *Muslim Conquest of Arabia*, says he began planning after his return from Tabuk.

39. Ibn Ishaq, 651–52.

40. Rodinson, *Muhammad*, 286.

41. Ibid.

42. Ibn Ishaq, 679.

43. Ibid.

44. Ibid.

45. Ibid., 680. See Weller, "Protozoan Infections: Malaria," 2:5.

46. Rodinson, *Muhammad*, 288.

47. Ibn Ishaq, 689.

48. Ibid.

13. MUHAMMAD'S MILITARY LEGACY

1. Hitti, *History of the Arabs*, 40.

2. In the same way that Paul of Tarsus influenced the development of Christian doctrine and helped bring about the spread and institutionalization of Christianity, so it appears that Abu Bakr influenced the doctrines of Islam on critical theological points. It was also Abu Bakr, not Muhammad, who was ultimately responsible for the spread of Islam and its institutionalization as a formal religion.

3. Shoufani, *Muslim Conquest of Arabia*, 71–73. For Western perspectives on the Riddah that challenge the religious perspective, see Wellhausen, *Skizzen und Vorarbeiten*, 6:7–8; Becker, "Expansion of the Saracens," in *The Cambridge Medieval History*, 2:335–36; Caetani, *Studi di Storia Orientale*,

3:349–52; and Lewis, *The Arabs in History*, 51–52. My own view is that Watt is correct in *Muhammad at Medina*, 147–48, where he argues that the Riddah proceeded from a combination of religious, political, and economic motives.

4. Shoufani, *Muslim Conquest of Arabia*, 62, citing Ibn Abi al-Hadid, 6:23.

5. Ibid. Al-Hadid provides a list of these commanders.

6. Shoufani, *Muslim Conquest of Arabia*, 111, citing al-Waqidi and Caetani, *Annali dell'Islam*, 2:587–88.

7. Shoufani, *Muslim Conquest of Arabia*, 109, citing Ibn Sa'd, II/i, 136.

8. My account of Abu Bakr's campaigns closely follows that of al-Tabari, vol. 1. Shoufani, who is the leading Arabic expert on the Riddah available in English, states that al-Tabari's account is the most complete and trustworthy.

9. Al-Tabari's list of Abu Bakr's field commanders during the Riddah can be found in Shoufani, *Muslim Conquest of Arabia*, 116.

10. Hitti, 141.

11. Ibid.

12. Shoufani, *Muslim Conquest of Arabia*, 118.

13. An example of the flexibility of Muslim armies under Abu Bakr is evident in the movements of Khalid al-Walid's army. Al-Walid marched from Dhu al-Qassah to al-Buzakhah, where he fought a major battle against a coalition of the tribes of Najd. After defeating the coalition, al-Walid pressed out in several directions until one of his columns engaged the enemy at Al-Butah against the Yarbu. Winning here, he was ordered to swing far to the southeast to rescue Ikrimah ibn Abu Jahl, who had been twice routed by the tribes of the Bani Hanifah. Al-Walid fought the largest battle of the Riddah at Aqraba dealing the Bani Hanifah a devastating defeat. He then turned northeast, crossed the remaining desert, and began raiding along the Persian border. Poised to cross the Euphrates, al-Walid was ordered by Abu Bakr to turn west, march across the Syrian Desert, and join the Muslim armies preparing to attack Palestine and Syria.

14. Gabriel, "Wars of Arab Conquest" in *Empires at War*, 2:639.

15. Ibid., 2:642–43.

16. It was the puritan caliph Umar who, fearing that the Arabs would loose their fighting spirit and fall into sin if they mixed with the infidels, decided to segregate the Arabs by establishing military cantonments for them to live in. Glubb, *Short History*, 55.

17. Crone, " Early Islamic World," 311.

18. Nicolle and McBride, *Armies of Islam*, 11.

19. The size of the Arab armies and their accompanying families is a matter of some debate. Glubb, *Short History*, 19, says that they numbered five hundred thousand, while Crone, "Early Islamic World," 314, says one hundred thousand. Using Yadin's method of calculation, this would mean that the Arab armies per se comprised between 25,000 and 125,000 soldiers, not a huge number in either case.

20. Nicolle and McBride, *Armies of Islam*, 12.

21. Crone, "Early Islamic World," 316.

22. Nicolle and McBride, *Armies of Islam*, 12.

23. Ibid., 13.

24. Gabriel, "Wars of Arab Conquest," 647.

25. Crone, "Early Islamic World," 318.

26. Those interested in pursuing the development of Muslim armies after the conquest period might consult Gabriel, "The Crusades," 791–836, and "Byzantines and Ottomans," 987–1030, both in *Empires at War* 3.

27. Firestone, *Jihad*, 37.

28. Ibid., 39.

29. Lane, *Arabic-English Lexicon*, bk. 1, pt. 2, 473.

30. Watt, "Islamic Conceptions of Holy War," in Murphy, *Holy War*, 141–56.

31. Firestone, *Jihad*, 50.

BIBLIOGRAPHY

The literature on Muhammad is vast. However, most of it either does not address Muhammad's military exploits at all or does so only in passing and is of little use to the military historian. This bibliography lists only those works I found most important to understanding and researching Muhammad's military life. It is not intended to address other areas of scholarly interest concerning Muhammad's life. The purpose of any bibliography is to help other scholars check one's work, criticize it, or build on it. I include in a separate section the original Arabic sources so that Arabic scholars and historians can use them in a similar manner as well. I have made occasional notes regarding those entries that I thought may be particularly valuable to the military researcher.

SOURCES IN ENGLISH

Arberry, A. J. *The Seven Odes*. London: Allen and Unwin, 1957. Valuable for the military facts that may be extracted from a very close reading of the material.

Becker, Carl. H. "The Expansion of the Saracens." In *The Cambridge Medieval History*, 2:332–38. New York, 1913. The classic Western view of the forces that shaped both the *Riddah* and the Arab conquests.

Beeston, A. F. L. *Warfare in Ancient South Arabia*. London: Luzac, 1976.

Bousquet, G. H. "Observations sur lat nature et les causes de lat conquete arabe." *Studia Islamica* 6 (1956): 37–52.

Breasted, James H. *The Development of Religion and Thought in Ancient Egypt*. New York: Harper and Brothers, 1959.

Brockelmann, Carl. *History of the Islamic Peoples*. Translated by J. Carmichael and M. Perlmann. New York: G. P. Putnam's Sons, 1960.

Buhl, Franz. *Das Leben Muhammeds.* Translated by H. H. Schaeder. Leipzig, 1930. A compact biography full of scholarly notes of great value.

Bulliet, Richard W. *The Camel and the Wheel.* New York: Columbia University Press, 1990.

Caetani, Leone. *Annali dell'Islam.* 10 vols. Milan, 1905–26. Probably the most comprehensive treatment of the history of the Arabs in which all then-extant Arabic sources can be found, year by year, quoted, analyzed, and compared. It has not been translated into English as far as I am aware.

———. *Studi di Storia Orientale.* 3 vols. Milan, 1911–14.

Crone, Patricia. "The Early Islamic World." In *War and Society in the Ancient and Medieval Worlds,* edited by Kurt Raaflaub and Nathan Rosenstein. Cambridge: Harvard University Press, 1999.

Doughty, C. M. *Travels in Arabia Deserta.* London, 1936.

Dupuy, R. Ernest, and Trevor N. Dupuy. *The Encyclopedia of Military History.* New York: Harper and Row, 1986.

Edwards, Michael. *Ibn Ishaq's Life of Muhammad, Apostle of Allah.* London: Folio Society, 1964.

Firestone, Reuven. *Jihad: The Origins of Holy War in Islam.* London: Oxford University Press, 1999.

Gabriel, Richard A. "Ancient India." In *Empires at War,* 1:235–52. Westport, Conn.: Greenwood Press, 2005.

———. "Byzantines and Ottomans." In *Empires at War,* 3:987–1030. Westport, Conn.: Greenwood Press, 2005.

———. "Charlemagne and the Empire of the Franks." In *Empires at War,* 2:659–700. Westport, Conn.: Greenwood Press, 2005.

———. "The Crusades." In *Empires at War,* 3:791–836. Westport, Conn.: Greenwood Press, 2005.

———. *Empires at War: A Chronological Encyclopedia.* 3 vols. Westport, Conn.: Greenwood Press, 2005. A basic reference for the major battles, armies, equipment, weapons, tactics, and commanders for wars fought in antiquity from 4000 B.C.E. to the fall of Constantinople in 1453 C.E.

———. *Gods of Our Fathers: The Memory of Egypt in Judaism and Christianity.* Westport, Conn.: Greenwood Press, 2002.

———. "The Japanese Way of War." In *Empires at War,* 3:837–72. Westport, Conn.: Greenwood Press, 2005.

———. *Jesus the Egyptian: The Origins of Christianity and the Psychology of Christ.* New York: iUniverse Press, 2006.

———. *The Military History of Ancient Israel.* Westport, Conn.: Praeger, 2003.

———. *Soldiers' Lives through History: The Ancient World.* Westport, Conn.: Greenwood Press, 2006.

———. *Subotai the Valiant: Genghis Khan's Greatest General.* Westport, Conn.: Praeger, 2004.

———. "The Swiss and the Rediscovery of Infantry." In *Empires at War,* 3:915–44. Westport, Conn.: Greenwood Press, 2005.

———. "The Wars of Arab Conquest, 600–850 C.E." In *Empires at War,* 2:639–58. Westport, Conn.: Greenwood Press, 2005.

Gabriel, Richard A., and Donald W. Boose, Jr. *The Great Battles of Antiquity: A Strategic and Tactical Guide to the Great Battles That Shaped the Development of War.* Westport, Conn.: Greenwood Press, 1994.

Giap, Vo Nguyen. *People's War, People's Army: The Viet Cong Insurrection Manual for Underdeveloped Countries.* New York: Bantam Books, 1968.

Glubb, Sir John. *The Life and Times of Muhammad.* New York: Cooper Square Press, 2001. Glubb was a professional soldier who lived and served with Arab units for many years. His experiences provide valuable insights in this small volume.

———. *A Short History of the Arab Peoples.* New York: Stein and Day, 1969.

Goldschmidt, Arthur, Jr. *A Concise History of the Middle East.* Boulder, Colo.: Westview Press, 1988.

Hamidullah, Muhammad. *The Battlefields of the Prophet.* Paris: Revue des Etudes Islamiques, 1939. Reprint, New Delhi, 1973. Mostly useful for the maps and terrain descriptions of the battlefields.

Hitti, Philip K. *History of the Arabs.* Hampshire, UK: Palgrave Macmillan, 2002. First published in 1937 and still one of the best historical sources available.

Hoyland, Robert G. *Arabia and the Arabs: From the Bronze Age to the Coming of Islam.* London: Routledge, 2001.

Huntington, Samuel P. *The Clash of Civilizations and the Remaking of the World Order.* New York: Touchstone, 1996.

Ibn Ishaq. *The Life of Muhammad: A Translation of Ibn Ishaq's Life of Muhammad.* Translated by Alfred Guillaume. Oxford: Oxford University Press, 1967. Perhaps the most important source and most easily accessible for understanding the detail and context of Muhammad's military life.

Kirsch, Jonathan. *Moses: A Life.* New York: Ballantine Books, 1998.

Lane, Edward. *An Arabic-English Lexicon,* bk 1. London: Williams and Norgate, 1865.

Laoust, Henri. *Les Schismes dans l'Islam.* Paris, 1965.

Lewis, Bernard. *The Arabs in History.* London: Grey Arrow, 1958.

———, ed. *Historians of the Middle East.* London: Holt, 1962.

Lings, Martin. *Muhammad: His Life Based on the Earliest Sources.* Rochester, Vt.: Inner Traditions International, 1983. An excellent narrative history based strongly in original sources.

Lowin, Shari. "Muslims and Circumcision," *JTS Magazine* 10, no. 1 (fall 2000): 18–21.

Lyall, C. J. *A Commentary on Ten Ancient Arabic Poems.* Calcutta, 1894.

Macdonald, M. C. A. "Hunting, Fighting, and Raiding: The Horse in Pre-Islamic Arabia." In *Furusiyya: The Horse in the Art of the Near East,* edited by David Alexander, 73–83. Riyadh: King Abdulaziz Public Library, 1996.

Murphy, Thomas Patrick, ed. *The Holy War.* Columbus: Ohio State University Press, 1976.

Nicolle, David, and Angus McBride. *The Armies of Islam, 7th–11th Centuries.* London: Osprey, 1982. A good source for descriptions of Arab military equipment.

Parry, V. J., and M. E. Yapp. *War, Technology, and Society in the Middle East.* London: Oxford University Press, 1975. A useful collection of articles dealing with Arab warfare at different periods with emphasis on technical detail.

Payne, James L. *Why Nations Arm.* Oxford: Blackwell Books, 1889. One of the first books published in the modern West that deals with Muhammad as a soldier.

Rodinson, Maxime. *Muhammad*. New York: New Press, 2002. Contains an excellent section on Muhammad's military exploits.

Roth, Jonathan P. *The Logistics of the Roman Army at War, 264 BC–AD 235.* Boston: Brill, 1999. Chapter 1, "Supply Needs and Rations," is particularly valuable for information dealing with the soldier's nutritional needs and the military capabilities of animals in war.

Shoufani, Elias S. *Al-Riddah and the Muslim Conquest of Arabia.* Toronto: University of Toronto Press, Arab Institute for Research and Publishing, 1973. The definitive work on the *Riddah* in English.

Watt, W. Montgomery. "Islamic Conceptions of Holy War." In Thomas Patrick Murphy, ed., *The Holy War*, 141–56. Columbus: Ohio State University Press, 1976.

———. *Muhammad at Mecca.* Oxford: Clarendon Press, 1953.

———. *Muhammad at Medina.* London: Oxford University Press, 1956.

———. *Muhammad: Prophet and Statesman.* London: Oxford University Press, 1961.

Weller, Peter F. "Protozoan Infections: Malaria." In David C. Dale and Daniel D. Federman, eds., *Scientific American Medicine*, 2:1–6. New York: Scientific American, 1999.

Wellhausen, Julius. *Skizzen und Vorarbeiten*, 6 vols. Berlin: 1884–89. Like Caetani's work, a classic in the field that deals with all the sources and the conflicts between them.

Yadin, Yigael. *The Art of Warfare in Biblical Lands in Light of Archaeological Discovery.* 2 vols. New York: McGraw-Hill, 1964.

ORIGINAL ARABIC SOURCES

Abu Yusuf, al-Kufi, Ya'qub ibn Ibrahim (731–98). *Kitab al-Kharaj.* Cairo, 1933.

Baghdadi, 'Abd al-Qahir ibn Tahir al- (d. 1037). *Al-Farq bayn al-firaq.* Edited by Muhammad 'Abd al-Hamid. Cairo, 1959.

Baladhuri, Ahmad ibn Yahya ibn Jabir al- (d. 892). *Ansar al-ashraf.* Vol. 1. Edited by Muhammad Hamidullah. Cairo, 1959.

Ibn Hisham, 'Abd al-Malik (d. 834). *Sirat al-nabi.* Edited by Muhammad 'Abd al-Hamid. 4 vols. Cairo, 1963.

Ibn Sa'd, Muhammad (d. 845). *Biographen Muhammeds* (known as *Al-Tabaqat al-kubra*). Edited by Edward Sachau. Leiden, 1904–40.

Maqrizi, Ahmad ibn 'Ali al- (1364–1442). *Kitab al-niza wa-al-takhasum fi ma bayn bani Umayyah wa-bani Hashim.* Cairo, 1937.

Tabari, Muhammad ibn Jarir al- (838–923). *Annales.* 15 vols. Translated into German and edited by M. J. de Goeje. Leiden, 1879–1901.

Tufayl, Amir al-. *The Poems of Diwan.* Edited by Sir Charles Lyall. London: E. J. W. Gibb Memorial, XXI, 1913.

Tufayl ibn 'Auf. *The Poems of Diwan.* Edited and translated by F. Krenkow. London: E. J. W. Gibb Memorial, 1927.

Waqidi, Muhammad ibn 'Umar al- (747–823). *Kitab al-Maghazi.* 3 vols. Edited by Marsden Jones. Oxford, 1966.

Ya'qubi, Ahmad ibn Abi Yaqub al- (d. 897). *Tarikh al-Ya'qubi.* 2 vols. Beirut, 1960.

INDEX

ALSO BY
RICHARD A. GABRIEL

The Ethnic Factor in the Urban Polity (New York, 1973)

(ed. with Sylvan H. Cohen) *The Environment: Critical Factors in Strategy Development* (New York, 1973)

Program Evaluation: A Social Science Approach (New York, 1975)

Managers and Gladiators: Directions of Change in the Army (Concord, N.H., 1978)

(with Paul L. Savage) *Crisis in Command: Mismanagement in the Army* (New York, 1978)

Ethnic Groups in America (New York, 1978)

The New Red Legions: An Attitudinal Portrait of the Soviet Soldier (Westport, Conn., 1980)

The New Red Legions: A Survey Data Sourcebook (Westport, Conn., 1980)

To Serve with Honor: A Treatise on Military Ethics and the Way of the Soldier (Westport, Conn., 1982)

NATO and the Warsaw Pact: A Combat Assessment (Westport, Conn., 1983)

Antagonists in the Middle East: A Combat Assessment (Westport, Conn., 1983)

Nonaligned, Third World, and Other Ground Armies: A Combat Assessment (Westport, Conn., 1983)

The Antagonists: A Comparative Combat Assessment of the Soviet and American Soldier (Westport, Conn., 1984)

The Mind of the Soviet Fighting Man: A Quantitative Survey of Soviet Soldiers, Sailors, and Airmen (Westport, Conn., 1984)

Operation Peace for Galilee: The Israeli-PLO War in Lebanon (New York, 1984)

Military Incompetence: Why the American Military Doesn't Win (New York, 1985)

(ed.) *Military Psychiatry: A Comparative Perspective* (New York, 1986)

Soviet Military Psychiatry: The Theory and Practice of Coping with Battle Stress (New York, 1986)

No More Heroes: Madness and Psychiatry in War (New York, 1987)

The Last Centurion (Paris, 1987)

The Painful Field: Psychiatric Dimension of Modern War (New York, 1988)

The Culture of War: Invention and Early Development (New York, 1990)

(with Karen S. Metz) *From Sumer to Rome: The Military Capabilities of Ancient Armies* (New York, 1991)

(with Karen S. Metz) *History of Military Medicine: Ancient Times to the Middle Ages* (1992)

(with Karen S. Metz) *History of Military Medicine: From the Renaissance through Modern Times* (1992)

(with Karen S. Metz) *A Short History of War: The Evolution of Warfare and Weapons* (Carlisle Barracks, Pa., 1992)

(with Donald W. Boose, Jr.) *The Great Battles of Antiquity: A Strategic and Tactical Guide to the Great Battles That Shaped the Development of War* (Westport, Conn., 1994)

Great Captains of Antiquity (Westport, Conn., 2001)

Warrior Pharaoh: A Chronicle of the Life and Deeds of Thutmose III, Great Lion of Egypt, Told in His Own Words to Thaneni the Scribe (Lincoln, Neb., 2001)

The Great Armies of Antiquity (Westport, Conn., 2002)

Gods of Our Fathers: The Memory of Egypt in Judaism and Christianity (Westport, Conn., 2002)

Sebastian's Cross (Lincoln, Neb., 2002)

Lion of the Sun: A Chronicle of the Wars, Battles and Great Deeds of Pharaoh Thutmose III, Great Lion of Egypt (Lincoln, Neb., 2003)

The Military History of Ancient Israel (Westport, Conn., 2003)

Subotai the Valiant: Genghis Khan's Greatest General (Westport, Conn., 2004)

Jesus the Egyptian: The Origins of Christianity and the Psychology of Christ (Lincoln, Neb., 2005)

Empires at War: A Chronological Encyclopedia, 3 vols. (Westport, Conn., 2005)

Soldiers' Lives through History: The Ancient World (Westport, Conn., 2006)